ALSO BY JACK MCCALLUM

FICTION
*Foul Lines: A Pro Basketball Novel* (with L. Jon Wertheim)

NONFICTION
*Unfinished Business: On and Off the Court with
    the 1990–91 Boston Celtics*
*Shaq Attaq!*
*Full Circle: An Olympic Champion Shares His Breakthrough Story*
*Seven Seconds or Less: My Season on the Bench with the
    Runnin' and Gunnin' Phoenix Suns*

# DREAM
# TEAM

# DREAM TEAM

How Michael, Magic, Larry, Charles,
and the Greatest Team of All Time
Conquered the World and Changed
the Game of Basketball Forever

## Jack McCallum

BALLANTINE BOOKS  NEW YORK

Published in the United States by Ballantine Books, an imprint of The Random House Publishing Group, a division of Random House, Inc., New York.

BALLANTINE and colophon are registered trademarks of Random House, Inc.

Library of Congress Cataloging-in-Publication Data

McCallum, Jack
Dream team : how Michael, Magic, Larry, Charles, and the greatest team of all time conquered the world and changed the game of basketball forever / Jack McCallum.
p.  cm.
Includes index.
ISBN 978-0-345-52048-7
eBook ISBN 978-0-345-52050-0
1. Basketball teams—United States—History.   2. Basketball Players—United States—Biography.   3. Olympic Games (25th : 1992 : Barcelona, Spain)—History.   4. Basketball—United States—History.   I. Title.
GV885.49.O43M35 2012
796.323—dc23                    2012006253

Printed in the United States of America on acid-free paper

www.ballantinebooks.com

9

Book design by Karin Batten

*To Donna, Chris, Jamie,
Jill, and Oliver
—my Dream Team*

"The older I get, the less interested I am in what's new, and the more interested I am in what endures."

—JAMES HYNES

"To live is to fly
Low and high,
So shake the dust off of your wings
And the sleep out of your eyes."

—TOWNES VAN ZANDT

"I don't know nuthin' 'bout Angola. But Angola's in trouble."

—CHARLES BARKLEY

# *1992 DREAM TEAM*

## THUMBNAIL SKETCHES

**BARKLEY, Charles, 6'4" forward;** TNT commentator whose fame has grown exponentially since retirement; boldly continues to play celebrity golf despite universally lampooned swing; leading scorer for Dream Team; known in Barcelona for rambling along Las Ramblas and elbowing an Angolan.

**BIRD, Larry, 6'9" forward;** at this writing still general manager of the Indiana Pacers but longing for golden years; limited by aching back in Barcelona that led to post-Olympics retirement; struck up unlikely Dream Team friendship with Patrick Ewing; engaged Chris Mullin in legendary H-O-R-S-E shootout.

**DREXLER, Clyde, 6'7" guard;** businessman/golfer/*Dancing with the Stars* veteran; wants to be NBA head coach; happy to have been Dream Teamer but unhappy he was added late; remembered for wearing two left shoes to practice and trying to get away with it; does not believe Michael Jordan was better than he was.

**EWING, Patrick, 7'0" center;** assistant coach with Orlando Magic and perturbed he's been unable to get interview for head coaching job;

much more popular with Dreamer teammates than with press; "Harry" half of Harry and Larry.

**JOHNSON, Earvin, 6'9" guard;** guiding force behind Magic Johnson Enterprises, having made good on long-ago vow to become big-time player in business world; sometimes irritated Dreamers with it's-my-team attitude but changed millions of attitudes worldwide about HIV and AIDS; at this writing, scheduled to be immortalized on Broadway, along with Bird, in play about their seminal importance to NBA.

**JORDAN, Michael, 6'6" guard;** chairman of the Charlotte Bobcats; trying to make it right after bad experience running Washington Wizards; serenaded aggravated Magic with "Be Like Mike" solo after legendary intrasquad scrimmage win; acknowledged by all Dreamers as team's alpha male and greatest of all-time . . . with Magic holding out just a little and Drexler holding out a lot.

**LAETTNER, Christian, 6'11" forward;** his BD Ventures, co-run with ex-Duke teammate Brian Davis, has had cash flow problems; at this writing wants to get into coaching; seems serious about changing spoiled-brat image; earned way onto Dream Team by being immortal college player.

**MALONE, Karl, 6'9" forward;** serious big-game hunter who wants back into NBA in some capacity; work ethic was inspiration to several other members of Dream Team; Jordan-Magic woof-fests at practice got under his skin.

**MULLIN, Chris, 6'6" guard/forward;** successful as ESPN commentator but might get another shot at front-office job after failure in Golden State; Barcelona sharp-shooting (.619 overall, .538 on three-pointers) affirmed selection to skeptics and Dream nod reaffirmed benefits of sobriety to him.

**PIPPEN, Scottie, 6'8" guard/forward;** has had serious money problems but, with commentating gig and reality-show wife, never far from public eye; hinted LeBron James was better than Jordan, then took it back . . . kind of; showed he belonged on Dream Team with world-class versatility.

**ROBINSON, David, 7'1" center;** runs private school in San Antonio called Carver Academy; faith-based activities govern his life; mostly outsider to other members of Dream Team but universally respected; teamed with a Marsalis for rooftop duet in Barcelona.

**STOCKTON, John, 6'1" guard;** full-time chauffeur for his family in his hometown, Spokane, and couldn't be happier; tutored star women's guard Courtney Vandersloot at alma mater Gonzaga; broken leg limited Dream Team play.

**DALY, Chuck, coach;** died of cancer in 2009; vowed never to take a time-out in Barcelona and didn't; everybody loved him, everybody misses him.

# CONTENTS

## 1 BEFORE THE DREAM

## 2 *THE DREAM UNFOLDS*

# INTRODUCTION

"You have a tape?" Michael Jordan asks. "Of that game?"

"I do," I say.

"Man, everybody asks me about that game," he says. "It was the most fun I ever had on a basketball court."

It is reflective of the enduring legend of the Dream Team, argurably the most dominant squad ever assembled in any sport, that we are referring not to a real game but to an intrasquad scrimmage that the Dreamers played in Monte Carlo before the 1992 Olympic Games. The United States engaged in fourteen games in that summer two decades gone—six in a pre-Olympic qualifying tournament and eight as they breezed to the gold medal in Barcelona—and the closest any opponent came was a fine Croatia team, which lost by 32 points in the gold medal final. The common matrices of statistical comparison, you see, are simply not relevant in the case of the Dream Team, whose members could be evaluated only when they played one another.

A video of that game is the holy grail of basketball, and the account of it is here, in Chapter 28.

A perfect storm hit Barcelona in the summer of the Dream Team. Everything came together. The team members were almost exclusively NBA veterans at or near the apex of their individual fame. The world, having been offered only bite-sized nuggets of NBA games, was waiting for them, since Barcelona was the first Olympics in which professional basketball players were allowed to compete. They were a star-spangled export for a country that still held a position of primacy around the world.

It couldn't have been scripted any better, and when the Dreamers finally released all that star power into a collective effort, the show was better than everyone thought it would be . . . and everyone had thought it would be pretty damn good. They were Johnny Cash at Folsom Prison, the Allman Brothers at Fillmore East, Santana at Woodstock. "If it would've happened today," says Larry Bird, "it would've been one of those reality shows."

The names (Michael Jordan, Magic Johnson, Larry Bird, Charles Barkley) remain familiar to fans two decades later, their cultural-relevancy quotient still quite high. It's not just that an engaging Dream Teamer who's now an A-list TV star partially inspired Danger Mouse and Cee Lo Green to christen their hip-hop duo Gnarls Barkley. Or that Magic Johnson (Red Hot Chili Peppers and Kanye West), Scottie Pippen (Jay-Z), Karl Malone (the Transplants), and Michael Jordan (impossible to count the references) have been subjects in song. Consider this: the name of John Stockton, a buttoned-down, no-nonsense point guard, is on a track in a 2011 release by Brooklyn rapper Nemo Achida, and the popular NBA 2K12 video game features Jordan, Magic, and Bird on the box cover, not contemporary players such as LeBron James, Dirk Nowitzki, and Derrick Rose.

The Dream Teamers are never far from the news, even the crime news. Not long ago a convict tattooed Jordan's Jumpman logo onto his forehead, and an accused rapist in Arkansas, in an interview after he was captured, described his run from the cops this way: "I was like Michael Jordan, man. Gone!" An armed robber asked that his sentence be increased from thirty years to thirty-three years to honor Larry Bird's number.

Yet the written record of that team and that time is not particularly large. The Dream Team, like the dinosaurs, walked the earth in the pre-social-media age. Beyond newspaper stories, there is no detailed daily log of their basketball activities ("Bird shot around today but his back is sore") and no enduring exclamations of chance meetings around Barcelona ("OMG, jst met ChazBark at bar & he KISSED me on cheek; hez not rlly fat LOL"). There is much of the story to be told in the fresh light of history.

There is little doubt that the Dream Team, like that red-haired lass you met years ago at a pub in Dublin, looks better in the soft-focus blur of nostalgia. "This is now the Dream Team of blessed memories," says NBA commissioner David Stern. "They were the guy with the piccolo and the scrappy band of revolutionaries marching off to war. They forget Charles elbowing the Angolan, Michael and the others covering up their logo, the cries of 'Why are we sending these teams? You're just trying to humiliate the other nations.' Over the years it's become beatified."

None of that is forgotten in these pages, Mr. Stern. The Dream Team was indeed forged amid conflicts athletic and bureaucratic and touched by tragedy and controversy when it returned home after an Olympics that, yes, was layered in a gauzy romanticism. All that is part of the story. The book is in fact a panoptic survey of that entire generation, in large part because the members of the Dream Team represented the central characters in the compelling drama of pro basketball from the mid-1980s to the early 1990s, a golden age for the NBA that ended when the fairy-tale world of the Dream Team itself ended in August 1992.

The narrative unfolds in roughly (emphasis on *roughly*) chronological fashion. It struck me as crucial to give definition to the players before they were Dream Teamers—Michael Jordan as the young hero of the 1984 Olympics, Scottie Pippen as the neophyte struggling to play alongside his infinitely more famous Chicago Bulls teammate, Charles Barkley as the unbridled wild child, and, of course, the 1980s rivalry of Magic Johnson and Larry Bird.

Then, too, the selection process—how the team came together—is in some ways more riveting than the games themselves. It was political theater, a kind of convention without the pom-poms, a process in which backstabbing and rivalries current and ancient all played a part.

But it was also important to provide glimpses of the players as they are now, some in their hometowns (Phoenix, Houston, San Antonio, Spokane), some in their places of business (Charlotte and Orlando). These are defined as "interludes." So there are stops and starts to the narrative, which emerges as more like a Magic yo-yo dribble than a Barkley straight-ahead, bowl-over-any-obstacle dash to the hoop.

Like all of us, in later life they have found failure, some as husbands or fathers, others as coaches, general managers, or businessmen. But from a basketball perspective they approached perfection. They are history writ large, the greatest team of all time by such a wide margin, says Dallas Mavericks general manager Donnie Nelson, who coached against them in the Olympics, "that I can't even think of who's in second place."

The best barometer of what this team meant to history is limned by the words of one of its most prominent members, a man who won five NBA championships, three MVP awards, one NCAA title, and an untold number of popularity contests.

"For me, the Dream Team is number one of anything I've done in basketball," says Magic Johnson, "because there will never be another team like it. There can't be."

· · · · · · · · · · · · · · · · · · · · · · · · · · · · ·

# THE DREAM TEAM GETS A NAME

*Barcelona, 1992*

I knew it was a bad idea from the beginning. I swear I did. But David Dupree, my friend and colleague from *USA Today*, kept pushing it.

"We've covered the Dream Team from the beginning," said David. "We should get our picture taken with them. It's no big deal. It'll be something to look back on."

Taking a photo with famous athletes seemed like the last thing David would suggest, but such was the overheated temperature of the times, when the phrase "Dream Team" was on the lips of everyone in the world, not just the sports world; when helicopters dotted the bleached Spanish sky like fireflies to protect the millionaire players; when snipers sat on the roof of their hotel in Barcelona to take down potential assassins wanting to enter the history books; when adoring fans congregated around the clock just to catch a fleeting glimpse of the twelve Americans who were in the process of storming to the gold medal and rewriting basketball history.

"I'll run it by Magic," said Karl Malone when we asked the Mailman about the photo. Karl, David, and I were having dinner in Barcelona. The other diners were staring at us. Staring at Malone, actually. I had gotten a restaurant recommendation from a friend—this was before the days of go-on-the-Internet-and-check-out-Zagat—and it was a bad choice. They brought out quail eggs for an appetizer.

"Man, I don't eat this shit," said Malone, a country boy from Louisiana who never hesitated to remind you of that fact.

"I don't, either," I protested. "Do I look like a quail egg guy?"

"I don't know *what* you white people eat," Malone said, winking at Dupree, also an African American.

When we finished, Karl promised to check on the photo op and get back to us. "We clear that stuff with Magic," said Malone. "He's the captain."

There was no better indication that the Dream Team had become one big happy family than Malone's unquestioned acceptance of Magic as ceremonial captain. Malone had never been a huge Magic fan, and just a few months later the Mailman would openly question whether Magic should be allowed to play in the NBA given the fact that Johnson had the AIDS virus. Then, too, there had been several times during that glorious summer of 1992 when Malone had tired of the relentless chatter of Magic, the go-to spokesman, a man who, as Scottie Pippen puts it, "always needs the microphone." And Malone wasn't the only one.

The days went by, the United States rolled up easy win after easy win, Barcelona and the world beyond continued to watch in slack-jawed awe, and the team continued to bathe in this heady marinade of adulation, testosterone, and 40-point victories. We heard nothing about the photo op until about a half hour before the Dream Team was to play the gold medal game against Croatia on August 8.

*"Now?"* I asked Brian McIntyre, the congenial and consistently competent head of NBA public relations. "Christ, they're going for the gold medal!" But Brian escorted David and me behind the

members-only ropes that led to the most famous locker room in the world just as the Dream Team was emerging to take the floor.

*"Let's go! Let's get it done! Let's take it to 'em!"*

I couldn't separate the voices, but there was much clamor and clapping; it suggested Croatia was about to enter a world of pain, which it subsequently did. Suddenly Magic halted the procession so that—I'm mortified even as I write this—Dupree and I could be photographed with the team. It was as if a band of brothers on the way to battle had been halted to share hors d'oeuvres with Anderson Cooper. There were several expressions of what-the-hell-are-we-doing? confusion, but the team stopped, Dupree and I slipped into the front row, and NBA photographer Andy Bernstein prepared to take the least compelling photo of his illustrious career.

And as we posed—my groin tight, flop sweat soaking my brow, praying that this moment would soon be over—I heard a voice from the back row, one with a distinctive Hoosier twang.

"Hey, Jack," drawled Larry Bird, "later on, you wanna blow us?"


If you'll permit a metaphorical extension of Bird's transitive verb—and who among you would not?—this was the most fellated gang of warriors since the Spartan army. As the members of the Dream Team, one by one, had accepted invitations to become the first NBA players to participate in the Olympic Games, they understood that they were signing on to something special. But from the first moment they came together to practice, in San Diego on June 21, 1992, they had been the central players in an unprecedented spectacle, an adoring public and almost-as-adoring media bestowing upon them attention that can only be described as pornographic. It's become so commonplace to describe them as rock stars that I won't even do it, although I guess I just did. They were Jagger mugging in an open limo, Princess Di flashing her come-hither smile at an Elton John concert, Liz Taylor air-kissing Michael Jackson at an AIDS benefit. By the time the Dream Team landed in Barcelona, thousands having gathered just to watch their plane touch down in twilight at El Prat de Llobregat Aeropuerto, they knew that they were on a march into immortality, not a footnote to sports history but an entire chapter.

An accident of timing—that most blessed breeder of success—put me in the middle of all this. From 1981 to 1985, I had been at *Sports Illustrated* as a kind of relief pitcher—long man more than closer—as the second, third, or even fourth backup on pro and college football, pro and college basketball, boxing, baseball, and track and field. In the winter of 1982 I wrote eight stories on eight different sports in eight weeks, including the World Championship of Squash, held in New York City at the Yale Club, to which I was denied access until I had purchased a sport coat and tie.

I am not suggesting that this equates to, say, walking through rice paddies and swiping leeches off your body to cover the Vietnam War, as the late David Halberstam, who became an NBA chronicler at a plane considerably elevated from my own, once did. It's merely to say that I needed a stable home, and in the fall of 1985 I got one when managing editor Mark Mulvoy put me as the number one man on the NBA beat.

It is the dirty little secret of journalism (maybe it's not such a secret) that you're only as good as your material, and man, I parachuted into a valley of material so rich and fertile that only the worst kind of hack could've screwed it up. Under Mulvoy, *Sports Illustrated* was largely a front-runners' magazine—that is, we wrote about winners and put winners on the cover. In the years before Barcelona, I wrote dozens and dozens of stories about these men, who were—as we realized even at the time—creating a kind of Golden Age of pro hoops.

Along the way I was accused by readers and friends of variously favoring Jordan and the Bulls, Bird and the Celtics, and Magic and the Lakers. (Years later, after he had become a general manager in Indiana, Bird would usually greet me with, "You blown Magic lately?" The man does like that verb.) I thought I did an adequate job of covering the beat honestly, tossing out criticisms along with encomiums. To varying degrees, stories I wrote in the 1980s and early 1990s angered Jordan, Barkley, Drexler, and Ewing, but part of what made this the golden age from a journalist's perspective was that these guys understood the implicit contract between athlete and writer, that it was not a crime against humanity when someone wrote something bad about them, that journalism was not to be confused with hagiography, even if they didn't know what hagiography is.

"It's a system of checks and balances," as someone described the relationship between athletes and the press to me not long ago. That was Michael Jordan.

I feel fortunate to have come along when I did, and I apologize in advance for making myself a small part of this story. "You can't help it," one editor told me. "You were along for the ride." I was a minor-league Cameron Crowe, *almost* almost famous, "walking in the shadow of a dream," as did Mr. Dimmesdale, Nathaniel Hawthorne's tortured minister in *The Scarlet Letter*.

I even had something to do with the nomenclature and explosion of the Dream Team phenomenon. In February 1991, well after the announcement that pros would be allowed into the Olympics but well before any player had publicly committed, I wrote a *Sports Illustrated* cover story projecting what the team could be and naming my choices for starters: Jordan, Magic, Ewing, Barkley, and Malone. I thought that they were the five best players in the game at that time. I would've had the thirty-five-year-old Bird on my starting team—though he hadn't made an All-Star team since 1988, it wouldn't have been a totally ceremonial choice, because the man could still play—but he had already made noises that his back was too creaky and he probably would not go to Barcelona. I took him at his word.

We gathered those five together at the 1991 All-Star Game in Charlotte for a photo that had taken months to set up, clearing the time with the players, their agents, and the NBA. I had been such a pain in the ass about it with the players that when Magic entered the room where the photo was to be taken, he looked at me and said, with some exasperation, "Okay, you happy now?"

With more prescience, I should've seen on that day what the U.S. Olympic team would become. Despite the fact that the shoot took place in a secured area, hundreds of onlookers pressed in when they caught glimpses of the players. They pushed against the door and tried to find a rear entrance to the room, hoping for just a glance at their heroes. It's beyond obvious that any individual fame the players had, which was considerable, had increased exponentially by their being together. (And in Barcelona it would increase exponentially *exponentially*.) But all I remember thinking was, "Hmm, now this is interesting."

The opening to my story in the following week's magazine read:

It's a red, white and blue dream: the five players who grace this week's cover playing together, determined to restore America's lost basketball dignity, in the 1992 Olympic Games in Barcelona. What's the chance of this dream coming true? Not bad. Not bad at all.

The cover photo was accompanied by the tagline "Dream Team," right up by the *Sports Illustrated* logo.

So there it was for the first time: Dream Team.

Years later, I was credited with coming up with that magical appellation, but I always tried to set the record straight: Yes, I had used the word *dream* twice, but an editor had put *dream* and *team* together on the cover. I even tried to find out exactly who had come up with it at the office but couldn't do it. *SI* cover lines are written democratically, by trial and error. Chances are there had been multiple possibilities: "Golden Dream!" "Red, White, Blue and Ready!" "Look Out, World!"

But Dream Team it was, and Dream Team stuck. To this day Barkley believes he was one of the first five players chosen by the committee because he was on the cover. (Trust me, he wasn't among the first five to be picked.) "Once in a while, something just clicks, and that was the case here," says Rick Welts, now the president and COO of the Golden State Warriors but then the NBA's resident marketing genius. "After that cover, the idea of 'Dream Team' really took off."

I'm proud of two things in my career: that the "This Week's Sign of the Apocalypse" that still runs in the Scorecard section of *SI* was my idea, and that I had something to do with coining the phrase "Dream Team." NBA commissioner David Stern said to me recently: "The fact that all of this took off was a delicious accident. We didn't even name it. Maybe, God forbid, you did."

In my office at home, I have only a few photos chronicling my years covering the NBA. The photo of Dupree and me with the Dream Team is clipped to a bulletin board, barely visible, a nearly capsized vessel floating in a sea of family photos. I never had it blown up. You can tell it's an afterthought photo, the kind in which everyone poses for a second or two, then keeps going. Christian Laettner gazes to one side, not even bothering to look at the photographer, and John Stockton is not in the frame at all; my guess is, he just continued onto the floor. I'm in the front row, partially obscuring Bird's face.

Though not, alas, his commentary.

# DREAM
# TEAM

# 1

**BEFORE THE DREAM**

CHAPTER 1

# THE INSPECTOR OF MEAT

· · · · · · · · · · · · · · · · · · · · · · · · · · · · · · · · · · · · · · · · · · ·

**Pros in the Olympics? It Was His Idea,
and Don't Let Anyone Tell You Different**

He first came to the United States in January 1974, dispatched by
his boss to study up on American basketball. He didn't speak the
language, didn't know the customs, and settled into the basketball
hotbed of Billings, Montana, because that's where he could secure
free lodging with a Yugoslavian family.

   This stranger in a strange land was named Boris Stankovic. He
was six months from his forty-ninth birthday and he had come on
behalf of FIBA. At the time not more than a dozen Americans knew
what it stood for (Fédération Internationale de Basketball), where it
was headquartered (at the time in an apartment in Munich, later in
Geneva), and what the hell it did (governed amateur basketball in
all parts of the world except the United States). "You cannot know
basketball if you do not know basketball in the United States,"
Stankovic was told by R. William Jones, who as secretary-general
ran FIBA with a bow tie, a lit cigar, and a dictator's fist. So Stankovic
came and was instantly seduced by the college games he saw

live—UCLA's redheaded phenomenon, Bill Walton, was his favorite player—and the NBA games he saw on television.

For much of his early adult life, Stankovic had been a meat inspector in Belgrade. "My job was to look over the meat and cheese and, as you do here, put a stamp on it," said Stankovic when I interviewed him in Istanbul in the summer of 2010. He is retired now but comes to many events as the éminence grise of international basketball. Stankovic had earned a degree in veterinary medicine in 1945 from the University of Belgrade. "It was natural in our country that veterinarians looked after the meat and cheese, because it has to do with animals, no?"

The type of meat Stankovic most liked to inspect, though, was the cured leather on a basketball. Even as he was arising at five in the morning to take up his meat stamp and lace up his white apron, basketball is what moved his spirit. He was an earthbound, fundamentally sound low-post forward who played thirty-six games for the Yugoslavian national team. One of his proudest moments was playing for his country in the first world championship organized by FIBA, which took place in Argentina in 1950. "We finished ninth," says Stankovic, chuckling, "and there were nine teams." One of his enduring regrets was that he never participated in the Olympics as a player.

The Yugoslavs were a tall, tough, and lean people, hardened by wars civil and foreign. In the Balkan area of Yugoslavia where Stankovic was born, the people measure eras not by "war and peace" but by "war and non-war." When Boris was nineteen, he and his father, Vassilje, a lawyer who fought for Serbian nationalism, were imprisoned by an invading Russian army. After two months Boris was released, but Vassilje was executed by firing squad and buried in a common grave; even today, Stankovic does not know where. Stankovic was put on a blacklist that later kept him from becoming a medical doctor, his desired profession, and forced him to veterinary school, his way of staying in the field of medicine. Like most of his countrymen from that generation, he identified with the Serbian rebels who had squirmed under foreign rule for five centuries. "They lived in groups and learned to cooperate, to work with each other," Stankovic said. "We grew up with that in our blood. We Serbians have never had much success in the individual sports, but our team sports are very, very strong. We have a proficiency in and an aptitude for sports that require a lot of teamwork."

Stankovic's knowledge of the game and overall intelligence—virtually anyone who talks about him invariably mentions his brains—enabled him to rise steadily as a coach and executive. By the time he was thirty he was the most important nonplayer in Yugoslavian basketball, even as he continued to inspect meat, and had already become active in FIBA.

In 1966 Oransoda Cantù, a team in the Italian professional league, came calling in search of a coach, and Stankovic left his homeland. "I went for the money," says Stankovic. "Italy was the richest league." He was reviled by many Italians as an outsider but later grew to be loved, as winners usually are, when his team captured the championship in 1968. That's when R. William Jones beckoned him back. Jones had seen the future of FIBA, and its name was Boris Stankovic.


Jones, who died in 1981, months after suffering a stroke during a dinner at the 1980 Moscow Olympics, was the kind of man for whom the term "grudging admiration" seems to have been invented. Born in Rome to a British father and French mother, he had earned a degree from Springfield College, where Dr. James Naismith hung up his first peach basket. Jones was "a very international guy" (Stankovic's words), a combination that made him an undeniable basketball visionary. But he was also the classic amateur-sport pasha, imperious and intractable. For basketball people in the United States, Jones left his enduring imprimatur by allowing the Soviets three chances to win the gold medal against the U.S. team on September 9, 1972, at the star-crossed Olympic Games in Munich.

Stankovic was a long way from being an established leader when he first came to the United States on that intelligence-gathering trip in 1974. He was just an outsider trying to learn the nuances of American basketball while also trying to learn how to order a hamburger. He was granted a papal audience with John Wooden—"We talked basketball, so it was easy to communicate," he says—but mostly he was left on his own, to watch, listen, and compare.

And what happened was that a basketball junkie was transfixed by the American players, college and pro. "It just seemed to be a different game," says Stankovic, smiling at the memory. "Faster but also fundamentally sound. You watched a guy like Bill Walton for one minute and you could see that his level was so much higher than anyone we had in Europe."

FIBA's rules at the time banned professionals from playing under the FIBA banner, and the rules of FIBA were the rules of Olympic basketball. So it was, so it had always been, and so, everyone thought, it would always be. The hypocrisy, of course, was that de facto professionals were playing anyway, since international basketball teams always comprised their country's top players, even if they were officially listed as "soldiers" or "policemen."

With the lone exception of Stankovic, there was no push to include American pros in the Olympics, since the supremacy of even American collegians was considered self-evident, the anomaly of 1972 notwithstanding. Plus, it was simply part of our sporting ethos that the Olympics were for our college players. The NBA and the Olympics were planets rotating in different solar systems.

But the Inspector of Meat, an outsider, didn't see it that way. As he watched the pro stars of the 1970s on TV—among them Oscar Robertson and Jerry West, plus his two favorites, Walt Frazier and Pete Maravich—it began to gnaw at him that America's best players would never participate in the Olympic Games. "The hypocrisy was what got to me," said Stankovic. "And there was a practical side. My concern was trying to make the game of basketball strong, to grow it, and yet there was this separation. It became impossible for me to tolerate."

There might've been a self-serving side, too. Stankovic saw himself as the messiah of hoops, the person to lift the game above King Futbol. And he was irritated by the fact that his organization—the We-Have-the-Final-Say Court of All Appeals for world basketball—came with an asterisk because it wasn't even a blip on the NBA's radar screen.

Whatever the variety of reasons, Stankovic came back to Munich and told Jones that dropping the amateurs-only clause, thus clearing the way for America's best players to compete in the Olympics, should be a FIBA goal—a truly anarchic idea, given the sociopolitical sports climate. The times might've been a-changin', but not in the International Olympic Committee (IOC), where Avery Brundage—a loathsome individual, a clear number one on the list of tin-pot despots who have run sports over the centuries—held fast to the concept of shamateurism.

Stankovic isn't sure what Jones really thought of his idea, but his boss's instruction was crystal clear. "He said, 'Don't bother,'" remembers Stankovic. "Or, as you say in America, 'Don't go there.'"

And for the next decade and a half, no one except Boris Stankovic went there.

Like many influential men and women throughout history, the Inspector of Meat is overlooked. He has never met Magic Johnson or Larry Bird, and the only time he has crossed paths with Michael Jordan was in the 1984 Olympics, in the pre–Dream Team days.

But whatever revisionist history might eventually be written, remember this: the Dream Team resulted from the vision of Boris Stankovic. It was not a secret plot hatched by David Stern to "grow the game," one of the commissioner's favorite phrases. It was not the result of a crusade by the NBA's marketing demons to sell $200 Authentics in Europe, even though that was an eventuality. It was not frustration built up by the increasing reality that inroads were being made on the United States' claim of basketball supremacy. The idea germinated in the mind of the Inspector of Meat from Belgrade.

# CHAPTER 2

# THE CHOSEN ONE

. . . . . . . . . . . . . . . . . . . . . . . . . . . . . . . . . . . . . . . . . . . . . . .

### Sneaker Porn Is Born

It was some rare time away from Bob Knight, their dictatorial Olympic coach, and two candidates for the 1984 U.S. team, Michael Jordan and Patrick Ewing, were taking advantage of it by horsing around in their dorm room. Wild in-room wrestling matches were a major diversion for the collegians, particularly Charles Barkley and Chuck Person, two Auburn teammates who went at it pretty hard before they ended up on Knight's very roomy chopping block.

Jordan, who had just completed his junior year at North Carolina, was heading for the NBA, while Ewing would be going back to complete his senior year at Georgetown. They were already good friends, having first met at high school all-star games and, more eventfully, in the 1982 NCAA final. It was there that a jump shot by North Carolina freshman Jordan led the Tar Heels to a 63–62 victory over freshman Ewing and his Georgetown Hoyas. Though no one realized the significance of it at the time, Ewing became the first of many great players to be stopped short of the finish line by Jordan.

The 6'6" Jordan had the 7'0" Ewing in a headlock. Neither young man was angry, but that didn't mean it wasn't semiserious: to Jordan, everything of a competitive nature had some degree of seriousness. Finally Ewing said uncle, and when the big center awoke the next morning, he couldn't move his neck.

Man, was *this* going to be a tough conversation.

"Coach, I can't practice this morning," Ewing told Knight after screwing up his courage.

"What happened?" said Knight, and Ewing was forced to tell the whole story, giving up Jordan as the culprit.

"So I sat out, and man, Coach Knight was *mad*," Ewing remembers years later. "But only at me. Michael? Nothing happened to him. Nothing *ever* happened to Michael."

Yes, the summer of 1984 was a glorious one for Michael Jordan, the first of many, despite the fact that he had been initially resistant to the idea of competing in Los Angeles. "I was a little intimidated by Coach Knight," Jordan told me in the summer of 2011. "I didn't like his tactics, heard he ragged players, swore at them, and I didn't want to spend the summer being berated by someone." So he sought the counsel of his coach, Dean Smith, with whom he had a kind of father-son relationship, although Jordan's own father, James, was a strong influence in his life.

"Coach Smith told me that all Knight wants to see is the fundamentals of the game of basketball," Jordan said. (Even in casual conversation Jordan uses the phrase "the game of basketball" almost as if he's describing holy writ.) "I had those fundamentals, so there shouldn't be a problem. And once I got there I just saw a man who demanded you play the game a certain way and don't make the same mistake twice. I didn't."

The summer was glorious, too, for the men who ran amateur basketball in the United States. The Olympic boycott of 1980, which had so soured them against President Jimmy Carter, was a distant memory. A solid team full of eager collegians—anchored by Jordan,

whose singular skills, if not known worldwide, were certainly recognized in the United States, where he had just finished a gilded
college career—was about to storm to the gold medal in Los Angeles. When the Soviets returned the 1980 favor by boycotting the
L.A. Games, it seemed not to matter all that much. The U.S. collegians would've beaten that group anyway, or so went the thinking.

Knight was right out of the amateur hoops handbook, a tyrant
of the first order but one of *them*, a dedicated (if sometimes out of
control) disciple of ABAUSA, the group that ran amateur hoops at
the time. "With Bobby in charge," says C. M. Newton, one of his assistants, "there was no hoopla. It was straight down the path."

Knight made the Olympic trials a Darwinian exercise from start
to finish. More than a hundred players were invited, and they got
cut twenty at a time. Karl Malone, a muscular but largely unknown
player from Louisiana Tech, remembers that the early cuts had an
impersonal feel. "You went through the lunch line in this big cafete-
ria, where they had a big bulletin board," remembers Malone. "If
your name was on the board, you were in." One day Malone's name
wasn't on the board. Eventually that freak of nature named Charles
Barkley was cut. So was a guard named John Stockton.

There was a segment of the basketball population that didn't
completely buy into Jordan when he was at North Carolina, where,
as common logic had it, the only one who could stop him was Smith,
a rigid fundamentalist whose teams often held the ball. Anyone
with one working eye and a semifunctional cortex knew that Jordan was going to be spectacular in the pros, but one supposition
was that he would be a Clyde Drexler type, referencing the University of Houston product who had just finished his first season with
the Portland Trail Blazers—that is, flashy but sometimes out of
control, a scorer but not a shooter, a fan favorite but not a coach's
choice.

Though that impression would endure in some quarters until
1991, the year Jordan won his first championship with the Chicago
Bulls, the basketball cognoscenti watching the L.A. Games saw
what it really had in Jordan. He was a player who could break a

zone with a jumper, lock down a high-scoring opponent, run the offense from the point if he had to. He could *please Bobby Knight*, for God's sake. "The 1984 Olympics," says David Falk, his agent, "was Michael's coming-out party."

Behind Jordan, the United States tore through the Olympic competition, winning its eight games by an average of 30 points and in the process drawing comparisons to the great Oscar Robertson–Jerry West team of 1960 that won gold in Rome. The United States beat Canada 78–59 in the semifinals and destroyed Spain 96–65 in the gold medal game, and the name Michael was on the lips of basketball fans everywhere.

It had become evident that Jordan was the Chosen One, and no one knew that better than Falk, who had already commenced endorsement negotiations with Nike that would forever change the way athletes are marketed. Jordan had always worn Converse, the sneaker of choice for both his college coach and the United States Olympic Committee, and the de facto historical choice of most hoopsters. Michael has since said that he, like many players, believed that Adidas made the best product. Had he gotten a decent offer, Jordan probably would've signed with either Converse or Adidas.

But Falk saw Nike as hungrier and more market-savvy than either of them. Both Magic Johnson and Larry Bird, the two biggest names in the pro game, wore Converse, but the company, coasting on its past rep, did almost nothing with them. Think about it: Magic had an immortal nickname, a thousand-kilowatt smile, a flashy game, a glitzy home base, and a championship resumé, yet in the early years of his career Converse didn't come close to capitalizing on his appeal, a decision that cost both Magic and the company millions. "Way before Michael came into the league," says Falk, "Magic could've owned the world."

At Nike, by contrast, executives such as Rob Strasser saw in Jordan a new horizon for the endorsement game. Plus, Nike needed to make a major move since the running boom of the 1970s had petered out. It was a company that prided itself on taking chances, so it had decided to blow its entire marketing budget, $500,000, on advertising that would feature Jordan, plus what it would have to pay him to wear the sneakers. Still, Jordan was resistant to Nike, which he had never worn and knew very little about. The night before he, his father, and Falk were to fly to Nike headquarters in Beaverton, Oregon, Jordan told his mom that he wasn't going. But she wouldn't hear of it.

"You will be on that plane, Michael," said Deloris Jordan. So he was on the plane.

At that first meeting, Peter Moore, Nike's head designer, showed Jordan and Falk the sketches he had made of Air Jordan shoes, warm-up suits, and apparel, all of it in black and red—"devil's colors," as Jordan told Falk. Jordan never blinked, never smiled, never said much of anything, and everybody in the room figured that he was underwhelmed. But after the meeting he admitted that he was swayed, and Falk negotiated a five-year $2.5 million deal that, like so many deals over the years, was supposed to bring the world to an end.

So was born Air Jordan.

At first Jordan hated the red-and-black shoe. "I'll look like a clown," he said. But he relented and wore them, after which the NBA ruled them illegal for some bizarre reason, fining Jordan $5,000 per game, a sum that Nike paid with a secret smile. A design compromise was eventually reached, and the major thing the fines had accomplished was to turn Jordan's shoes into one of the biggest stories of the 1984–85 season and gather worldwide attention for Nike.

Rod Thorn, the Bulls' general manager at the time, asked Falk, "What are you trying to do? Turn him into a tennis player?"

"Now you get it," said the agent.

# CHAPTER 3

# THE COMMISSIONER AND THE INSPECTOR OF MEAT

. . . . . . . . . . . . . . . . . . . . . . . . . . . . . . . . . . . . . . . . . . . . . .

## The NBA Sticks a Tentative Toe into International Waters

Late in 1985 David Stern and Russ Granik, commissioner and deputy commissioner of the NBA, received the Inspector of Meat in the league's New York offices. The FIBA boss could hardly believe his good fortune. "You have to understand where I came from," Stankovic told me recently, reflecting back on the meeting. "It was considered almost criminal just to communicate with the pro league. The amateur way was that we were not supposed to speak to them. And here I am sitting with the commissioner and we have a normal relationship." He was positively beaming at the memory, sounding like Sally Field receiving her Best Actress award at the 1984 Oscars: *You like me!*

Stern did like him. Both men are attracted to power the way moths are to light, but there is a similar air of informality about them, too. They're not exactly regular guys, but they're smart enough to know that they should *act* like regular guys. And

Granik—cool, careful, collected, a lawyer who had started at the NBA in 1976—was the perfect complement to Stern, who could be quick-tempered, even volcanic.

After a few get-acquainted moments, Stankovic went right to the point. "I don't believe in these restrictions about who should play and who shouldn't," he said. "The best players in the world should be playing in everything, including the Olympics. But I can't do that alone."

In some revisionist histories, Stern—all-seeing, all-knowing—instantly grasped the importance of aligning with FIBA, envisioning a day when NBA players were the toast of the Continent and the league was flooding Europe and Asia with sneakers, T-shirts, and hoodies. Nothing could be further from the truth, and Stern, to his credit, has never claimed otherwise. It wasn't that the idea of NBA players in the Olympics slipped onto the NBA's back burner; it wasn't even on the stove. Yes, Stern saw the hypocrisy in the rules against competition—Germany's Detlef Schrempf, who played in the NBA for about $500,000 a year, was considered a professional, while Brazil's Oscar Schmidt, who played in Italy for about $1 million a year, was considered an amateur and eligible for Olympic play. Everyone saw the hypocrisy except the empty suits who ran the Olympics. But the commissioner couldn't imagine adding the Olympics to an already full plate.

"David and I thought that global basketball came with as many burdens as benefits," says Granik today, "and that's what we told Boris."

However, when Stankovic suggested a competition that would include an NBA team and a couple of FIBA teams, a kind of first step, Stern said yes. "We'll host it," he said immediately. It was out of that meeting that the first McDonald's Open, which was eventually held in Milwaukee in 1987, was born. But it was never Stern's plan to get his players into the Olympics, in large part because he faced far more pressing issues.

The tide was beginning to turn by the time of Stankovic's visit, but the NBA was still on relatively shaky ground. The popular how-bad-was-the-NBA? nugget to offer is the 1980 NBA Finals, which was on tape delay even though it pitted the Los Angeles Lakers (rookie Magic Johnson, superstar Kareem Abdul-Jabbar) against the Philadelphia 76ers (Julius Erving). But there are other ways to measure the NBA's low-water marks. When Rick Welts was hired in 1982 to head up sponsorship—"Like all of David's guys back then, I was perfect for the job because I was young, dumb, and poor," Welts says today—the NBA literally had no business plan. It sold nothing to no one. Welts and the other young, dumb, and poor soldiers found a nation that not only didn't care about the NBA but downright loathed it.

"The perception was that the NBA was mismanaged, too many African Americans, too many drug accusations, too many teams going out of business," Welts told me in 2011. "I'd call advertising agencies, and to get a return call was remarkable if you had NBA attached to your name. The priority was NFL, Major League Baseball, and college sports. The NHL would get the calls before they'd even think of investing in the NBA."

As his young band of committed warriors tried to chip away at the NBA's image, it was always Stern cajoling, conniving, caterwauling. "The power of everybody saying the same thing over and over again is pretty significant," says Welts. "I'd come home beaten and battered after twelve hours of rejection, and the phone would ring in my room at the Summit Hotel on Lexington Avenue at ten o'clock. It would be David, and after fifteen minutes I'd be charged up and ready to go again."

Stern is so commonly called the best sports commissioner ever that he has all but retired the term, but there was certainly a bit of serendipity in his rise. It was under his watch, after all, that Michael/Magic/Larry descended from the heavens, and at the end of the day, the only thing a marketing man can do is shine a brighter light on the stage. If the people don't like what they see, nothing is going to happen. But Stern and others in his office figured out how to maximize the appeal of these players and leverage their popularity.

And while he didn't see the full road ahead of him, the commissioner always kept an ear open to the sermons by the Inspector of Meat, who thought that great things would happen if the United States was able to put its stars together, bundle them up in red, white, and blue packaging, and send them off to play under a sacred set of rings.

# CHAPTER 4

# THE LEGEND

· · · · · · · · · · · · · · · · · · · · · · · · · · · · · · · · · · · · · · · · · ·

### "I'm the Three-Point King"

Larry Bird stood on the floor of Reunion Arena in Dallas on the morning of February 8, 1986, where eight hours later he would compete in the NBA's first three-point shooting contest during All-Star Weekend. Standing nearby was Leon Wood of the New Jersey Nets, who is now an NBA referee but who was then one of the favorites in the competition.

"Hey, Leon," Bird said, "you changed your shot lately? It looks different."

That was nonsense, of course. But Wood, a second-year player known for his three-point range—he wasn't shy about attempting shots from a couple of feet behind the three-point line—looked stricken. *Man, if Larry Bird says my shot has changed, I wonder if . . .*

Then Bird started talking about the red-white-and-blue balls, the ones that would be worth two points (instead of one) at each of the five racks of five balls that were set up for the competition. Bird said they felt slippery. Wood looked stricken again.

Scratch Leon Wood from the list of potential winners. The others would come later.

At this point in time—midseason, 1986—Larry Joe Bird was the undisputed king of the NBA. He was on his way to his third straight Most Valuable Player award, and his Boston Celtics were on their way to the NBA title. But it went beyond that. It was Bird's bravado, his utter belief in himself, his trash talk (legendary around the league, if largely unknown to the general public, since Bird did it subtly), the street game that came wrapped in a pasty package that made the early-to-mid-1980s *his* game, *his* time.

Bird's package of skills—shooting, rebounding, passing, court savvy, competitiveness—had been there since his rookie season, 1979–80. We tend to think of him as the ultimate workaholic, endlessly polishing a shooting stroke that he had fabricated back in his high school days, and to an extent he was. But he was also a natural, someone to whom, as he always admitted, the game came easily. He just *saw* it differently from most everybody else.

Bird well knew that at age twenty-nine and seven years into his Hall of Fame career, there was nobody like him. And that was even taking into account his creaky back, which he first injured in the summer of 1985 when he was shoveling gravel at the home he had built for his mother in his native French Lick, Indiana. Even early in that marvelous 1985–86 season, Bird had sometimes needed the magic hands of his physiotherapist, Dan Dyrek, just to get out of a prone position. A month into the season Dyrek had been called to Bird's suburban Boston home and couldn't believe that the star was in that much pain. But the back gradually improved—it would never really get better—and Bird was on his way to another transcendent year.

Shortly after All-Star Weekend, *SI* sent me to write a story about whether Bird was, in fact, the greatest player ever. Magazines love these greatest-ever stories—men, in particular, are inveterate list makers, adept at wasting hour after hour in fervent arguments about whether Keith Moon or John Bonham was the greater drummer or whether *Taxi Driver* or *Raging Bull* was the greater De Niro vehicle—and, predictably, I got into the spirit and pretty much decided that Bird was the greatest ever, backed up by several quotes from unbiased observers, one being John Wooden. "I've always considered Oscar Robertson to be the best player in the game," the Wizard of Westwood told me. "Now I'm not so sure that Larry Bird isn't."

(Never mind that the following season I would find a different all-time best, Magic, and a couple of years after that another, Jordan. That's how it goes in the list-making business; you have to have a short memory.)

I recall several things from that Bird story, beyond him telling me that *Bonanza* was his favorite TV show. Chuck Daly, later his Dream Team coach, told me that Bird deliberately "once knocked me ass over tin cups" after he drilled a jumper in front of the Detroit Pistons bench. Celtics teammate Danny Ainge told me that Bird was so good that from time to time he deliberately dribbled into trouble just to increase the degree of difficulty on the play, something that Bird confirmed. (Years later Kobe Bryant would be crucified when Phil Jackson claimed that Kobe did the same thing.) Bill Walton related a night when Bird dribbled into the corner, drew a triple-team, then zipped him a pass that traveled through Joe Barry Carroll's legs.

Bird was also not shy about professing his proficiency at other sports, something that always fascinates me about pro athletes. (Jordan always mused about how well he could've done not only in baseball, a question to which we later got an answer, but also at sports such as track and football.) Bird told me, in all seriousness, that he was as adept at backyard badminton as he was at basketball. He also said that he wasn't "weight-room strong but cock-strong," a farmer's expression that has nothing to do with the penis. And he loved to brag about his softball skills (a sport he enjoyed playing with his brothers for Terre Haute's Platolene 500–Carpet Center team) as a power hitter and first baseman/outfielder. Bird had shattered a knuckle in a softball injury he had suffered years later and always claimed he couldn't feel the basketball as well after that. I never knew whether to believe that.

I was particularly intrigued by Bird's ambidexterity, which went well beyond his ability to dribble with his left hand. Bird looked utterly comfortable shooting left-handed, as he did from time to time, and he both ate and signed autographs with his left. He just grew up that way. He says that he always picked up a pencil and wrote with his left, yet when a teacher sent him to the blackboard to write he used his right hand.

There was about Bird the mystique of a street hustler, always with something up his sleeve, always some kind of trump-card chicanery at the ready. Quinn Buckner, a former Bird teammate who would later be on the committee that would select the Dream Team, tells of Bird's wizardry during a practice shooting game called Knockout. "You'd be ready to win, and all of a sudden—I'm not making this up—Larry would throw up a shot that would not only knock your ball away from the basket but would also *go in itself*," says Buckner. "The man could play pool and basketball at the same time."

Buckner conjures up a moment during a game when he was streaking downcourt and Bird wound up to throw him a long pass despite the fact that a defender was directly in the line between them. "So Larry throws this thing that starts way out to the left, veers around the defender, and curves *right into my hands*," Buckner says. "Nobody in history—nobody—threw those kinds of passes."

That Bird had even agreed to compete in this 1986 three-point contest was a triumph for the NBA because no one was quite sure how that particular sideshow was going to turn out. But Bird had signed on for a few reasons. It appealed to the gunslinger aspect of his game—he loved the pre- and post-practice shooting games in which he engaged with teammates Ainge and Jerry Sichting. He loved the idea that, as talk about the three-point contest heated up, he was not necessarily considered the favorite since players such as Craig Hodges, Dale Ellis, and Wood were long-distance specialists. With a game on the line, Bird was everybody's choice, of course, but that was not necessarily the case in an exhibition, where his relatively slow delivery would be a liability. Bird wanted to show that such an analysis was flawed.

And so, a few minutes before the competition in Dallas was to begin and seven of the eight players who would be participating in the three-point contest were gathered in a locker room, suddenly the door burst open and in strode Bird, asking, "Who's comin' in second?" Then he reiterated his feelings about the slippery red-white-and-blue balls.

It was pretty much over at that point. Bird didn't even remove his warm-up jacket for the first two rounds—he always insisted that it was not a fuck-you move but just how he felt comfortable—and went up against sharpshooter Hodges in the final. It was no contest. Now in his absurdly bright red East All-Star uniform, Bird drained nine shots in a row at one point and even deliberately banked in the red-white-and-blue ball near the end.

Bird was ecstatic. His first comments were directed to his Boston teammates who had kidded him that he wouldn't win, and specifically to veteran M. L. Carr, who used to claim that he was the "three-point king." So Bird stole his line. "I'm the three-point king," Bird yelped, over and over. "I'm the three-point king." Even later in his career, it would bring a smile to his face when someone called him the three-point king. He was, too, in a way that Bird didn't even intend at the time. He probably wasn't the first great three-point shooter, a title that might belong to Dale Ellis. But he was the first true superstar to incorporate the three-point shot into his game, and he remains the greatest combination of player and three-point shooter in NBA history.

Bird would win the contest the next two years, too, but there was something about that first one. It came in the middle of a championship season, and it seemed to say everything about Bird—the deadly concentration, the balls-out confidence, the pure joy he got from playing the game better than anyone else. There was just something about Larry, something that earned him the sobriquet of "Legend" even if we allow for the fact that Jordan was a better all-around player and Magic (five championships to Bird's three) was a greater winner.

We cannot, ever, divorce Bird from his ethnicity. The fact that millions of white youngsters all over the world gravitated to Bird, found him almost godlike, is not racist, but it is certainly racial. Ditto for the millions who detested him purely because he was white, theorizing that his fame, trumpeted by a mostly white press, was chimerical.

But those who knew him knew that his grittiness was hard-earned, legit, that his darkness-on-the-edge-of-town upbringing (his alcoholic father committed suicide when Bird was eighteen) was the foundation of his character.

Years later Patrick Ewing told me everything I needed to know about what other players thought about Bird. Though Ewing grew up in Cambridge, Massachusetts, and idolized Celtics legend Bill Russell, he was not a fan of Bird or the contemporary Celtics. He didn't explain why. He didn't have to. The Celtics were the white team and Bird the white leader. "All through high school," says Ewing, "my friends and I *hated* him and *hated* his team."

But something changed when Ewing entered the league and faced those flinty eyes of the Hick from French Lick. So he picked up the phone and dialed his friends.

"You know all that shit we were talking back then?" Ewing told them. "Well, forget about it. This motherfucker right here is the *truth*."

# CHAPTER 5

# THE OUTCAST

. . . . . . . . . . . . . . . . . . . . . . . . . . . . . . . . . . . . . . . . . . . . . . . . . . .

## Isiah Throws It Away . . .
## Then Throws It *All* Away

He had it in his hands, right there, the whole game, the whole season, his long battle to make the NBA's Terrific Triumvirate a Fantastic Foursome . . . all of it. *Right there!* His Detroit Pistons were leading the Boston Celtics by one point in Boston Garden in Game 5 of the 1987 Eastern Conference finals. There were only five seconds left, and all Isiah Thomas had to do was successfully in-bound the ball to a teammate and victory was his. Easy. Isiah was then, by his reckoning, the smartest guy in the room, all the time, every time. And he wasn't far wrong.

But then the situation started to devolve. Coach Chuck Daly motioned for a time-out, which the Pistons had, but nobody saw him. None of the veterans on the court, including Joe Dumars, Bill Laimbeer, Adrian Dantley, or Thomas himself, thought to do it, either.

Isiah's best option was Laimbeer, a good foul shooter, and Larry

Bird knew this, too. So Bird faked as if he was covering Dantley and darted toward Laimbeer just as Thomas, now pressed by the five-second clock, threw it in that direction.

This was classic Bird, who always had trouble staying in front of his own man but, like a classroom busybody, was a master at horning in on everyone else's affairs. Bird thought for a moment about fouling Laimbeer, but, as he said later, Thomas's pass "seemed to stay in the air forever." Bird made the steal, then immediately whirled, found teammate Dennis Johnson streaking down the lane, fed him a perfect pass, and watched as Johnson banked in a layup that gave the Celtics a 108–107 victory and a 3–2 series lead.

It was not then that Thomas severely hurt his chances of being on a Dream Team that wasn't even born yet. It was a few minutes later.

Thomas was caught in what was then the worst place for an NBA player who had just lost a tough one—the visitors' locker room in ancient Boston Garden, one step up from a junior high lavatory, complete with tepid water, open stalls, and the aroma of a prison mess hall. It was crowded, the air thick with tension, the season all but gone, and much hostility toward the Celtics already roiling in Isiah's system. Indeed, a fight between Bird and Laimbeer, Isiah's good buddy, had erupted during Game 3, a 122–104 Pistons victory. Laimbeer had been fined $5,000 for taking Bird down, and Bird $2,000 for throwing the ball at Laimbeer.

Dennis Rodman, a rookie, then (as far as we know) dressing only like a man, decided to offer an opinion on Bird. I wasn't there for the beginning of the conversation, but Rodman said that Bird was "overrated" and had won three straight MVP awards "just because he was white." The attention then turned to Thomas, which was when I arrived. Thomas was asked about Rodman's comments and said he "had to agree with Rodman." Then, his brain, evidently in full lockdown mode, added: "Larry Bird is a very, very good basketball player. But if he was black he'd be just another guy."

Then Isiah did the Isiah laugh, familiar to anyone who had been around him, a little chuckle, accompanied by the part-angel, part-devil Isiah smile.

Days later, when he went on an ask-for-absolution tour that culminated at the NBA Finals in Los Angeles, Isiah, standing next to an obviously uncomfortable Bird, would offer up the laugh as proof that he was joshing. But the laugh, then as now, never comes across that way. It is inscrutable, one that could mean he was joking or could mean he was as serious as a priest at high mass. It was impossible to tell. Isiah was, and remains today, a solipsist, his reality the only reality.

At the press conference Isiah made some legitimate points about how black athletes are sometimes adjudged differently than white athletes. Whites are frequently called "heady" and "hardworking," while blacks are presented as just naturally talented. There is something to that, but it was a subject for a different time and, in any case, should not have included Bird. Better that Isiah's defense would've been: *I blew it. I was mad. You ever stand half naked in Boston Garden in front of an audience and been asked about a hated rival?*

But he didn't. Though there were other reasons that Isiah never ultimately made the Dream Team—many point to the alleged All-Star Game freeze-out of Jordan, which had occurred two years earlier, and others pointed to the backroom politicking he had done during the 1988–89 season to force the Pistons to get rid of Adrian Dantley in favor of his buddy Mark Aguirre—I think that this was the major strike.

Detroit still had hope, even after Isiah's double gaffe. The Pistons beat the Celtics 113–105 at home to tie the series but, predictably, lost back at Boston Garden in Game 7, 117–114.

So what Isiah should've said when asked lo those many years ago whether Bird was overrated was what Patrick Ewing said to the boys back home: *Rodman was wrong. This motherfucker right here is the truth.*

# CHAPTER 6

# THE MAGIC MAN

. . . . . . . . . . . . . . . . . . . . . . . . . . . . . . . . . . . . . . . . . . . . . .

## With a Junior Skyhook, He Claims
## His Place on Top

Just a few weeks after Isiah made the ill-advised pass that came to
(partly) define his career, Magic Johnson, Isiah's best buddy (so they
both told us), also stood with the ball at Boston Garden, the game in
his hands, as it had been in Isiah's. The stakes were higher for Magic
than they had been for Isiah because this was the Finals. Johnson's
Lakers trailed the Celtics 106–105 with about ten seconds left, and
this was Game 4. A Boston win tied up the series.

    The Lakers called time-out and the ball came in to Magic, which
was no surprise. He caught it near the left baseline about twenty
feet from the basket as long-armed Kevin McHale jumped out to
guard him. Magic stutter-dribbled, then continued into the lane as
Bird and Robert Parish converged on him. Magic would frequently
dish off at this point, but from my perspective along the baseline, he
seemed to be shooting all the way. About eight feet from the basket
Magic softly released the shot that was later proclaimed to be, by a

jubilant Johnson, "the junior, junior skyhook," playing off the name given to the hook shot that was the specialty of teammate Kareem Abdul-Jabbar. It went in, giving the Lakers a victory and a 3–1 series lead, which proved to be crucial when they won the title in L.A. in Game 6.

It was at that moment—one year after the Celtics and Bird owned the league, and three years after McHale had referred to Magic as "Tragic Johnson" for his poor play in the 1984 Finals—that Magic stood on the top rung of NBA players. Picture Bird and Magic on side-by-side elevators somewhere around midseason. They stopped for a while on the same floor while others below them, including youngsters such as Michael Jordan, could only gaze at them up there on high, saviors of the league, guardians of all that is holy in hoops—skill, unselfishness, imperviousness to pressure. Then Bird slowly, ever so slowly, started on his way down, grimacing with back pain, and Magic ascended. Here's how good Johnson was in the 1986–87 season, which earned him the first of his three MVP awards: he increased his scoring by an average of 5 points per game while still controlling the offense with his passing.

The reversal of fortunes was sudden but not altogether unexpected. If you listened to Bird closely at the end of the Celtics' 1986 championship run, he was already looking into a hazy future. He knew his back was getting worse, and he also worried about the health of Bill Walton, whose sixth-man play had energized the team. And how many games did Walton, plagued by an ankle injury, play in 1986–87? Better to measure it in minutes: 112.

If Magic was ever the optimist, Bird was ever the realist.

The popular belief is that Magic was a ton of laughs and the Lakers Showtime caravan was the linchpin of the joie de vivre that took place in the NBA during the 1980s. That was not the case. Abdul-Jabbar brought new meaning to the word *dour*; I approached his locker in the Forum the same way I would've approached an open viper pit. James Worthy kept his own counsel. Byron Scott

always seemed a little nervous, as if he were on permanent audition, subject to rebuke from coach Pat Riley's hook or Abdul-Jabbar's
scowl. A. C. Green was not a stirring conversationalist once you
got past the subject of his virginity, on which I never lasted long.
(Gordon Edes of the *Los Angeles Times* memorably quipped that
Green's idea of a one-liner was John 3:16.) Pat Riley was (is) a
smart man whose company I enjoyed, but somewhere along the
line he was overtaken by paranoia and is the person most responsible for instituting closed practices and a football-coach mentality
in the NBA.

The broad strokes used to define the teams—the Lakers franchise as Entertainment Central, the stodgy Celtics as the *MacNeil/
Lehrer News Hour*—were simply wrong. Celtics practices at Hellenic
College in suburban Boston were entertaining affairs, a kind of basketball vaudeville. Coach K. C. Jones was rather like a substitute
teacher winging it without a lesson plan. McHale zinged one-liners
at Walton, Bird stuck it to anyone and everyone, and Danny Ainge
performed daily in the role of a Mormon Beaver Cleaver. Walton,
never averse to hyperbole, called the intrasquad scrimmages "spiritual," filled as they were with what he considered the essence of
basketball—the unbridled joy of competition.

Something funny always seemed to happen when you hung
around the Celtics. Such was the case one night in L.A. during the
'87 Finals when I opened my hotel room door to find Celtics reserve
forward Darren Daye sticking a bare foot into my Portabubble, an
unwieldy portable computer terminal with huge couplers on which
I wrote and transmitted my stories.

"Darren, what the hell are you doing?" I asked.

"Uh, what's your last name?" he said. "McCallum? Oh, see, I
asked for McHale's room key at the front desk and they gave me this
one. I thought this was the foot-stimulator machine Kevin was
using."

Without a McHale, an Ainge, and a Walton, the Lakers were not
so outwardly comical. They had their moments—karate-chopping
a teammate's newspaper while he was reading in an airport lounge

or in the locker room was a team obsession for a while—but the Lakers, so flashy on the court, were more about outward propriety.

There was always Magic, of course, and the man could talk the shell off a hard-boiled egg. But the idea that he was the eternal Mr. Sunshine, at least during his playing days, is overblown. After his exquisite junior-skyhook/MVP season of 1986–87, the game became a little less fun for him, the result of the Lakers' enervating crusade to repeat as champions in 1987–88. Riley, who had "guaranteed" a repeat after the '87 Finals, pushed them endlessly. I went out to L.A. before the playoffs and Riley pulled out a computer printout showing that the performances of Magic, Worthy, and Abdul-Jabbar had all gone down from the season before. Riley then put Magic in the context of Jordan and Bird, hauling out another stat sheet to reveal that Johnson's plus-minus rating was third in the league, below the metrics of the other two. Coaches and players hate when journalists make comparisons based on statistics, but they do exactly the same thing.

"Last season Earvin was a driven player," Riley told me. "He was driven to win the MVP award and finally get his due. He did it by constantly pushing himself to shoot, to penetrate, to take over a game. This year, for whatever reason, he hasn't done it." Riley couldn't have been any more obvious that he was sending a message if he pulled out an envelope and a stamp.

Those comments forced Magic to don the mantle of victim. He sighed heavily when presented with Riley's opinions and stats. "I think it's just going back to the same way it was before, to taking me for granted," he said. "'Magic? He's *supposed* to get a triple-double. He's *supposed* to have all those assists. He's *supposed* to be leading the best team in basketball.' Does it bother me? Yes, a little. It hurts my chances for recognition as an individual, no doubt about it."

You never got sighs and I'm-a-victim from Bird. You might've gotten a fuck-you-I-don't-want-to-talk-about-it. But not sighs and I'm-a-victim.

The Lakers did indeed repeat that season, the first team in two decades to go back-to-back. But the strain cleaved the relationship between Riley, who subsequently left after the 1989–90 season, and Magic, who was no longer so much the Sunshine Warrior.

Magic's effulgent personality was a bit off-putting at times, but the man was a great, great player, the point guard on most everyone's all-time team, his 6'9" size giving him a clear advantage over the 6'5" Oscar Robertson. One could argue to exhaustion about whether he or Bird was the greater player . . . and then you could keep arguing some more. But over the twelve years when he was on top of his game, Magic almost always put it on the line when it counted. The man finished with thirty triple-doubles in the playoffs, a record that might never be touched. (Bird had ten. Of the other Dream Teamers, only Charles Barkley and Scottie Pippen are on the list, with four each.) And since both Magic and Bird defined their careers by rings—I heard Bird say "win a championship" so often that it began to sound like one word, *winachampionship*—my contention is that Magic had the better career. He had five rings, Bird had three. Yes, Johnson had a great supporting cast, but so did Bird.

Purely as a basketball player, Jordan was better than either of them. (More on that later.) But Magic comes out on top in a singular aspect of the game—being influential on offense without needing to score. Hundreds of cases support that, but none better than this: in Game 6 of the 1982 Finals, Magic, who would win the series MVP, took exactly four shots yet totally dominated the game. He scored 13 points, grabbed 13 rebounds, and handed out 13 assists in a 114–104 win that closed out the Philadelphia 76ers.

Johnson did two things better than any other player who ever lived. One was his ability to control and conduct the half-court offense. Owing to his height, he ruled from on high, his court vision unobscured, like a lighthouse operator scanning the horizon for fog. And those who tried to steal the ball from him met with a strong arm bar. In effect, the defense could never pressure the quarterback. Second, he executed full-speed, completely-under-control spins that weren't for show but, rather, for eluding the defense. He gets very little credit for that.

The rivalry between the Lakers and the Celtics (and therefore between Magic and Bird) was not nearly as protracted as one might believe. Their only truly epic mano-a-mano battle was in the 1984 Finals, when the Celtics won in seven games, a memory that still furrows Magic's brow. By the time that Magic and Bird met again in the 1987 Finals, they had become more like bicoastal teammates, selling sneakers together and singing mutual hosannas, and by 1992, when they co-captained the greatest team ever, they were marching lockstep into history.

# CHAPTER 7

# THE SHOOTER

. . . . . . . . . . . . . . . . . . . . . . . . . . . . . . . . . . . . . . . . . . . . . . . . .

## Mullin Puts Down the Bottle
## and Puts Up the Numbers

Chris Mullin was comfortable being alone. The first sport at which he was proficient back in his native Flatbush was swimming, stroking away in the local Boys Club pool in the early-morning, chlorine-scented fog that hid the world. He was a sprinter—"a 25-meter guy," in his words—and probably would've gone on to be a really good one.

But he liked being part of a team, too, so when the Catholic Youth Organization (CYO) coach at St. Thomas Aquinas told him he had to give up swimming if he was going to be really good in basketball, he said okay. He enjoyed the solitary aspects of basketball, too, and that's why he got good. "I liked being in the gym alone," Mullin told me recently. "No, I *loved* it. I'd put a tape player or radio near the floor, put on some Springsteen, really blast it, shoot it, get your own rebound, shoot it, get your own. I loved that. Or I'd go full-court thirty minutes by myself. I had no problem with that."

So he never minded drinking alone, either.

Drinking was part of the family culture. His dad, Rod, a customs inspector at Kennedy Airport, was an alcoholic—a gentle one, but an alcoholic nonetheless. The mood swings scared Chris a little bit, but basically Rod always came out on the positive side. He was a "good drunk," never a "mean drunk."

Chris could drink at home, but he could be a club guy, too. Throughout his gilded years at St. John's, 1982 through 1985, when players such as Mullin, Georgetown's Patrick Ewing, and Villanova's Ed Pinckney put the Big East on the map and sent three teams to the Final Four, Chris could be spotted in New York City bars, always part of the crowd but never making a scene, the quiet star leaning on the bar. But if he had to drink alone, back in his room, he could do that, too.

It had become easier to drink alone after the Golden State Warriors drafted Mullin with the seventh pick in 1985. Oakland, California, was a world away for a kid from Queens who was the epitome of old-school New York basketball. First and most basic, he could shoot. "I started doing it in my yard and took to it," he says. "I just *grabbed* it, like a golfer grabs a great stroke. One day I made twenty, so the next day I had to make twenty-one. Then it became more shots and more makes." As a shooter, Mullin was a prodigy, the way some kids are prodigies at chess or the violin. He won the national Hoop Shoot title when he was ten.

Mullin also learned the rudimentary geometry of basketball—the angles, the jab steps and quick cuts that would get him open. He loved playing one-on-one, then two-on-two, then three-on-three, the last of these the most fun because you could screen away, flare, always get yourself open. "I was taught how to *negotiate* the other guys on the court," says Mullin. And he knew the physics of basketball, too, all the spins and caroms and applied English, sending up more junk than Fred Sanford, much of it ending up in the basket.

"I'd go into the city and play some street ball," says Mullin, "and that would help me some. But then, back home, my CYO coach would go '*nhhh*' [Mullin makes a sound like a buzzer going off] and get me back to fundamentals. So my game became a combination of the two."

Fundamentals and team play were not what was going on in Oakland, California, circa 1985. Mullin came to a team defined by a big center named Joe Barry Carroll, who existed primarily as a punch line for *New York Post* columnist Peter Vecsey, who memorably rechristened him "Joe Barely Cares." And Oakland itself was disorienting, three thousand miles away from his family, his long-time girlfriend, Liz Connolly (later to be his wife), who had worked on the St. John's stat crew, the unspeakably bad sweaters of his beloved college coach, Lou Carnesecca, and the overall warm familiarity of New Yawk ball. Oakland was a different culture—a drug culture, not a beer culture, and widely recognized as the cocaine capital of the NBA, which at the time was saying something. I remember Atlanta Hawks coach Mike Fratello deciding to keep his team in Los Angeles for an extra couple of days instead of staying in Oakland for a game with the Warriors. "I'd rather have them fuck themselves to death in L.A.," Fratello reasoned, "than spend one night in Oakland."

Cocaine was never Mullin's problem. Beer was. He drank it in bars and he drank it alone, and he grew heavier and slower and less of a player in the eyes of coach Don Nelson, who had expected so much more of him.

In early December 1987, Mullin, the kid who would shoot a thousand jumpers alone in a darkened gymnasium, missed a couple of practices, and Nelson suspended him. Nellie knew what was going on from years of missed practices with other players, and he gave Mullin a message: *Get yourself to rehab.* Mullin had motivation. He knew that his father had given up the booze years earlier when he came to realize that it was doing himself and his family no good. But Chris was resistant. He said no to Nelson, they argued some more, and then Nelson got a report from a fan that Mullin was out boozing it up after a game. Nelson confronted him again, and finally Mullin said yes and entered an alcohol rehab clinic.

Back home, the *New York Post*, which once celebrated Chris

Mullin as the ultimate playground star, a kid with both street smarts and textbook fundamentals, put Mullin's face over a Heineken bottle in reporting the story. He was a long, long way from the Olympic glory he had experienced three years earlier, in 1984, and which he would find again four years hence.

The rehab part of the Mullin story is not dramatic, not Lohanian in any way, shape, or form. Mullin went in dirty and came out clean. He says there was no relapse and no return, and I never met anyone who believes differently. Mullin just beat it, and his career turned around immediately. It was that sudden. He averaged 26.5 points per game in his first booze-free season (1988–89) and 25.1 and 25.7 in his next two, the ones that mattered when Dream Team candidates were being identified.

"It seems like maybe there should be a lot more to tell," Mullin said to me years later. "But . . . you know, I always wanted to beat it. I wanted to be a great player and booze was keeping me from being one. Now? Being sober is like a blessing I'd like to share. I'd like to tell everybody how good I feel."

# CHAPTER 8

# THE CHRISTIAN SOLDIER

. . . . . . . . . . . . . . . . . . . . . . . . . . . . . . . . . . . . . . . . . .

## The Admiral Takes an Olympic Fall

He grew up between two worlds, a self-described "oddity." He'd be invited to a party, and when spin-the-bottle came up, someone would say, "Okay, David, you can be the referee."

David Robinson still feels that sting. "'Yeah, well, okay,' I used to think," said Robinson. "'They're cool with me.' But only to a point."

*They* were the white kids, the ones with whom he shared the advanced math classes and the elevated SAT scores. Among that company Robinson hit the social glass ceiling in his high school years.

Then he would go to the playground and the basketball camps, and it would be time to deal with the black kids, and he wasn't comfortable there, either. "It was fun up to a certain point," says Robinson, "but we might be talking trash and . . . well, if you speak a certain way and act a certain way, they'll call you an Uncle Tom, tell you that you're not black enough."

The trash talk, at least the tone of it, never felt right to Robinson, which is easy to understand when you learn that his father, Ambrose Robinson, an imposing naval officer, used to open the dictionary to a random page to test his son's spelling. "Why are we doing this, Dad?" David would ask, and his father, a sonar technician and an E-8, one step below the highest rank an enlisted man could reach, would answer that it was to keep him "focused." When they weren't doing that, they were assembling small televisions. You know, the usual father-son stuff.

Robinson relates all this two decades later in a tone best described as wistful, and I suggest that it couldn't have been that bad, since at the very least he could always play, dominate the competition.

"Not when I was young," Robinson answers quickly. "I wasn't any good. It wasn't like I had basketball to pick me up and get me in good standing. I didn't do anything until my senior year of high school."

By then Robinson had grown to 6'7" and made enough noise to be recruited by schools including Virginia Military Institute and George Washington, which were near the suburban Maryland area where he grew up. It was practically ordained, though, that he would get an appointment to the United States Naval Academy.

He flourished at Annapolis and continued to grow, eventually reaching 7'0". He looked all of seven feet, too, since he walked with textbook posture, his bearing a metaphor for the shoulders-straight, eyes-forward way he tried to live his life. The nation began to hear about his college board scores, his aptitude for gymnastics (he could do backflips and handsprings, and he could walk the length of a basketball court on his hands), and his punctilious manner; his public comments were unfailingly lucid, literate, and carefully chosen.

But even as he swatted away shots and got Navy to the regional finals of the NCAA tournament, there was resistance to Robinson. The basketball public looked at him the way the black kids used to back at Osbourn Park High in Manassas, Virginia. Nobody could be *that* smart and also tough. Yes, pro players such as Michael Jordan and Magic Johnson had also come from stable two-parent families, but, from the beginning they demonstrated a wolfish rapacity on the court that Robinson didn't have. Plus they weren't nearly as smart. Nobody was as smart as David.

Georgetown's John Thompson was selected to be the 1988 U.S. Olympic basketball coach, which didn't mean that he was particularly popular among the hierarchy of ABAUSA. Thompson didn't have much international experience and didn't care about studying the game beyond our shores, something he had in common with many American basketball coaches at the time. He was independent to the point of arrogance. He brooked no interference from officials and defied them by making Mary Fenlon, Georgetown's academic advisor, an assistant Olympic coach.

Still, he was the predictable Olympic choice, having established the Hoyas as a national power through dint of pure will and a knack for getting the most out of the tough kids who came to play for him. There was a clear line of coaching succession within ABAUSA, almost as rigid as the monarchial line in Great Britain. The Olympic coaching job was just *conveyed* upon the most likely candidate, the one who had paid his dues. North Carolina's Dean Smith in 1976, Providence's Dave Gavitt in 1980 (he was named although the boycott kept the United States home), and Bob Knight in 1984—that's how it went. You signed on, you formed your team from the best available collegiate players, and you kicked ass.

When David Robinson, fresh from two years as a civil engineering officer at a submarine base in Georgia, reported to Thompson for Olympic duty, he had already been the first pick in the 1987 draft and had already earned the sobriquet "the Admiral," though in point of fact the highest rank he attained was lieutenant. The Admiral told Thompson that he would probably be out of his rhythm for a while considering that while on naval duty he had not scrimmaged against anyone taller than six-feet-one. "But, Coach,

I'm going to work hard, just like I did in college, and I'll become a dominant player again," Robinson told Thompson.

The coach looked him over and said: "Son, you're not going to make this team." Thompson then went through the list of what he considered Robinson's weaknesses. "You can't handle the ball, you can't pass, your basketball skills are minimal."

What Thompson really had against Robinson was that he didn't see him as tough enough. "He thought I was a spoiled, not-from-the-hood type of guy," says Robinson. "Coach Thompson likes those guys that . . ." Robinson stops, probably trying not to sound racist himself since Thompson's teams were the victim of stereotyping, though maybe not as often as Thompson thought. "The type of guys who would run through a wall if he asked them," Robinson continues. "But, see, I'm the type of guy who says, '*Why* are we running through this wall?'"

Robinson eventually made the team—Thompson wasn't crazy enough to leave off a player who even before his first NBA game was one of the most multitalented big men in the world. But the burden of Olympic success fell most heavily upon Robinson . . . and fall it did.

At that point in time, the rosters of the Soviets and the Yugoslavs were filled with players who would go down as their nation's all-time best. They were extremely well coached, too, the Yugoslavs by a strategic master named Ranko Zeravica, the Soviets by the immortal Alexander Gomelsky, about whom someone should make a movie.

Gomelsky, who died in 2005, was known as the "Silver Fox." He was a mysterious character, rumored to be a Russian secret agent, which is possibly true, although the KGB hated him, too. No one ever knew exactly what the Silver Fox was up to. He was supposed to coach the national team at the Munich Olympics in 1972, but the state confiscated his passport, fearing that, as a Jew, he would defect to Israel. He was always involved in this deal or that deal—for

a while in the early 1980s he was suspended from coaching for alleged smuggling—yet managed to be the major figure in the rich
history of Soviet basketball.

Two days before a semifinal showdown in Seoul against Robinson and the United States, Gomelsky began visiting the Soviet players for personal pep talks. Sarunas Marciulionis, the Lithuanian
star, remembers three visits from the Silver Fox, all of them with the
same message: *You have to believe in yourself. The Americans are not
gods. They are only college players.* Plus, the Soviets, at least players
such as Marciulionis, Arvydas Sabonis, and Alexander Volkov, had
an extra incentive: *Win the gold medal,* they were promised, either
implicitly or obliquely, *and you can leave the country to play in the
NBA.* "We considered the Olympics our freedom ticket," says Marciulionis. *That* is serious motivation.

Then, too, Gomelsky was prepared for Thompson's stifling
press, which had intimidated and shut down so many collegiate opponents. Gomelsky worked on little else during the practice sessions
in Seoul, insisting on an elaborate set of screens to free Marciulionis
and get open shots for players such as Sabonis and Volkov. He didn't
want backcourt turnovers to be converted into dunks. "Don't let
them fast-break dunk," Gomelsky told his charges. "When they do
that, their arms turn into wings." The man knew his way around a
phrase.

The Soviets won 82–76, thus becoming somewhat the Dar-
win's finches of worldwide basketball, the marker of the evolution-
ary changes that had come upon us. Unlike 1972, this loss to the
Soviets was no fluke, no give-'em-three-chances-to-win. The United
States just got beat.

The Admiral averaged a respectable 12.8 points and 6.8 rebounds in Seoul, but he didn't dominate, didn't snarl his way
through the competition. And he took it very hard. "I thought, obviously, I had missed my one and only chance to get a gold medal,"
he says today. "And it was an embarrassment because I thought we
were good enough. The '72 team was robbed. We just got beat. And
man, I grew up with the Olympics. I loved the Olympics. This was a
big, big black mark."

In the United States, the 1988 team is still looked upon as an abject failure. That is wrongheaded. With a different approach, yes, the United States *could've* won, but its defeat wasn't necessarily an upset. That was the message conveyed by anyone who had his eyes open.

Gold medal: the Soviet Union. Silver medal: Yugoslavia. Bronze medal: the United States.

*We're number three! We're number three!*

Nobody in charge ever wanted to see that again. But, seemingly, there was nothing that could be done about it.

Robinson was disappointed and discouraged that he had been blamed. But he wasn't all that surprised. He had played on touring U.S. teams before and seen the growth in European basketball, his nimble mind uncovering the fact that, though he himself was athletically blessed, there was more to this game than running and jumping.

And there was more to life than basketball. It was around this time that Robinson began feeling the first stirrings of discontent with his life's path, not the basketball so much but the spiritual part of it. He felt empty inside, and he began searching for something else.

CHAPTER 9

# THE CHOSEN ONE

. . . . . . . . . . . . . . . . . . . . . . . . . . . . . . . . . . . . . . . . . . . . . . . . . . . . .

### And So Does a Fork Become a Holy Relic

On the morning of May 7, 1989, I came down to breakfast at a suburban Cleveland hotel, the same one at which the Chicago Bulls were staying for their semifinal Eastern Conference series against the Cleveland Cavaliers. The deciding Game 5 was that afternoon. At breakfast I chatted up coach Doug Collins and his assistants, Johnny Bach and Tex Winter, both of whom spun more stories than Scheherazade, and I even collected a quote or two from Jordan. That sort of impromptu meeting rarely happens these days. While reporters may graze away at the make-your-own-waffles station, players are eating in a private room or skipping breakfast altogether. But the Bulls in those days were a young team—Jordan, Pippen, Horace Grant—and they made their own waffles.

Jordan was in his fifth season, engaged in the heavy-lifting process of trying to get a championship ring. He had no peer as a player, but there was still a resistance to him. Was he a *winner*, like Bird and

Magic? He had become the individual face of the NBA, so seemingly comfortable in the spotlight that few people remembered that he had once been a tongue-tied kid who in 1985 was so nervous that he couldn't get through his lines in his first McDonald's commercial.

Although Jordan was cordial, he was not particularly enamored of me at that moment. About seven weeks earlier I had come to Chicago to do a story on Jordan, and he invited me to his suburban townhouse to hang out with him and his boys. One of the delightful aspects of Jordan's life at that point was how close he had remained to his boyhood chums, who included Adolph Shiver, Fred Whitfield, and Fred Kearns. It was a variation on the customary leader-of-the-pack syndrome that so often gets star athletes into trouble. Some athletes cannot or will not disentangle themselves from their past and end up giving too much money and too much power to guys who shouldn't be around. But Jordan's circle consisted of good guys and solid citizens, the whole scene a kind of early *Entourage*, African American style, without the Cristal and the blow. (Whitfield is today president of the Charlotte Bobcats, the franchise partially owned and run by Jordan.)

At the end of the afternoon, a young lady, Juanita Vanoy—who later became Mrs. Michael Jordan, and, years after that, the very rich ex–Mrs. Michael Jordan when she received about $168 million in a divorce settlement—came down the stairs holding a baby. I was astonished because I hadn't heard that Jordan was a father, and we spent the next thirty minutes billing and cooing over the kid.

Later that night, at the game at Chicago Stadium, Tim Hallam, the Bulls' PR chief, collared me and said: "You know, Michael expects that you won't write that he has a son." Tim was just doing his job.

"But, Tim, I saw the baby," I answered. "We talked about diapers and stuff like that. He didn't say anything about not writing it."

"Well, he told me to tell you that. A couple other guys know it and haven't written it."

To me, it was a journalistic dilemma, not a moral one. The list of human beings who have had children out of wedlock is quite long and includes friends and relatives of mine. What did I care? But I didn't see how I could hide the fact that Jordan had a baby—what was he going to do, store Jeffrey Michael in a closet?—so I put it in that week's story as the last paragraph.

I was criticized in Chicago both for burying it and for writing it at all. And Jordan let it be known that he was upset. But those were different times, when détente was possible between journalist and subject, and he let it go.

Anyway, at breakfast that morning in Cleveland, the Bulls left, and a teenager stealthily approached the table and grabbed a utensil.

"Look!" he shouted. "Michael Jordan's fork! Michael Jordan ate with this fork!" He stuck it in his pocket and walked out of the restaurant.

I've thought about that fork from time to time. Does he still have it in a collection somewhere? Is it on eBay? Encased in glass at his law office?

When you hung around Jordan, your story quite often almost wrote itself. A year earlier during a visit to Chicago, I was waiting for Jordan after practice, and he told me to jump into his car so he could dodge the autograph hounds. As we cruised through the parking lot of a shopping center in his Porsche 911 Turbo, two cars just about cut him off, forcing Jordan to brake. A man jumped from one car holding a sweatsuit to which he had affixed an Air Jordan logo, while two autograph seekers leaped from the other. Jordan dutifully signed his name and took the sweatsuit guy's card, all of that theater supplying invaluable material for a journalist.

As for the fork, well, it became a collectible after Jordan stuck a metaphorical one in the Cavaliers. That was the day he made an impossible double-clutch jump shot (his 43rd and 44th points of the game), with 6'7" Cavaliers defender Craig Ehlo hanging all over him, to give the Bulls an absurdly dramatic 101–100 victory and the series. My favorite part of the clip, which you've seen about a thousand times, is Ehlo wistfully throwing up his hands, as if to say, *This just isn't fair*. Which it wasn't.

Before the Bulls broke from the huddle, Jordan had whispered to his teammate Craig Hodges, "I'm going to make it." The Bulls frequently ran what Bach called "the Archangel Offense," defined by the assistant as "getting the ball to Jordan and saying, 'Save us, Michael.'" After this game, Doug Collins, who looked more exhausted than Jordan, said this about the play, "That was the give-the-ball-to-Michael-and-everybody-else-get-the-fuck-out-of-the-way play." Jordan cracked up but looked embarrassed that Collins had used the *F*-word. Indeed, at that time, in casual conversation Jordan would say things like "Eff you" and "that MF-er." There was an innocence about him, and I always thought that it might never have been better for him than it was on that day in Cleveland, his star rising, his future bright and unclouded, his breakfast utensils sacred tokens.

# CHAPTER 10

# THE OLD GUARD

. . . . . . . . . . . . . . . . . . . . . . . . . . . . . . . . . . . . . . . . . . . .

## Here Today . . . Gone Real Soon

In April 1989, about a month before Jordan made his oft-replayed shot over Ehlo, the Inspector of Meat got his wish. Boris Stankovic had never wavered in his crusade to get open competition into the Olympics, not even after his first attempt at passing the resolution, at the FIBA Congress in Madrid in 1986, failed. Getting the NBA into FIBA had by this time taken on a pragmatic aspect for Stankovic, too: After the 1980 Moscow Games, the Olympics boycotted by the United States, FIBA had been hemorrhaging money and was heading for bankruptcy. It needed both the sizzle and the steak that would come with the addition of NBA players.

So at a specially convened FIBA Congress in Munich, which had been preceded by much behind-the-scenes arm-twisting, a resolution passed that allowed NBA players to participate in the Olympics. The vote was 56–13, the United States and the Soviet Union being among the nay votes.

"We knew it was going to pass," said Commissioner David Stern, "but we were absolutely not enthusiastic about it. It was sort of like, 'Okay, what do we do now?'"

That's a slight exaggeration, but it's absolutely true that no full-scale mobilization was under way at the NBA offices in midtown Manhattan. In fact, the vote got relatively scant attention in the United States because many observers believed there was no practical application. Nobody would ever get NBA players to go to the Olympics. Among the most skeptical was college hoops commentator Billy Packer, who said that NBA owners would not let their players play, and anyway, selfish NBA players would not want to give up their vacation. The late Al McGuire, a commentator of whom you couldn't make any sense but whom you liked to hear talk anyway, said the same thing. Besides, this was spring, the opening of Major League Baseball, and, more than ever, there was Michael Jordan. Who could think of something that might or might not happen at the Olympics three years in the future?

In one corner of the United States, however, there was considerable interest. Immediately after the Final Four in Seattle, a group of men from ABAUSA, the body that governed amateur basketball in the United States, flew to Munich for the FIBA meeting. Their official role was to cast a no vote on the resolution, a vote they all knew was pointless because it was obvious that the Inspector of Meat would not have called the meeting if he didn't have the votes.

Dave Gavitt had just been elected ABAUSA president and, as such, would be the official voter. He voted no, but what he really wanted to say was yes. By that time, Gavitt had already paid a visit to the NBA offices, where he told Stern and Granik: "Look, we're going to vote no, but it's going to pass. You better get ready to decide how you want to handle this."

Stern had an idea: the NBA would simply buy the Olympic team from ABAUSA.

"It's not for sale," Gavitt told him. "It's the country's team. What you need to do is become part of ABAUSA, and I promise you that in putting together the committee we will protect you and make sure you have the majority of representation coming from the NBA."

It was Gavitt's insistence that the NBA buy in lock, stock, and barrel that made all the difference in the end. While others feared the coming of the monolithic NBA, Gavitt saw the advantages. For one thing, the amateur organization—which depended primarily on funding from the U.S. Olympic Committee (USOC) and a half-assed contract with Converse that was worth about $300,000, a sum that Nike was tucking into the soles of Jordan's shoes by then—was nearly broke. The NBA, its Michael/Magic/Larry renaissance still building, was awash in cash. Gavitt suggested that if NBA Properties could step in and do the marketing, everyone would benefit. Stern said okay.

In amateur basketball circles, Gavitt had done it all, seen it all. He had been a successful and respected coach and athletic director, one of the masterminds behind the creation of the Big East Conference, and, most impressive, the moving force behind the expansion of the NCAA basketball tournament into a billion-dollar bonanza. Soon after the amateur vote, the Boston Celtics would come calling, naming Gavitt CEO. Like many college guys who went to the pros in some capacity—Rick Pitino, Jerry Tarkanian, John Calipari, Lon Kruger, Leonard Hamilton, Tim Floyd, and that is not the end of the list—Gavitt would find that jump a long one, Beamonesque in its difficulty. But that would have no bearing on his importance in what was to become a sea change in Olympic basketball. "In many ways, Dave was the classic college guy," says Russ Granik, "but he was also someone who saw the whole picture."

About basketball, Gavitt was both visionary and romantic. He died at 73 in September of 2011, but in 2010, during a memorable lunch in his hometown, Providence, he conjured up a long-ago evening from the mid-1970s, when he was coaching a college all-star team in Athens. "We were playing a night game and there must've been thirty thousand people there and the Acropolis was in the background with a full moon," Gavitt remembered. "I had chills."

Gavitt never spoke from a bully pulpit. He was smooth, a

work-the-room diplomat who played both sides and from the beginning knew which side was going to win. Still, Gavitt had to mute his enthusiasm for the idea of open competition, for he was, after all, heading a group that was observing its own extinction.

"For me it was kind of simple," Gavitt told me. "I felt that people in our country should have the same rights to represent their country as everyone else. I never bothered to lobby the college community with that opinion because they were squarely against it. They were against pros playing in the Olympics. Period."

After Gavitt had cast the no vote on behalf of the United States and the resolution had passed, he asked for the floor. "Now that we've done this," Gavitt told the FIBA reps, "you need to realize a few things and help us. We're dealing with a powerful organization in the NBA, and we're going to have to get your cooperation with dates and things like that."

There were questions from other nations about how the United States would get its NBA players to participate—it wasn't only Packer and McGuire who thought the idea of pros giving up their summer was folly. But Stankovic would have none of it. "That's not our problem," the Inspector of Meat told the delegates sternly. "That's the problem of the United States. What we have to do is the right thing, and then let them work it out."

After the vote, the U.S. delegation had a layover in Amsterdam on their way back. Gavitt had dinner with Bill Wall and Tom Mc-Grath, the executive and assistant executive director, respectively, of ABAUSA. The future was uncertain, particularly for Wall, who had run the organization since the mid-1970s. That's when ABAUSA was created to supplant the Amateur Athletic Union (AAU), the confederation of stuffed shirts and clueless bureaucrats who, with an infuriating arbitrariness, had run amateur sports in this country for decades.

McGrath was an ABAUSA guy all the way, but he was younger than Wall and more politically nimble. He might've resented the NBA intrusion, but he saw the future and knew that much of the old organization's resistance came from, as he puts it today, "not wanting to vote ourselves out of office." Wall could see that his time was up and absolutely resented it. At the 1986 FIBA Congress, when the resolution of open competition was first brought up by Stankovic and soundly defeated, Wall had spoken out passionately against admitting pros, and he still felt the same way. Wall was aligned with George Killian, a politician of the first order who would later become a U.S. delegate to the International Olympic Committee. Gavitt and Killian never got along, so Wall didn't get along well with Gavitt, either.

But Wall did grasp the irony, too: the NBA was about to do to ABAUSA exactly what his group had once done to the AAU—turn it into the Edsel.

"You have to understand how much change this was for the college guys, and I was one of them," said C. M. Newton, who, like Granik and Gavitt, was an important person in keeping the peace between the college types and the pro types. "Charter flights and exclusive hotels and the idea that we were going to train in Monte Carlo? These were things that David [Stern] and Russ [Granik] insisted on, and they were foreign to us."

There would be talk later, from both Wall and McGrath, about how well the NBA had treated ABAUSA. But much of that is attributable to the fact that it's not wise to piss off David Stern, not then, not now, not ever. Make no mistake about it: by the time the vote for open competition had been taken, the NBA had angered the amateur organization. The McDonald's Open, for example, should've been an ABAUSA operation, but it turned into largely a Stern-Stankovic operation. The two men—oligarchs both, masters of their respective kingdoms—had become simpatico and done much of the planning and negotiation with their own people, their eyes now on a joint prize.

But at that dinner in Amsterdam, there was still business to discuss, as hazy as the future might be. Wall wasn't out yet, and he, Gavitt, and McGrath began talking. Nobody could be sure of how substantial the NBA participation was going to be. The group finally reasoned that six NBA players, probably none of them top-flight stars, would sign on. They figured that elite NBA players would never sacrifice playing time for the sake of pursuing a gold medal.

There was also the matter of a coach. All discussions were premature, but none of these men thought for a moment that the monarchial progression would not take place, which meant that, in all likelihood, Duke's Mike Krzyzewski would be the 1992 Olympic coach in Barcelona. Of course it would be a college coach, for aren't they the resident geniuses of American sport?

Of all the myths in sports, few are as entrenched—and as absolutely ridiculous—as the idea that college basketball coaches are better coaches than their counterparts in the NBA. With a longer game, more time-outs, constant matchup changes, doubling defenses, better athletes, and five-games-in-seven-nights drudgery, an NBA coach does more coaching in a week than the college coach does in an entire season. College coaches coach programs; NBA coaches coach games. The fact that pro coaches lose jobs as often as tulips lose petals does not disprove the point; it supports it. Yes, many NBA coaches do their job with a scythe swinging overhead, but still they design the plays during time-outs and find another way to get somebody open on a back screen with two seconds on the clock—and *then* they get fired. Doesn't mean they can't coach the hell out of this game.

When the men returned to ABAUSA headquarters in Colorado Springs, questions about players and a coach had to take a backseat to more pragmatic agenda items. The name of the organization, for example, had to be changed to get "Amateur" out of it. So it became, simply, USA Basketball. The constitution had to be amended to provide for membership and representation of the NBA. Eventually Granik would come aboard as vice president, and, though he, like Gavitt, was a conciliator, a diplomat, the old guard could always feel the invisible presence of Stern behind him. Almost from the first meeting, Wall could see that he was gone.

"The essential tension that existed between USA Basketball and the NBA came about because of the way the amateur organization had done business for twenty years under Bill's guidance," said Jeffrey Orridge, who was the staff attorney for USA Basketball and is now the executive director of sports properties for the Canadian Broadcasting Corporation. "The vision and the level of business acumen, the sophistication the NBA had about growing the game . . . it was far, far different than the way USA Basketball had done it."

Orridge remembers one of USA Basketball's first trips to New York when the management team went in to meet with Stern and Granik. "We weren't rubes or anything like that, but there was an almost overwhelming atmosphere to the whole thing," says Orridge, a native New Yorker himself. "Now, you combine that business sophistication with the fact that I never met harder-working, harder-driving people than NBA people, and you could see it was inevitable that the NBA was going to take over. They drove the whole thing, make no mistake about that."

And Wall, hardheaded and tough but also a realist, had to get out of the way of these mad drivers from New York City.

"How should I say this?" Wall says today from his home in the California desert. "I didn't like some of the stuff I saw coming, and they wanted to get rid of somebody who was going to say no. And it was probably my time."

It was. It was time for the NBA to come in and start throwing money around. The question nobody knew the answer to was this: who would sign on to play?

CHAPTER 11

# THE SHADOW MAN

. . . . . . . . . . . . . . . . . . . . . . . . . . . . . . . . . . . . . . . . . . . .

**For the Kid from Nowheresville, Arkansas, Playing Alongside Michael Could Be a Real Headache**

Scottie Pippen was blinking furiously, trying to focus, trying to will away the pain of a migraine headache minutes before his Chicago Bulls went out to play the Detroit Pistons in Game 7 of the NBA Eastern Conference final at the Palace of Auburn Hills in 1990.

Michael Jordan was no doubt rolling his eyes. Another hard game, another disappearing act by Scottie, another one-man battle against the cold, cruel Pistons, who were, to Jordan, the anti-Cavaliers. Jordan had Cleveland's number, all the time, every time, but the Pistons had his, all the time, every time.

For the first three years of his career, it was debatable whether Scottie Pippen was the luckiest player ever, having been drafted by Michael Jordan's team, or history's most unfortunate player . . . having been drafted by Michael Jordan's team. Jordan was already the game's ascendant star when Pippen—little known, a seeming creation from the secret laboratory of Bulls general manager Jerry

Krause—came aboard in 1987. His multitude of talents and his sometimes astounding athleticism—I'm convinced that Pippen could've been world-class in track (400 meters? long jump?) had he directed himself to that—instantly made him the Sundance Kid to Jordan's Butch Cassidy. But he always came up short in comparison, and who wouldn't have at that point in time? No matter what Pippen did, he was consigned to that dark spot on and off the court, the shadow cast by Jordan.

Even the positive things Pippen did were the little things, the shadow things that only experienced eyes could discern. I remember Jim O'Brien, then a New York Knicks assistant coach, describing a subtle play that Pippen made in his second season. The Knicks, trailing the Bulls by one with about ten seconds left, were trying to get a simple turnaround jumper for Patrick Ewing on an inbounds play from the frontcourt. But Pippen applied heavy pressure to his man, the target of the inbounds pass, forcing him to get the ball much higher than he wanted. That in turn fouled up the entry pass to Ewing, who now turned in desperation to shoot. By that time, guess who had come over to double? Jordan. He blocked the Ewing shot and drew the plaudits. But it was the Shadow Man who had made the shadow play.

During Pippen's first three years, he was the subject of much analysis by Jordan and the Bulls' coaches. Doug Collins, then the head man, thought that Jordan, while the ideal role model in some ways (skill level, competitive temperament, practice habits, etc.), was a hard act to be around because of his superhuman ability to compartmentalize. I'd watch Jordan in the locker room an hour before the game, schmoozing with Jesse Jackson and doling out ticket instructions to ballboys ("Kid 'n Play get these") even as he kept up a lucid running commentary about the game he was about to play. Then he'd drop, oh, 45, on the opposition. Collins believed that Pippen and the Bulls' other young buck, Horace Grant, would watch Jordan's example and believe that they could approach the game the same way. But unlike the Chosen One, Pippen couldn't multitask while getting ready to play, so his focus and preparation were always a concern.

When Jordan talked about Pippen he did it with a kind of benevolent bemusement, the way Wally Cleaver used to talk about the Beaver. He recognized and praised Pippen's talents but wasn't always surprised when Scottie, who had that infantile first name, didn't deliver.

Pippen was sometimes shy around Jordan, letting the big brother direct the conversation, even though Pippen, a 6'8" athletic specimen who walked with an erect and almost noble bearing, was the more striking of the two. But that was understandable; it was Jesse Jackson, after all, who was begging for face time with the Chosen One, not the other way around. One night on a team bus in Los Angeles, the Bulls players were talking about celebrities they knew. Jordan, always holding the trump card, picked up his cell, left a message for Janet Jackson, and flashed a triumphant smile when she called back thirty seconds later.

Pippen is about two and a half years younger than Jordan, but in many ways he never fit the little-brother role. Pippen had seen so much more, been through so much more, than the Carolina Kid, whose most cataclysmic childhood moment was famously being put on the junior varsity instead of the varsity at Laney High School in Wilmington, North Carolina.

The men who would constitute the 1992 Dream Team were all over the sociological lot. I don't pretend to know every detail of their childhoods, but it roughly breaks down this way: Jordan, Magic, Robinson, Stockton, Mullin, Drexler, Ewing, and Laettner came from two-parent homes. None was rich, particularly Magic, Drexler, and Ewing, but all had relatively stable domestic lives. Malone and Barkley came from households dominated by strong matriarchal figures. They were anything but flush, but they got a lot of love. This is not to say that Bird and Pippen weren't loved. But they had it much rougher than any of their Dream Team counterparts. Bird was one of six children of an alcoholic father who would eventually commit suicide; Pippen, the youngest of twelve, was brought up in the dusty mill town of Hamburg, Arkansas, which was redolent with the smell of pulp from the Georgia-Pacific plant. In some ways Hamburg was the Arkansas counterpart of Bird's French Lick.

Pippen talked to me not long ago about that childhood. I began by saying, "Of all the guys in the Hall of Fame, you have to have come from—"

"The lowest?" he interrupted me.

And something he said right after that stuck with me.

"Two in Pampers," he said, shaking his head. "Man, that was rough. My mom took care of two in Pampers."

By the time Pippen was in kindergarten, his father, Preston, a Georgia-Pacific employee like almost every other adult male in the town, was all but disabled by arthritis. Several years later Preston Pippen had a stroke, recovered slightly, then had another, more incapacitating one. (He didn't live long enough to see his son become a champion.)

When Pippen was eleven, an older brother, Ronnie, was paralyzed when a classmate fell on him during a wrestling match. Ethel Pippen stepped in. "Everybody told her there wasn't nothing could be done for them," Pippen says, referring to both his father and his brother. "That's how they treated those things back then. So my mother took care of them. Fed them, put them to bed, changed their diapers."

Unlike Bird, who looks back fondly (for the most part) upon French Lick, and certainly unlike John Stockton, who treasures the place where he grew up, Spokane, Pippen has ambivalent feelings about Hamburg.

"It was sort of a racist town," he told me in 2011. "I just always had the feeling that the coaches were pulling more for the white kids. I don't want to say they didn't *allow* the black kids to succeed, but they weren't going to allow a black kid to be the star basketball player, the star receiver on the football team, and then be on the track team. It just wasn't going to happen."

Without a major college scholarship—he was a 6'2" point guard in high school—Pippen went to Central Arkansas on a work-study grant, figuring he would eventually get a chance to play. The most enduring part of the Pippen lore is that he was the team manager, which is not exactly true. "From the time I got there, my grant was going to be working with the basketball program," says Pippen. "So some people threw the word 'manager' out there. Tell you the truth, I never even handed out a towel. It just made for a good story."

Still, he had to talk his way into getting a scholarship, which became easier after he sprouted five inches to 6'7" in a sudden burst (he eventually made it to 6'8") and discovered the benefits of weight training. And he remained a point guard, his added height only boosting his abilities at the position, à la Magic. Still, even after he became a National Association of Intercollegiate Athletics (NAIA) All-American, he never got the big-time postseason exposure. "We didn't even make it to Kansas City," Pippen says, referring to the site of the NAIA tournament.

Consequently, the Central Arkansas campus during the Pippen era was not a stopping-off point for NBA scouts. Except for one—Bulls general manager Jerry Krause. He knew about Pippen. And he wanted to keep it quiet.

"Jerry was like a little cat burglar around me," says Pippen, laughing at the memory. "Everything was done as a big secret. He didn't want anyone to know that he even knew who I was."

What started as mere interest turned into an obsession after Pippen shone in postseason camps, the primary vehicle for border-lines and unknowns to audition for NBA jobs. Whether or not Krause's secrecy was necessary is a matter of opinion, but the deal he worked to get Pippen at number five in 1987, switching picks with the Seattle SuperSonics (who took Olden Polynice), stands as one of the canniest draft-day head fakes ever. These days YouTube videos of Pippen would have been all over the Internet before the draft, and one can imagine the taglines: "Another Magic Surfaces at Obscure NAIA School!" "Central Arkansas Sure to Produce Lottery Pick!" Krause wouldn't have been able to keep Scottie to himself.

Twenty-two years later, it's still known as the "Migraine Game." Kareem Abdul-Jabbar and Maurice Cheeks were among NBA players who suffered from debilitating headaches, but Pippen, who never had another one, has the clearest association with the word *migraine*. In that infamous Game 7 in 1990, Pippen played forty-two minutes, which is the most amazing stat of all since he says that at times he had trouble distinguishing his teammates from the opposition. He took ten shots and made only one. He had just four rebounds, one steal, and two assists. The Bulls lost 93–74, and, later, in the locker room, Pippen shed tears.

But from the ashes of that game, the Bulls rose, Pippen in particular. Scottie had this eureka moment in the 1991–92 season when he just *got* it, figured out how to be Jordan's teammate: take the shots when Michael was off, play distributor when Michael was on, and always—*always*—do the tough jobs defensively. They were so good together that it was hard to remember that they had not always been a fibrous and lethal combination. Just months after the Migraine Game, in the fertile soil of a new season, the Bulls would be heading toward their first NBA championship, and a few months after that, Scottie Pippen was targeted as one of the prime "gets" on the greatest basketball team ever. Not bad for someone who did his work in the shadows.

# THE SHADOW MAN

. . . . . . . . . . . . . . . . . . . . . . . . . . . . . . . . . . . . . . . . . .

## "Michael Got Away with a Lot of Things"

*Fort Lauderdale, Florida*

Scottie Pippen strides through the lobby of the hotel, bearing still noble, posture still erect, Roman nose still distinctive. If Michael Jordan has the jangly, tippy-toed walk of the ex-jock, Pippen carries himself with the easy, unhurried grace of a patrician.

In the years since he retired in 2004, Pippen has from time to time been the subject of headlines that haven't been glorious. He was not happy when his wife, Larsa, signed on as a regular on *Real Housewives of Miami,* though it was on the show that the world—or whatever portion of it watches dishing housewives—learned that Scottie had been chosen to enter the Naismith Memorial Basketball Hall of Fame. I'm still checking, but I'm pretty sure that's a first for an NBA superstar.

Pippen has had continued financial problems, and a "yard sale" at his suburban home near the Bulls workout facility was daily newspaper fodder in Chicago for a while. ("Boxes of Beanie Babies!" noted one story.) That explains why Pippen ended his career not in Houston, where he played (and feuded) with Barkley for one season, not in Portland, where he played for four, and not in Chicago, to which he returned for twenty-three ill-advised games (karmic alert: that's Jordan's number) in 2004, but in Helsinki, Finland, in 2008, playing for a team called ToPo. I'm still checking, but I'm pretty sure that's also a first for an NBA superstar.

"Yes, some of the problems remain," concedes Pippen. "But I don't work, right? And I drive a Rolls, right? Some of these things were just out of my control, not my fault."

Pippen seems to nestle comfortably within the bounds of an athletic archetype: the kid who came from nothing and can't stop spending money when he finally gets it. But that doesn't precisely fit Pippen, who early in his career fretted about money and says, "You won't find a more conservative money guy than me." That's an obvious exaggeration. But what cost him millions late in his career was a combination of ill-advised spontaneous investments and the advice of bad investors, not a steady orgy of profligate spending. Granted, that might be a distinction without a difference and one that didn't help his bottom line.

At any rate, in the 2011 postseason Pippen was back working, as an analyst for Comcast SportsNet Chicago, when he suggested that LeBron James might be "the greatest player to ever play the game." That caused the predictable firestorm because it seemed to demean Jordan. (When I asked Jordan about it in the summer of 2011, he just shook his head and said, "Jealousy.") Pippen later did some backtracking, but, honestly, I didn't think what he said in retreat was all that different from what he said in the first place—that James could *someday* surpass Jordan. I don't happen to agree, but the man is entitled to his opinion, whatever its wellspring.

So it goes for the Shadow Man. Since 1987, when he came to Chicago, Pippen has had very little reality outside what can be framed within the all-consuming force that is Jordan. Over the years I must've had three hundred conversations with coaches, GMs, and other players about Scottie Pippen, and I honestly wonder if any of them ever proceeded without a mention of Jordan. Here's what Chris Mullin perceptively said when we talked about Pippen: "I'm not going to say that Michael *made* him. That's too strong because Scottie had a lot of game. But if Scottie plays with another guy, I'm not sure whether it's not just the gifts that wouldn't have come out, but also the drive."

And so my conversation with the Shadow Man turns, as it inevitably would, to being Jordan's teammate.

"To me, our team was always about chemistry," says Pippen, pushing around some scrambled eggs, "and we never could develop chemistry because of Michael. He didn't believe in his teammates. It was hard for us. We got accused of standing and looking because he would always . . . do the Kobe." (He means showing visible anger to his teammates, as the Lakers' Kobe Bryant often does.)

"When Phil [Jackson] came, it made all the difference to Michael. Phil convinced him to believe in his teammates, and I think I was the first one Michael really trusted. We didn't have to worry about Michael coming down and pulling up one-on-five. We could just play.

"Look, there was pressure on Michael. Obviously. But it always turned out good for Michael, win, lose, or draw. He was getting the headlines no matter what happened—'Jordan scores 35 or 40 or whatever, and the team didn't back him up. Michael did this but the team didn't do that.' That's how it was for a long time."

I ask Pippen if Jordan would ever admit that.

"No way," he says. "The great ones don't tend to admit things were their fault. He's going to say, 'We were going to get beat by 25, so I did what I had to do.'"

When it's all said and done, I ask, is he glad he played with Jordan?

"Of course I'm glad I played with him. But I had to figure out how to do it. You have to understand that Michael is a scorer. He has a will to score, and he had three years in the league without me. He knew what he could get done without me.

"Defensively, we did it together. I can't take the credit and he can't take the credit. In '91 [the Finals against the Lakers] I got some credit for defending Magic, but Michael defended him, too. We wore Magic down together.

"See, we had good defensive chemistry. We had areas on the court where we just knew we were going to trap. We didn't even talk about it. We let them cross half-court and get them in that corner. Or on an inbounds play, if a guy caught it at a certain spot, we knew we had him nailed. Or on our way up court, Michael would stop his guy, I would come, and we would catch him there. We were always in tune of how to double-team the ball."

So, I ask, who was the better defender?

Pippen smiles. "Well, I guess everybody would say Michael," he says.

But what does Pippen say?

"Well, Michael got away with a lot of things," says Pippen. "Let's just put it that way. He was the icon of the game for the world. And remember, that means for the opposing coaches, the officials, the opposing scorekeepers. *Everybody* was in awe of Michael Jordan. There's never been another player like this in professional sports.

"I mean, officials are saying to me, 'Ask Michael if I can have his shoes after the game.' Are you kidding me? All that made a difference. Michael goes into the backcourt, mauls Joe Dumars, and steals the ball. What, Joe Dumars is going to get a call? Nobody wanted Joe Dumars's shoes after the game."

(Man, what the Pistons of the "Bad Boys" era wouldn't have given to hear Scottie say that twenty years ago.)

"But, hey, they were great perks if you were playing with him. They worked to our advantage and they worked to Michael's advantage."

When Pippen was inducted into the Hall of Fame in 2010, he asked Jordan to stand with him onstage. Scottie was as emotional as any player I've ever seen up there, truly overwhelmed by the moment, and he was extremely complimentary about Jordan. It was hard playing in the Jordan shadow, but in his heart of hearts I think he understands how much it helped him.

I also know that he was extremely happy when, as I walked him to his car, a man looked up and said: "Hey, it's Scottie Pippen! No Scottie . . . no rings for M.J."

# CHAPTER 12

# THE COACH

· · · · · · · · · · · · · · · · · · · · · · · · · · · · · · · · · · · · · · ·

## A Man of Both Style and Substance

Minutes before tip-off of a postseason game in 1990 at the Palace of Auburn Hills in suburban Detroit, Pistons coach Chuck Daly leaned over to whisper some words of wisdom to me and my court-side companion, David Dupree of *USA Today*. We listened intently—perhaps it would be some strategic nugget we could use later.

"See the subtle gold pinstripe in this suit?" Chuck said. "Notice how it's the perfect match for the gold coloring in my tie?"

That, in a nutshell, was why Charles Jerome Daly ended up coaching the Dream Team.

Daly wasn't serious, of course. Oh, he was serious about his wardrobe—"Nobody ever looked bad in a blue suit," he told me once, offering one of his life principles in a sober voice, much like my father, who, cautioning me to drink booze neat, told me, "It's those mixers with all that sugar that'll kill you"—but Daly was having fun with his own wardrobe obsession, not to mention slowly opening the valve on the pressure-cooker reality of the occasion. Try to imagine, say, Bill Belichick acting that way before a playoff game; actually, try to imagine Bill Belichick noticing that his pinstripes matched his tie.

The idea of having a college guy coach the '92 team did not go down without a fight. Krzyzewski, who almost certainly would've been the coach, said that he came to accept the decision early, while others say that his was the most strident voice about the necessity of having a college coach for Olympic competition. Whichever account is correct, his opinion deserved to be heard . . . and was doomed to failure, since the selection committee was stacked with NBA general managers.

Daly was not the first name out of everyone's mouth. Quite early, Don Nelson volunteered for the job, and the names of two other predictable suspects, Pat Riley and Larry Brown, were bandied about. It was committee member Billy Cunningham who first brought up Detroit coach Daly, who had been Cunningham's assistant when the Philadelphia 76ers won the NBA championship in 1983.

At this point, sometime after the 1988–89 season, Daly was coming off a championship sweep of the Lakers, and he would win another, against the Portland Trail Blazers, in the summer of 1990, before the committee would make its decision. Daly had coached in high school, in college (at Penn, where for six years in the 1970s he co-dominated the Ivy League with Princeton), and the NBA. Most important, nobody didn't like Chuck.

Perhaps it had to do with Daly being a latecomer who had clearly paid his dues. He was already forty-eight when he got his first NBA job as Cunningham's assistant. He was fifty-one when he got his first head coaching job (with the Cavs), fifty-one when he first got fired (from the Cavs), fifty-three when he got hired by the Pistons, and fifty-eight when he won his first NBA championship. He was no phenom, and perhaps that made him aware that it could all go away tomorrow. He wasn't gloomy, but he did have a dark side that balanced out that nobody-looks-bad-in-a-blue-suit hauteur. The *Boston Globe*'s Bob Ryan, the dean of NBA writers, had christened Daly the "Prince of Pessimism." In contrast to, say, Red Auerbach, who would light his victory cigar as soon as he felt his Celtics had the game under control, Daly would be sitting on a 20-point lead with ten seconds left and fret about the 21-point play the opposing coach had up his sleeve.

Daly was the kind of guy who looked like *somebody* even if you didn't know exactly who. With his dark suits and carefully coiffed hair, he seemed to have stepped out of the pages of *Guys and Dolls*, a man who knew how to make the deals or knew someone who knew how to make the deals. But he never got lost in all that Hugo Boss. He was from a small town called Kane, Pennsylvania, about a hundred miles northeast of Pittsburgh, a land of snow and ice and slush. Here's what his high school coach, C. Stuart Edwards, was like. I called Edwards for a profile I was writing about Daly, and after hearing the words *Sports Illustrated*, grumbled, "I'm not interested in buying any magazines," and hung up the phone. It took two more calls to get Edwards back on the line.

Chuck's first coaching job was at Punxsutawney High, in the town best known for pulling a groundhog out of a basket every February and asking it to predict the weather. With those roots, it's hard to take yourself seriously, and this helps explain why Daly managed the neat trick of coming across as both blue- and white-collar without being a poseur.

He had all sorts of set pieces he pulled out to charm you. "Ya owe me any money?" he used to say when he pumped your hand to say hello. He described NBA coaching as "dealing with twelve individual Fortune 500 companies." He never overtalked during time-outs; sometimes he got his point across by saying nothing. "You know how some business executives hate meetings and say they're ineffective?" Daly used to tell me. "Well, think about my job. Before the game you meet with the team and that's a meeting. Every time-out . . . meeting. End of a quarter . . . meeting. Halftime . . .

meeting. After the game . . . meeting. Next day at practice . . ." It was a brilliant shtick, and it rang true.

Daly had remained a popular figure despite the fact that his physical Pistons, who wore the tag "Bad Boys" with pride, were controversial. Every night of his Pistons coaching life, Daly did a Wallenda on a very skinny rope. He had a subtle way of humanizing his hated team. Isiah Thomas was always "Zeke." Laimbeer was always "Billy." Feisty forward Rick Mahorn (a funny and terrific guy off the court, by the way) was always "Ricky." Throw in "Vinnie" Johnson, the Pistons light-it-up third guard, and the Bad Boys sounded like a collection of precious cherubs rather than one of the most physical and intimidating teams in NBA history.

Though Daly would never, ever sell out his players, he somehow detached himself from the on-court mayhem the Pistons created. It was almost as if he were the feckless father in a sitcom, unable to stop his sons from breaking the furniture, rather than the architect of the "Jordan Rules," an armor-plated defense that doubled and tripled Jordan and gave him a strategic shove or elbow even when he didn't have the ball. "Chuck's ego," says Rod Thorn, an NBA executive who helped pick the Dream Team coach and players, "was not as big as his team's."

In short, Daly didn't have warts—"He didn't bring any baggage," as Thorn put it—and, in the end, the committee decision was an easy one. On Valentine's Day, 1991, a limo picked up Daly before a game in Milwaukee and whisked him to O'Hare Airport in Chicago, where he was told that he was the choice to coach the 1992 Olympic team. Daly said he was surprised, but who knew if that was true? He was a poker player of the first order. He was also told that Lenny Wilkens was the choice for first assistant, and that was fine with Daly, too.

As an organization, the Pistons took the official position that they were happy for Daly. The reality might've been something else. The team had clearly lost its edge over the Bulls by then, yet there was Daly getting a "promotion" that had nothing to do with Motown. Isiah Thomas was battling a wrist injury that kept him out of action for ten weeks, and several weeks after Daly was announced as the Dream Team coach, the Pistons' captain went off on everyone. "Nobody gives a shit around here anymore and that includes the coaches," Thomas said after a home loss to the lowly Cleveland Cavaliers. "We've become comfortable with losing."

Perhaps that was Isiah's audition for the Dream Team, an effort to demonstrate how important winning was to him. Perhaps it was legitimate anger. Perhaps it was both.

USA Basketball wanted to announce a team by September 1991, ten months before qualifying competition would begin, and felt comfortable that it had gotten the right man as coach. Quite early in the process it was decided that the time-honored Olympic tryouts—those enervating ordeals that enabled tyrants such as Knight to rage and fume and hold the stage for weeks on end, and which in the U.S. track and field world are still held sacrosanct—weren't going to happen. *Listen, Michael, could you get in that layup line over there? We wanna get a good look at you.* There was a lot of work to do to fill the roster, and the committee charged Daly with creating a list of the players he'd want, broken down by position, a half dozen or so in each category.

For Daly, that was the easy part. That was the big list, and anyone could've made one with the usual suspects—Jordan, Magic, Bird, Barkley, Malone, Stockton, Mullin, Drexler, and so on. Daly included four of his own players on that list—Isiah (obviously), Joe Dumars, Rodman (just coming into his own as a player who would become one of the greatest rebounders of all time), and Laimbeer, who didn't have a snowball's chance in hell of making the team but was an exceptionally smart player who had been a big part of Daly's two championship teams.

Seeing all those names on the board—players such as James Worthy, Kevin McHale, and Dominique Wilkins, all of whom were unlikely to be chosen—had a profound effect on the college guys on the committee. In casual conversations, the idea of a team with six

NBA players and six college players had gradually given way to an eight-and-four breakdown. The college guys prepared to dig in at eight and four.

Then the hard reality set in. "I'll never forget the day we put the names from the big list on the board," says C. M. Newton, one of the college guys on the committee. "We were talking about eight pros and four college kids at that point, and then you looked at the NBA names . . . and there was literally no one to leave off. We all knew at that point, and it was pretty early, that it was just about all over for the college kids."

The more interesting list that Daly provided, though, was his wish list, which included the names of the players he felt were most essential for success. I never saw that list, and as far as I know Chuck never showed it publicly before he died from cancer in May 2009. Perhaps he never even wrote down the names. Or perhaps somewhere in Chuck's files there is a scrap of paper still to be unearthed. The memories of the committee members do not completely coalesce on the names, but, after some investigation, I stand behind the names I wrote in *Sports Illustrated* at the time: Jordan, Magic, Pippen, Robinson, Mullin, Malone, and Ewing.

The order is deliberate. Michael and Magic are the obvious one-two. Daly wanted Pippen for his long-armed, cover-the-court defensive abilities and his offensive versatility. True, he had seen his own team turn Pippen into a shell of a player many times, but the Bulls sideman had upped his game considerably during the Bulls' '91 championship run. Players are often damned with the faint praise of being "complementary," but Pippen was perhaps unique in this respect: he was a superstar complementary player.

Daly loved Robinson's shot blocking and Mullin's shot making. Reggie Miller's name came up early, but Daly saw Mullin as more of a classic zone breaker. The coach wasn't completely enamored of Malone but considered the Mailman a dependable low-block scorer and a shot-clock bailout. Ditto for Ewing, though Daly had far more affection for Robinson's game than he did for Ewing's.

The name of Isiah Thomas was not on Daly's list. Exactly why not is a subject for later (Chapter 14), but Daly constantly sold the idea that he was only the coach. "The committee picks the players," he said, comparing it to the situation in the NBA—general managers get the players, and coaches coach them. That was technically true but pragmatically hogwash. Had Daly walked into the room and said, "I want Isiah Thomas on this team," the committee would've had a much tougher time with the selection process. I didn't express that opinion at the time, and neither, as far as I know, did anyone else. In part I excuse myself for not writing about it because there was no Internet and no SI.com and therefore no great volume of stories about the selection of the Olympic team. But another part of the reason I didn't write it was my respect for the tough position that Daly was in.

"Chuck's the one who really skated on the Isiah issue," says Jan Hubbard, who did the most aggressive reporting about the Olympic selection process for *Newsday*.

Isiah had another supposed ally on the committee in Detroit general manager Jack McCloskey, a respected voice in the NBA. If Isiah felt uncomfortable lobbying Daly for a spot on the team—and he did—he certainly could tell McCloskey that he wanted in on the Barcelona festivities. "Isiah felt that he couldn't put pressure on Chuck," says Dave Gavitt, "but he put big-time pressure on Jack."

Thomas once had political capital around the league, back when he was a kid whose killer crossover was matched only by his killer smile. But that capital was diminishing—the Jordan freeze-out, the Bird insult, the Pistons' physical play. As Gavitt puts it, "It quickly became obvious that Isiah was not the most popular dude."

"At that particular time, we were the past," says Laimbeer, Isiah's best friend on the team and the Bad Boy least likely to mince words. "It would've been interesting to see what would've happened if the Olympics had come along two years earlier, when we were in the middle of our run. The Olympic team was a political battle, and if there was one team and one player that wasn't going to win a political battle, it was the Detroit Pistons and Isiah Thomas."

Two notable names that were not on Daly's wish list were those of Larry Bird and Charles Barkley. Bird had already made noises about being too old and too beset by back problems. And Charles . . . well, Charles was another matter, even to someone like Daly, who had coached more than his share of space cadets.

CHAPTER 13

# THE JESTER

· · · · · · · · · · · · · · · · · · · · · · · · · · · · · · · · · · · · · · · · · · · · · · · ·

**Sir Charles Wants to Be an Olympian . . .
He Just Doesn't Always Act Like One**

On the evening of March 26, 1991, as USA Basketball's Olympic selection committee was getting serious about whom they were going to invite to play on the team, Charles Barkley of the Philadelphia 76ers was getting irritated during a game against the New Jersey Nets. Even Barkley's detractors had to give him points for getting amped up in New Jersey, in an arena devoid of animation and energy. Barkley would later say that an older male fan was yelling things like "Fat ass!" and "Asshole!" at him; in some stories the insults were said to be racial. The latter was never proven, but suffice to say that back then racial epithets were hurled during games. They weren't directed at me, obviously, but I heard them.

At any rate, Barkley turned to spit at the fan, but, as he said later in a memorable disquisition on the incident, "I didn't get enough foam," and his spittle landed on an eight-year-old girl named Lauren Rose, who was at the game with her parents. As

soon as he realized what he had done, Barkley was properly mortified, issuing heartfelt apology after heartfelt apology, and, as was
and is his style, eventually befriending the girl and her family.

But spitting on a fan? A young girl? That was considered by
many to be the public relations strike that would keep Barkley off
the Olympic team, of which he desperately wanted to be a part. A
few weeks earlier, at the NBA All-Star Game in Charlotte, he had
run into C. M. Newton, who was on USA Basketball's selection
committee and who had been an assistant coach on Bob Knight's
gold medal team from which Barkley had been cut, partly because
Knight didn't like him, to be sure, but partly because Barkley grew
bored with the enervating trials and more or less dared Knight to
axe him.

"Don't hold 1984 against me," Barkley said to Newton. "I really
want to be on this team!" That was the All-Star Weekend to which
Barkley, acknowledging the first Persian Gulf incursion, wore a cap
that read "Fuck Iraq."

At the time, the should-Charles-be-chosen? debate was one of
the hottest among the committee members. On pure ability, Barkley
was a lock, "one of the top three players in the world at that time,"
as Mike Krzyzewski, a committee member, described him. Barkley
could score, run the floor, and shoot well enough to bust zones (if
that was necessary); most important, he could rebound. He is probably not the greatest rebounder of all time, but he's in the conversation. His rebounding stats, in the double figures per game, are taken
for granted, but what was extraordinary was the number of offensive rebounds he got—four per game for his career and almost five
per game during a five-season stretch early in his career. Yes, Dennis Rodman got more offensive rebounds, but the Worm was averaging in single figures in scoring, compared to 25 points per game
for Barkley.

Barkley was less easy to classify than any of the other reigning
superstars at the time. Jordan's ability was nonpareil, but at least
you could explain it: he was hardwired for success, talented and te-
nacious, gifted with a body that was both strong and supple. Magic

was a giant at his position. David Robinson was a seven-footer with gymnast's skills, Isiah Thomas an elusive jitterbug with lightning reflexes, Karl Malone a muscleman who had refined his shooting touch.

But what was Barkley? He was 6'4", yet played almost exclusively under the basket. He looked fat, but he could jump out of the gym. He rebounded like a madman, but he never boxed out; Roger Banks, an assistant coach back at Auburn, told Barkley, "Just go for the ball," so that's how he rebounded, from the first day to the last day of his NBA career. He looked like he couldn't beat the ballboy in a race, but few people ever caught him when he went end to end with the ball.

Chris Mullin remembers the first time he met Barkley. It was the summer of 1982, and the two were bunking up prior to a tour on a U.S. junior team. They were both going into their sophomore year, Mullin at St. John's, Barkley at Auburn. Mullin, his head and his heart in eastern basketball, had never heard of Barkley.

"He was sitting on the bed with his shirt off," says Mullin, "and I'll never forget it. He was real . . . inquisitive. Asking me about New York, real interested that I came from there, almost like—I hesitate to say it—a fan. I swear to God, I thought he was working for the basketball organization or something, maybe like a manager. I did not know he was a player.

"So the next day, the first day of practice, we split into sides and there on my team is Charles. I could not believe it. And then we started playing and here's this fat kid jumping out of the gym and . . . I mean, I never saw anything like it. The only thing I can compare it to was years later when I saw [7'7"] Manute Bol for the first time. Just this extreme . . . *physicality*. Two things stuck in my mind: How freakin' *good* is this guy? And can he maintain because of how hard he comes down on dunks?"

I compare Barkley to Bird, strictly in a during-the-game sense. That is strange in one respect because the ability to elevate, one of the keys to Barkley's game, had nothing to do with Bird's success. But they both jumped quickly, if to markedly differing altitudes, and they both had strong hands when they seized a rebound. Bird was a student of Barkley's game and loved analyzing it. "Charles jumps from side to side, not just straight up," Bird told me once. Bird jumped side to side, too, thereby clearing a path while almost never getting whistled for it.

There was a street-smartness to Barkley's game, too, a Bird-like elemental rawness. I was at a game during the 1988–89 season when Barkley was standing near Portland Trail Blazers rookie Mark Bryant, who held the ball on the baseline. "Yo!" Barkley shouted to him suddenly, and apparently convincingly, because Bryant passed him the ball, which Barkley took to the other end for a dunk. Bird pulled off some kind of similar street theft a dozen times in his career.

But as far as the men choosing the Olympic team were concerned, Barkley brought baggage way, way, *way* over the fifty-pound limit. After all, it wasn't like Barkley had lost his virginity with the spitting incident. Before he was drafted, he was considered in some quarters to be an NBA question mark, which didn't stop him from going on an eating binge in an effort to discourage the 76ers from drafting him. (Philadelphia owner Howard Katz wanted Charles to go from 282 pounds to 275; instead Charles ballooned to 291.)

He once slapped a fan in the face for verbally abusing him. He told an elderly female fan in Boston, "Shut up, you bitch." He got in trouble with the league office for pretending to lay bets during the game with the New York Knicks' Mark Jackson. In August 1988, Barkley was arrested for illegal possession of a handgun after being pulled over for speeding. He had a permit to carry in Pennsylvania but not in Jersey. When I brought it up during an interview, asking the inevitable non-gun-owner's question about whether it was loaded, Barkley responded, "Of course it was, *fool*! What's the use of carrying a gun that ain't loaded?"

He trashed teammates, cursed out referees, exchanged punches with opponents, and angered every kind of minority group possible, which was mitigated by the fact that he angered majority groups too. Indeed, it is impossible to find another player who was at once praised for his honesty yet made so many contradictory statements. What he said on Tuesday might go against what he said on Monday, but that didn't matter because he'd say something else on Wednesday. "You never know what Charles is going to say," David Stern says, "because he doesn't know himself." Barkley would talk about team unity, for example, then rip his teammates, as he did in *Outrageous!*, which came out in December 1991. After that he made publishing history by declaring that he had been "misquoted" in his own autobiography and didn't really mean to criticize teammates Armen Gilliam, Manute Bol, and Charles Shackleford, as well as 76ers owner Katz.

He talked endlessly about the leadership lessons he had learned from Julius Erving, Maurice Cheeks, and Bobby Jones, the 76ers veterans who ran the club when he came aboard in 1984, and he waxed nostalgic for the days when he was required to bring Erving the morning newspaper at 7:00 a.m. and fetch Andrew Toney a glass of warm milk at night. Yet his own leadership style would never have been even remotely mistaken for the ones demonstrated by those diplomats. He didn't always practice hard and sometimes showed up late, a precursor to another 76er, Allen Iverson, who went on a memorable rant about practice, believing, as Barkley did, that the measure of a man was how hard he busted his ass in the forty-eight minutes that really mattered.

But—and there is always a but with Barkley (not to mention a butt)—I loved coming to see him. There is not another athlete in history who could do the things that Barkley did and still remain beloved to a good portion of the population.

After the spitting incident, Rod Thorn, in his position as the NBA's vice president of operations, fined him $10,000 (it would be much, much more today, not to mention a lengthy suspension) and said all the predictable things about how disappointed the league was in Barkley. At the same time, Thorn, in his position as an influential member of the USA Basketball committee assembling the Olympic team, was lobbying for Barkley's inclusion.

Whenever I came to see Charles, I would promise myself that I would wade through the muck of his contradictions and make him answer for some of the double-talk that came out of his mouth. He would invariably go on some kind of rant about the media, which, in his version, had started to treat him unfairly after the gun incident. The charges in that case were eventually dropped after a judge ruled that the car had been illegally searched, but Barkley professed at the time to have been fundamentally changed by the incident, claiming that the media had overreacted to the story. I suppose that was the case in some instances, but by and large the media were Barkley's ally. If they hadn't been, nobody could've gotten away with what he did and still emerge as a popular figure.

No matter how much you thought he deserved to be skewered, the man would wear you down with his antic charm. All of the Dream Teamers were friendly and polite when they met my family, but Charles was the one to bear-hug my sons and tell my wife, feigning confusion, "You seem like a nice woman. What the hell's the matter with your judgment?" He was like Claude Rains's Captain Louis Renault in *Casablanca*, a figure who would round up the usual suspects yet somehow remain likable.

The committee's job was to weigh the benefits of Barkley's abilities (they did love his rebounding) and general popularity (all of the top players in the league liked and respected him, especially Jordan, for whom he had good-naturedly caddied during a charity golf tournament in the summer of 1990) against the possibility that he would start World War III. "The question we had to answer," says committee member Donnie Walsh, "was whether Charles was too much of a nut."

The two most powerful NBA voices on the committee were divided on Barkley. Had it been up to Russ Granik, the committee probably would've said no to Charles. Had it been up to Rod Thorn, it would've said yes to Charles. "The basketball people are always petrified that they don't have enough good players," said Stern, and Thorn was a basketball guy. By contrast, executives such as Granik are always more concerned about the knucklehead factor. They have to be. Neither man would've gone to the mat with his position, and gradually Barkley the basketball player started gaining traction over Barkley the knucklehead.

Then again, he hadn't yet downed a drunk with a left cross thrown outside a Milwaukee bar at two-thirty in the morning.

# CHAPTER 14

# THE COMMITTEE AND THE DREAM TEAM

· · · · · · · · · · · · · · · · · · · · · · · · · · · · · · · · · · · · · · · · · · ·

**Okay, Superstars, Prepare for
Deification. . . . Uh, Isiah? Not So Fast**

There's back story here, and, even two decades later, much broken-field running by everyone who was involved in the final decision about who was invited to play on the 1992 Olympic team and who was not. It's one of the stickiest subjects in the history of the NBA. But let's cut to the bone before we sort through all the meat.

Isiah Thomas was not a member of the Dream Team primarily because of two men, Michael Jordan and Chuck Daly. If we want to put a finer point on it, it was really one man—Jordan.

Throughout the spring and summer months of 1991, the business of USA Basketball's Olympic selection committee was carried out rather like the business of the Politburo. Bits of news leaked out from time to time but quite often were wrong, as when the *Chicago Tribune* reported that Isiah had been offered a spot. USA Basketball was not unlike a schoolgirl planning a sweet-sixteen party. They wanted the cool kids there, but if the cool kids weren't coming, they needed to get the next-coolest kids there to fill the quota. But sometimes the coolest kids were the ones who were coy about coming, so they had to let the next-coolest kids know that they still had a chance without raising their hopes too much.

Fortunately for the committee, cool kid Magic Johnson wasn't coy. After getting an early call from Russ Granik, the first official one made by the committee, Johnson jumped in with both feet, thereby becoming a kind of baseline selectee. "Magic really helped us," says Dave Gavitt. "He set a tone, that being on the Olympic team was the thing to do."

Rod Thorn, who as general manager of the Bulls in 1984 had drafted Jordan, was assigned the most important task: pulling the prize catch into the boat. Thorn called Jordan directly sometime during the summer, after the Bulls had won their first championship. (In fact, all of the invitations were extended directly to the athletes, not through agents; Granik, who as a league exec had fought numerous nasty battles with agents by that time, had insisted on that.) So let's be clear right now about what Jordan said in that first phone call.

"Rod, I don't want to play if Isiah Thomas is on the team," Jordan said.

I wrote that in *Sports Illustrated* at the time, not because Jordan confirmed it, which he didn't, but because at least two reliable sources did. At the time, Jordan more or less denied that he would stand in Isiah's way.

But he did confirm it to me in the summer of 2011. "I told Rod I don't want to play if Isiah Thomas is on the team." That's what he said.

Thorn knew his part. I don't know how explicitly he said it—and Thorn won't say—but he made it clear that no one would be on the team if Jordan didn't want him on the team. No one on the committee had to communicate that to Daly because Daly knew it himself, as Jordan had told the coach in an early phone call, *I don't want to play if Isiah Thomas is on the team.* And Chuck let it be known that he wouldn't fight for Isiah.

Was Jordan wrong? Well, you can call him spoiled and talk about how this was "America's Team" and all the rest of it. But he was hesitant to give up his summer time in any case and definitely didn't want to do it if it involved making nice with a man he despised. "Michael was all about who was going to be on the team," Magic told me years later. "It was more important . . . no, make that *just* as important, for Michael to have a good time as it was to play the games." No, Magic, stick with what you said first—it was *more* important.

A more interesting question is whether Daly was wrong. A number of people say that he was, all but one of whom didn't want his name attached to that opinion. The exception was Clyde Drexler (see the interlude following Chapter 18). But to those who say that Daly politicized the process by letting one man dictate what a committee should've decided on, and to those who would castigate the committee for caving to the dictates of one player, ask yourself what you would have done. Would you have selected Isiah Thomas over Michael Jordan in the summer of 1992? Or any other summer?

Even though he had assurances that Isiah would not be on the team, Jordan continued to be coy. Magic played the role of ambassador, calling Jordan from time to time. As late as August 19, when they shared the podium at Magic's annual summer all-star game in L.A. to benefit the United Negro College Fund, Jordan was still playing footsy. But I still maintain that Jordan knew early on that he was playing, once it was clear that Isiah would not be invited and that Daly would leave sufficient time for golf. From the beginning, Jordan was set; he just wasn't *set* set, as screenwriter William Goldman once wrote in *Adventures in the Screen Trade* about the peculiar way that deals were set up in Hollywood.

Bird was another matter. That task, less crucial than landing Jordan but ceremonially significant, fell primarily to Gavitt, who by then was in his first year of running the Boston Celtics. The committee didn't *need* the thirty-four-year-old Bird in the way that it needed the twenty-eight-year-old Jordan, who was in the prime of his career. But the members desperately *wanted* Bird, which was almost the same thing.

The extent to which Jordan, Magic, and Bird formed a subset within the universe of great players cannot be overestimated. Magic and Bird had been measured against each other for over a decade by that time, and Jordan had come along to join them; the three formed the golden tripod on which the NBA was standing strong. No one else could join this exclusive club. Some players, like Barkley, understood this and carved out a comfortable position outside the tripod but friend to all three. Others, like Malone, may have resented the primacy of Michael/Magic/Larry but remained on the outside, smoldering but seemingly unconcerned.

Isiah was different. It was an enduring frustration for him that he could not break into this select society, that, as great as he was, he was on the outside looking in. Had he been as tall as Magic or Larry, or even Michael, yes, perhaps it would've been a Big Four. (Isiah would make that point, in typically ham-handed fashion, years later.) But at 6'1" he just couldn't dominate like the others, and it gnawed at him that he was, in his view, perpetually unappreciated. What hurt more was that Magic, his old friend, was growing closer and closer to Jordan, his enemy. Most of us are familiar with, and perhaps even subject to, this dynamic . . . in junior high.

Gavitt thought he had a chance with Bird. They had hit it off when Bird returned for the 1990–91 season and saw that Gavitt, now the Celtics CEO, had upgraded the facilities at Hellenic College, the old-school venue where the Celtics practiced. "Hey, we're serious about winning again, huh?" Bird said to him.

Gavitt first broached the subject of Barcelona at Bird's house in Needham, Massachusetts.

"Larry, we want you to be on the Olympic team," he said.

"I'm past history," said Bird. "It's for the young guys."

Gavitt let it go. There would be time.

Bird desperately did not want to be a token, but his aching back was forcing him to conclude that that's exactly what he would be. I was around him a lot in those days, writing a book on the Celtics' season, and Bird's aching back was the defining leitmotif of that season. *How is Larry? Will Larry announce his retirement? Is Larry getting treatment? Is Larry answering questions today?*

Gavitt, his political powers tested to the max, decided that all missives about Bird would come from him. To this day, when I see Celtics trainer Ed Lacerte (who was also the Dream Team trainer), I'll ask him, "Any update on Larry?" and Lacerte, the nicest of men and the most capable of trainers, will smile and say, "Dave will have a statement soon."

In truth, the issue of Olympic participation was pushed to the background by Bird, who had worries that his career was over. Midway through that 1990–91 season, as I went to work on what became the "Dream Team" story in *Sports Illustrated*, Magic let it be known that he would not appear on the cover without Bird.

"But Larry says he's not playing," I told him.

"I'm going to check myself," said Johnson.

A couple of dozen phone calls transpired before Magic finally said okay, convinced that Bird was not going to Barcelona.

Looking back at Bird's storied career, one could do worse than studying the 1990–91 season to capture the man's greatness. There were mornings that he could barely walk. I saw it with my own eyes. That doesn't make him a messiah, a saint, or a war hero, but it makes the numbers he put up that season over 60 games, much of them played in pain, quite remarkable. He averaged 19.4 points, 8.5 rebounds, and 7.2 assists and mixed in an epic game or two along the way, one of them against Jordan's Bulls on the last day of March, when he scored 34 points as the Celtics won 135–132.

"Man can still play," said Jordan, shaking his head after the game.

Aside from the Golden Tripod, the committee had a few easy choices. Robinson and Ewing were locks, considering the dearth of quality centers. Karl Malone was a lock. Pippen had by then distinguished himself on the way to the Bulls' championship, and he was a lock. Some committee members didn't think quite as highly of Mullin as Daly did, but Mullin's smarts and his ability to play both shooting guard and small forward turned the tide. He was in.

There was much discussion about Barkley, who had been charged with a misdemeanor count of battery stemming from the incident in Milwaukee after a game against the Bucks. Barkley contended that a group of men followed him for a city block, taunting him, and eventually one of them, a twenty-five-year-old named James R. McCarthy, walked up to him with a balled fist. Charles hit him.

*Okay,* thought some of the committee members, *we can overlook that.*

But then there was Charles's presence at a nasty incident in the lobby of a Chicago hotel when teammate Jayson Williams had smashed a glass beer mug against the head of a Chicago man, who, according to the players, had advanced upon them in a threatening manner. Barkley wasn't charged—as a matter of fact, Williams wasn't, either—and the incident took on its sharpest focus years later when Williams was revealed to have a capacious dark side. (Williams pleaded guilty in 2010 to reckless manslaughter in the death of his limousine driver in an ugly 2002 incident that dragged on for years.)

*Well,* thought some of the committee members, *we can overlook that, too.* Eventually the "great-player" people won out over the "good-citizen" people, and Barkley was in. Let me go on record as saying I agreed wholeheartedly with the decision; in some ways, Barkley turned out to be the most important Dream Teamer.

But always there was the Isiah question. Nobody wanted to come right out and say that Jordan didn't want him. At one point C. M. Newton stood up and said: "Wait a minute. We have a team that won two straight championships and a coach who coached that team, and we're *not* taking the best player from that team?" Another committee member said: "Chuck won two championships. I don't recall him winning them by himself." The Isiah question was always the unspoken subtext, the piece of unpleasant flotsam wobbling just under the surface.

Isiah never called Magic directly, but he did lobby with Magic through Matt Dobek, the Pistons' PR man. But Magic did not speak up for him, partly, Magic says now, because Isiah had questioned his sexuality after he revealed he was HIV positive. Magic discussed it in *When the Game Was Ours*, Jackie MacMullan's bestseller about Magic and Bird.

"He questioned me when I got my HIV diagnosis," MacMullan quotes Magic as saying. "How can a so-called friend question your sexuality like that? I know why he did it, because we used to kiss before games, and now if people were wondering about me, that meant they were wondering about *him*, too."

(Magic confirmed all of it to me in 2011. Not that he needed to—unlike Barkley, Magic's not the kind of guy to be misquoted in his own book.)

There was something else, too, one more Isiah misstep that committee members could use to justify his exclusion. As the seconds counted down on Detroit's four-and-out loss to Jordan and the Bulls in the 1991 Eastern Conference finals, a few members of the Pistons got off the bench and walked off, deliberately passing the Bulls bench and refusing to acknowledge them, never mind congratulating them. To this day, people think that it happened at Isiah's instigation. It did not.

"It was my idea," says Bill Laimbeer, "and I don't regret it for a minute. The Chicago Bulls were the biggest whiners in the world. They said things about us that went beyond the court, that we were dirty and bad individuals. We just happened to play a style of basketball that they didn't like."

Laimbeer also says that Daly pleaded with them not to do it. "He told us, 'Take the high road,'" remembers Laimbeer. But they went low.

Though it wasn't Isiah's idea, he was next to fall in behind Laimbeer. He could've stopped and said, "Billy, we're not doing this." He was the captain, the leader, the best player. But Isiah didn't do that, so it became an Isiah-engineered deal all the way.

Perhaps that figured in the committee's ultimate decision. Perhaps it just supplied more justification to ignore a pariah who would've been ignored anyway. Perhaps it didn't matter at all. But, ultimately, Isiah's phone was not going to ring.

Ultimately, Jordan and Bird said yes, the former finally convinced that Daly, himself a member of the species *Golfus degeneratus*, would allow enough time for recreation, the latter convinced that he was more than a token. Bird knew he was retiring by then—almost no one else did—and he knew he hardly needed to burnish his image as one of the greatest players in history and one of the most important. But maybe at last he realized the significance of the whole thing. Maybe the thought of playing in the Olympics, which he had watched back in French Lick "on those old rabbit-ear antennae," as he said later, seized his soul. Maybe he saw the Olympics as the logical capstone. Maybe he was tired of taking Magic's calls. Maybe all of those things.

On September 21, Bob Costas hosted *The Dream Team: The USA Basketball Selection Show* on NBC. The USA Basketball committee had decided to pick ten NBA players and leave the remaining two roster spots open, thereby staging a de facto tryout that would take place over the 1991–92 season. In order, here's how the players were announced: Magic Johnson, Charles Barkley, Karl Malone, John Stockton, Patrick Ewing, David Robinson, Larry Bird, Chris Mullin, Scottie Pippen, and—for ultimate suspense—Michael Jordan.

By that time, though, Jan Hubbard had listed the ten names in *Newsday*, and the show, the first production ever done inside the new NBA Entertainment facilities in Secaucus, New Jersey, was kind of a dud. It was supposed to be revelatory as well as celebratory, but really, the only true headline was: why wasn't Isiah on the team? As various bits of Pistons news drifted across the airwaves, Barkley was blunt in his assessment: "Pistons! I hate those motherfuckers." Yet moments later, with no apparent irony, he talked about how eagerly he looked forward to playing for Daly, further evidence of Daly's tightrope mastery.

Shortly after the show, Magic released a statement through the

Lakers' public relations department that expressed his disappoint-
ment that Isiah was not on the team. "I sincerely hope the selection
committee awards one of the final two remaining roster positions to
Isiah," it read. "I say this not because Isiah is my friend, but because
I believe he will assist the team in winning the gold medal."

Jack McCloskey, the Pistons' general manager, resigned from
the committee to protest its exclusion of Isiah, after which Hubbard
exposed the fact that McCloskey had never spoken up strongly for
Isiah when he could have. Thomas did not make a loud protest
about his exclusion. In fact, Dennis Rodman, whom some reported
as having gotten more consideration than Isiah—"If Rodman's
name came up at all, and I don't remember that it did," says Rod
Thorn, "a dozen voices right away said, 'Noooo!'"—complained
louder. But Thomas was devastated. When he saw Matt Dobek at a
wedding that summer, he said, "Your boy Chuck left me off." Even
Daly, always uncomfortable with the subject, conceded: "Can I
guarantee that this will not affect them during the season? I don't
think so. I know Isiah is hurt. That's not going to go away."

Years later we discovered, though it was hardly a shock, that
Magic's support of Thomas was bogus, too, another example of
why you should treat "official statements" from a team as fruit from
the poisonous tree. In MacMullan's book Magic says: "Isiah killed
his own chances when it came to the Olympics. Nobody on that
team wanted to play with him. . . . Michael didn't want to play with
him. Scottie [Pippen] wanted no part of him. Bird wasn't pushing
for him. Karl Malone didn't want him. Who was saying, 'We need
this guy'? Nobody."

There was an assumption by many that Thomas would be the
eleventh player chosen nine months hence. But those in the know
realized by then that it was all over for Isiah, that he had lost out not
only to his enemies but also to those who were supposedly his
friends.

# CHAPTER 15

# THE CHOSEN ONE

. . . . . . . . . . . . . . . . . . . . . . . . . . . . . . . . . . . . . . . . . . . . . .

## Michael Seems to Have It All . . .
## But "All" Comes with a Burden

It was a Friday afternoon late in September, shortly after the announcement of the first ten Dream Teamers, and I was backstage at
*Saturday Night Live* with Michael Jordan. If that sounds cool, which
it was, you should also know that Jordan was probably sick of me,
and, truth be told, I was a little sick of him, too. I had spent the last
couple of months of the NBA season chronicling Jordan's first
championship run, which, since it bears repeating, took him seven
arduous seasons. Jordan had appeared on the cover of *Sports Illustrated* for three straight weeks, still unprecedented. (As is the number of times he's been on the cover—fifty-six at this writing, eighteen
ahead of runner-up Muhammad Ali.) I had coaxed every morsel,
exhausted every angle, tapped dry every well concerning Jordan
and the Bulls' season.

Chicago had won the championship in five games, finishing off
the Lakers in L.A. on a Tuesday night, which gave me until Sunday

to file my story. Jordan was supposed to meet me on Thursday but stood me up. Friday, same deal. To be honest, I didn't really blame him, and I can only imagine that he was celebrating in his own way. Finally, on Saturday morning, he dragged himself into one of his downscale breakfast haunts in suburban Chicago, an hour or so late.

"Alarm clock malfunction," said Jordan, sliding into the booth. "Can you believe I missed my first tee time? The official beginning of the golf season?"

We talked for a while, and I could see the relief on his face now that he had officially joined the list of winners that included Magic, Bird, and his hated rival, Isiah.

"Personally, I always felt that in terms of intensity and unselfishness, I played like those type of players," Jordan said as he pushed waffles around on his plate. (He meant players who had won championships.) "Some people saw that, but many others didn't. And the championship, in the minds of a lot of people, is a sign of, well, greatness. I guess they can say that about me now."

On a Friday afternoon in September 1991, backstage at *SNL*, it was hard to believe that anyone else could own the world the way Michael did. He was more avatar than athlete, the center of his and many other universes, clowns to the left of him, jokers to the right. Months earlier he had vanquished the hated Pistons in the Eastern finals, then dispatched Magic in the Finals even as he joined him on the NBA's Mount Rushmore. Part of the championship series turned into a lovefest between Magic and Michael, mostly at Magic's instigation. "I told Michael, 'We can't be separated like this,'" Magic said. "'I respect you too much, and I'm sure you respect me.'" Jordan wasn't nearly as sappy about it—it's hard to out-sap Magic—but he said: "Before, we hadn't known each other as people. Then we got to know each other, and that's when the friendship began."

After the Finals, Jordan had disappeared, as he had in past Julys and Augusts, into the world's finest fairways, sand traps, and clubhouses. But he reappeared with a vengeance in September. A week before his *SNL* appearance, he was toasted and roasted in an NBC special called *A Comedy Salute to Michael Jordan*, a benefit for Comic Relief and Jordan's nonprofit foundation. The show was hardly Emmy material—neither would be his *SNL* appearance—but it did demonstrate conclusively that he had become America's pet rock and its national hero around whom everyone could rally.

Then came the Dream Team announcement. That was followed by his annual black-tie gala in Chicago for the United Negro College Fund. The next day a seven-mile stretch of I-40 near his native Wilmington, North Carolina, was dedicated in his name. Around that time Marketing Evaluations Inc. released its Q-ratings, and Jordan was number one not only in the United States but also in Canada, meaning that he was more popular north of the border than hockey immortal Wayne Gretzky.

To recap, he had become an NBA champion, an Olympian, a humanitarian, a highway, and a cultural touchstone. That's not a bad lifetime's work, and it had taken Jordan all of three months.

Backstage at *SNL*, the younger cast members, some of them Jordan worshippers from their days in Chicago's Second City comedy troupe, gravitated toward him, testing his capacity for horseplay, which was high. At one point Jordan pantsed the rotund Chris Farley, then snuck up behind him to block a shot that Farley tried to take on a small basket. When Dana Carvey missed a cue that led to Jordan's botching a line, veteran Phil Hartman gave Carvey a withering look. "Dana, get it right," Hartman said. "Michael Jordan's a big, international star. You're just a little comedy act." (It's hard to think about that scene without realizing that both Hartman and Farley are dead.)

Still, there was reality, and in his cramped *SNL* dressing room Jordan was tired and cranky. An enervating live-to-tape show awaited him in twenty-four hours; it was killing him that a beautiful Friday afternoon was going by and he wasn't playing golf. There was a tap on the door and in came cast member Al Franken, now the junior senator from Minnesota. Franken was bearing a basketball, a sweatsuit, a few pieces of paper, and a sheepish grin.

"Uh, Mike," said Franken, "I told you I wouldn't ask you to autograph a lot of stuff, but . . ." Jordan looked up from the TV and asked, "But you want me to autograph a lot of stuff, right, Al?"

When he left Jordan confessed to having some trepidation about a sketch he was to do with Franken in the role of Stuart Smalley, a helpless self-help guru.

"That's a funny character," I said.

"You would like it," Jordan said.

I was never sure what he meant by that; perhaps that it was a sketch attuned to fortysomething Caucasians, of which I was one at the time.

Rehearsals had been hard. The writers had wanted to do a bit about Jordan's keeping Isiah off the Olympic team, but he wouldn't go for it. He had missed one of his shots in a scene about carnival basketball, so the writers had cut it. (It seemed to me that it might be funnier to have Jordan play against type and be unable to hit any shots, but who am I to second-guess *SNL* sketch writers?) He wasn't sure of his lines and was a little wooden when he did nail them.

We talked for a while, and the conversation turned to Sam Smith's soon-to-be-released book, *The Jordan Rules*. I had read excerpts that were sent to *Sports Illustrated*, and though the book wasn't nearly as negative as Jordan took it to be, it did eventually cause a sensation, as it laid out Jordan's sometimes heartless competitiveness, expressed mostly in rage toward his teammates, who never quite knew how to act around him. (It also showed glimpses of his compassion and was clear in its depiction of his alpha-superstar status.) "I know what's in there," Jordan said. "I know it's going to be negative." He shrugged but looked angry, as if this were part of a continuing crusade of negative publicity against him. Jordan had been nicked here and there, but he had basically been on a seven-year honeymoon with the press—ten years if you count his time in Chapel Hill.

In *The Jordan Rules*, Smith wrote of a moment during the season when Jordan said to his teammates: "Five more years. Five more years and I'm out of here. I'm marking these days on a calendar, like I'm in jail. I'm tired of being used by this organization, by the league, by the writers, by everyone." That from a man who had a love-of-the-game clause written into his first contract that allowed him to play pickup anytime, anyplace.

I wasn't aware of that quote then, but it struck me on that Friday afternoon that Jordan seemed to know what lay ahead, the burdens of fame. He was happy, of course, and felt vindicated that he had sent a message to all those who said he was just a shoot-first-second-and-third player who would never win. But he was wary, too, hardened, much less the happy-go-lucky kid who had taken the sports world by storm. That was inevitable, but it didn't mean it hadn't come along quicker than I thought it would. And it was a little sad.

On the way out, I knocked on Franken's door and asked him what it was like to have Jordan host. He thought for a moment and said, "It was like having Babe Ruth host in 1927."

# CHAPTER 16

# THE SPOKANE KID AND THE OUTCAST

. . . . . . . . . . . . . . . . . . . . . . . . . . . . . . . . . . . . . . . . . . .

## Isiah Sends an Olympic Message . . . and the Mailman Follows with a Special Delivery

John Stockton was a wide-eyed Gonzaga Prep kid back in 1978 when he journeyed to an AAU basketball tournament in Huntington, West Virginia. Stockton was not a recognized star, even in Spokane, and says today that his parents participated in AAU fundraisers "only because they were convinced it would be my last chance to play." Stockton, who would later lead the NBA in assists, steals, and expressions of self-deprecation, loves to tell the story of a Salt Lake City television station interviewing a former grade-school teammate on the occasion of some Stockton milestone with the Utah Jazz. "The guy told him, 'Stockton was really nothing special,'" remembers Stockton.

For the first eighteen years of his life (not to mention the final chapters, still to be played out), Stockton's world was circumscribed by the city limits of Spokane, a town where people have their heads on straight, a town of sensible shoes, a town where his paternal grandfather, Houston Stockton, was a football legend. Stockton was small, 5'5" as a high school freshman and barely six feet when he graduated. What made his career in basketball were his abnormally large hands and his abnormally large capacity for self-improvement. Stockton had a quiet confidence. He says he realized quite early that the battle didn't always go to the biggest or the swiftest. "I felt that if you played the right way you could win," Stockton says. "The other guys, when you looked at them, maybe they *should* win. But we *can* win."

So there was no reason that he couldn't win at that AAU tournament in Huntington. When the team arrived Stockton studied a tournament program that included a grainy photo of a player from the Chicago team. "I remember thinking, 'How good can this guy be?'"

The guy, Isiah Thomas, who was about Stockton's size, turned out to be pretty good. Team Washington hung in with Isiah's Chicago for three quarters until Isiah decided to take over. "We had been pressing them pretty effectively and it looked to me like Isiah just decided he wasn't going to do what the coach wanted," says Stockton. "So he just dribbled through us like we were nothing. Dribble through, pass . . . somebody dunked. Dribble through, pass . . . somebody dunked. Dribble through . . . Isiah layup. He just killed us. One guy. He *killed* us.

"Now, I went back to my room and normally I was a pretty smiley kid, but I was frowning that day. I couldn't believe anyone was that good."

Anyone who has played sports remembers that moment of stark realization when someone proves to be *that* much better than you. The question is, what do you do about it? What Stockton did was set a new bar for himself. He had to get as good as guys like Isiah Thomas. There was a new universe out there.

Athletes like Stockton are often referred to as embodiments of the American dream. Undersized and undervalued, driven by doubt, they go on to achieve great things in a sport that doesn't seem designed for them, their own extraordinary athletic gifts (hand-eye coordination, endurance, competitive drive, balance, ambidexterity) not necessarily the gifts associated with their sport.

Too often, we forget that a player like Isiah represents the American dream, too, just not the white-bread version that's been hammered into our heads. Yes, Isiah probably had more natural talent than Stockton in terms of quickness and jumping ability. But he had many, many, many more ways to go wrong. His odds of reaching the NBA were every bit as formidable as Stockton's.

Three Thomas brothers surrendered to the temptations of the street. One of those, Gregory, an intravenous drug user, died of AIDS. Isiah's heroic mother, Mary, chased away drug dealers, gang bangers, and thugs of all stripes so that her youngest of nine, Isiah Lord, could escape, make a life for himself. Isiah spent hours in isolation, dribbling a basketball off a milk crate, and rode a bus ninety minutes from his home on the West Side of Chicago to attend a Catholic school in Westchester, Illinois, where the bangers couldn't get at him. St. Joseph was to Isiah what Gonzaga Prep was to Stockton.

Isiah's game was both street and textbook, the perfect marriage of the West Side and St. Joseph, just as Chris Mullin's game would be the perfect marriage of the playground and the CYO gym. "I always considered myself a smart player, thinking maybe one step ahead," says Laimbeer, Thomas's closest friend on the Pistons. "That's the only way I could make it. But Isiah was always one step ahead of me. He saw what that guy was going to do, but he also saw what the other guy was going to do when that guy did that."

And so it was—to use the favorite word in our vernacular—ironic that these two flip sides of the American dream, these two combatants from an AAU tournament in West Virginia, came to be the major sticking point for the Dream Team selection. Had Isiah not been so unpopular among other players and committee members, he would've made the Dream Team, and Stockton would've been left out. That's just a fact.

My own opinion was that Isiah deserved to be on the team over Stockton, and I wrote that in a column for *Sports Illustrated*. Lo and behold, in the week that that opinion was due to appear, I was covering a game in Los Angeles and ran into Stockton at a deli where we were both catching a late-night sandwich.

"John, I don't know whether you read *Sports Illustrated*, or whether you really give a damn," I told him, "but I want to let you know that I wrote that Isiah should've been on the Olympic team." I don't think I had the guts to add *instead of you*, but the implication was there.

"Sure, okay," he said. "A lot of people feel that way."

"You know how much I respect your game," I said. "It's just that—"

"Don't worry about it," he said.

We sat down and ate.

On November 15, 1991, two months after Isiah discovered that he was not one of the first ten choices for the Dream Team and could only make it as a dreaded "add-on," the Utah Jazz came to the Palace of Auburn Hills. As Laimbeer remembers it, "Isiah didn't say anything before the game. He just had that *look*."

Armed with a vendetta, few players in basketball history are more lethal than Thomas, who could score on almost anyone when he put his mind to it, and Stockton was just another in a long line of players who could not stay in front of Isiah. Thomas owned Stockton on that night, scoring 44 points in a Detroit victory, forgetting his role as team quarterback in the service of demonstrating that he belonged on the Dream Team.

Years later, I talked to Stockton about that night. This is all he would say: "Isiah figured he should've been on the Dream Team, and I guess I was the clear target."

What's forgotten is that Stockton was pretty good, too, with 20 points and 12 assists, fulfilling what Bill Simmons said about him, in a backhanded-compliment way, in *The Book of Basketball*: "For

Jazz fans, watching Stockton was like being trapped in the mission-ary position for two decades. Yeah, you were having regular sex (in this case, winning games), but you weren't exactly bragging to your friends or anything." Over the course of their careers, Stockton ac-tually played quite well against Thomas, as did Thomas against Stockton.

A month later, Detroit came to the Salt Palace in Utah, a notori-ously hostile place for rival teams. Isiah went at Stockton again, scoring six early points. That's when Karl Malone decided he had seen enough.

This was the Mailman's seventh season with Stockton and they had grown close, bonded by mutual respect and the realization that they made each other better. (They remain that way today; Stock-ton and his wife, Nada, are godparents to one of Malone's daugh-ters.) They were as hard as mahogany, and they liked it like that. At this writing, Malone has committed the second highest number of fouls in NBA history (behind Kareem Abdul-Jabbar) and Stockton ranked at number fourteen, the only true guard on the top-twenty list. (While Malone will take his rep as a tough guy to the grave—just look at his body—succeeding generations may not remember that, in his own way, Stockton was considered a bully, too, someone who wasn't afraid to throw an elbow or stick out a knee in the middle of a scrum. Years later I asked Stockton if he was a dirty player. At the time we were standing high above the Spokane Falls in his home-town and I thought maybe he was going to push me over. "Abso-lutely not," he snapped. "I would never intentionally hurt anybody and in nineteen years I never did. The only reason they said that was that they couldn't think of anything else to say. They just fig-ured that a little guy couldn't have set so many screens any other way.")

Malone and Stockton had friendly debates on the team bus to and from games, particularly about hunting. Stockton was no fiery liberal but he just couldn't understand why Malone enjoyed gun-ning things down. (Malone's home in Louisiana is a taxidermist's wet dream. About a hundred mounted big-game animals hang unsmilingly from the walls and ceiling, including what he calls "the grand slam of sheep," the Dall, the Stone, the bighorn, and the desert bighorn. I had bad dreams about being eaten alive after spending a few hours in their company.)

Stockton also didn't approve of Malone's habit of nocturnal snowmobiling, believing that careening pell-mell down a mountain in darkness had a somewhat risky aspect to it.

They were extremely comfortable with each other. I walked them out to their cars after practice one day in Utah and said to Stockton, "Well, John, I bet you have something controversial to say as usual, right?"

"Not much," deadpanned Stockton. "Only this homosexual problem we've got on our team." He jerked his chin toward Malone. "And it's worse among our black players. Typical." Malone cracked up.

Until their dying days, Stockton, Malone, and ex-coach Jerry Sloan will be the very definition of Utah Jazz basketball, though a nasty public fight has erupted between the Mailman and Jazz CEO Greg Miller, son of the original owner, the late Larry Miller.

Anyway, late in the first quarter of this game, Laimbeer set a high pick on Stockton and Isiah set off down the lane on the right side, streaking by center Mark Eaton and heading for the basket. Malone left his man and met Isiah in the lane, chopping his right arm down on Isiah's face. Isiah flew through the air like a rag doll and landed on the floor, blood pouring off his face, "like a boxer who had taken a punch," as the play-by-play announcer described it at the time. By chance, Utah's orthopedic surgeon had gone outside to answer a page, so it was left to the Jazz podiatrist to see if he could help the trainer with the profusely bleeding Thomas. His suggestion was to put a cervical collar on Isiah and take him out on a backboard. But Laimbeer, his eternal protector, said that his buddy wasn't going out in such ignominious fashion, so he picked up Isiah himself, as easily as an adult picks up a three-year-old, and carried him into the locker room.

Malone was ejected from the game, and years later I asked him if he hit Isiah on purpose.

"Of course," he said.

But unless you're holding a scalpel and your target is lying on an operating table, you can't arrange *that* kind of hit, right?

"Look, I tried to hit him," Malone answered. "I wanted to hit him. But that hard? No, you don't have time to plan that. But I hit him, I know that."

Had Malone's victim been someone other than Isiah, league reaction might've been massive outrage. Accusations that Malone was a dirty player were nothing new, and the best reaction came, of course, from Barkley, who mused about what would happen if Isiah were added to the Dream Team roster. "I have no problem with Isiah being on the Olympic team," said Barkley, "but there would be at least three guys he wouldn't be roommates with. Michael and Scottie don't want to, and I guess Karl's out of the picture now. I'd wind up rooming with him by default." (The idea of the players actually having to bunk with someone was hilarious in itself.)

For me, the most interesting part of Malone's hatchet job was Chuck Daly's reaction. As soon as Isiah went down, the Pistons' coach flew off the bench in a rage, charging over to the scene of the crime. It was absolutely not an act—his captain had gone down and Chuck was mad. But what could he do? Rip off his custom sport jacket and challenge Malone to a fight? Pick one with his Jazz counterpart Jerry Sloan, a bare-knuckles brawler from way back? In the end, what Daly did was go ballistic in the time-honored I-want-to-hit-somebody-but-I-don't-know-whom-to-hit manner that we've seen from so many coaches.

Perhaps because Stockton was so sensitive to the Isiah issue, and because he also respected him as a player, Stockton never said anything remotely negative about Thomas. (Then again, Mostly Silent John never said that much anyway.) And Thomas, for his part, never hung Stockton out to dry. There is no doubt that Isiah considered himself the superior player, but he never denigrated the Jazz point guard, and after the Dream Team business had finished, Isiah placed a phone call to Jack and Dan's Bar and Grill in Spokane and asked to speak to the owner.

"I just want to let you know, Mr. Stockton," Isiah said to John's father, Jack, "that anything I had to say about the Dream Team had nothing to do with your son. He's a great player."

Neither Stockton nor his father ever forgot that call. And when Stockton was inducted into the Hall of Fame in 2009, he asked Isiah to stand onstage and represent him. It may have been 50 percent theater, but it was 50 percent legit.

When Daly was asked after the game about the Malone foul, he did the customary bobbing and weaving. He had to stick up for his captain and star, but he didn't have much to gain by trashing a player he would be coaching in Barcelona. "They ask if it was a flagrant foul, and Isiah had forty stitches, fifteen inside and twenty-five outside," Chuck answered. "The league office will determine how malicious."

Before Chuck died, I never got a chance to ask him, after years of reflection, whether he regretted not advocating for Isiah to be on the Dream Team. I know he agonized about it at the time, even though "It was tough . . . really hard . . . I really wanted him, but . . ." was about all I managed out of him. But as I watched him kneel over the bleeding Isiah, I wonder: did he wish at that moment that he had pushed harder for the inclusion of this complex kid from Chicago, this lightning rod who had brought him two championships and so many magic moments?

# CHAPTER 17

# THE DUKIE

. . . . . . . . . . . . . . . . . . . . . . . . . . . . . . . . . . . . . . . . . . . . .

### Wanted: College All-American . . . Must Perform Scut Duty on Summer Vacation

With the exception of Michael Jordan, Magic Johnson, and Larry Bird, one could argue that Christian Laettner, who turned out to be the least important player on the twelve-man roster, was the next surest player to be an Olympic invitee. In the earliest stages of negotiating among the committee members who would pick the team, the idea that college players would have equal representation was quickly squelched. Then eight and four bit the dust. The idea of ten pros and two collegians remained alive, but—with players such as Isiah Thomas, Clyde Drexler, and Dominique Wilkens not among the initial ten chosen—it soon became clear that only one collegian would be among the twelve roster players, "the gift to the college guys," as committee member Donnie Walsh put it.

And it became clear who that guy was going to be.

"Nobody said it out loud," says C. M. Newton, "but Christian Laettner was going to be on this team."

Certainly his college coach, Mike Krzyzewski, a committee member, pushed that idea. Laettner says that early in his senior year, 1991, Coach K told him, "They're going to take one collegian. Your goal should be to be that guy. And you *will* be that guy if we have a great season and you play great."

Duke did have a great season and Laettner did play great, and if there were still some holding out throughout the winter months for Shaquille O'Neal, the man-child from Louisiana State University, that all changed on the fateful afternoon of March 28, about two months before the committee would announce the final two players. That was when Christian Laettner became a legend.

In the Eastern Regional final at the Spectrum in Philadelphia, a game that would determine one Final Four entry, Kentucky led Duke 103–102 with just 2.1 seconds left. "We're gonna win," Krzyzewski told his team in the time-out huddle that would precede a full-court pass. That's what a coach is supposed to say, of course, but Krzyzewski felt he had a chance. Everyone knew the final shot would go to Laettner, and there was a precedent for success; two years earlier, in a regional final against Connecticut, Laettner had hit a lunging, twisting double-pump jumper to win the game and put Duke into the Final Four.

Krzyzewski designated Grant Hill to throw the pass. Hill's father, Calvin, had been an NFL star with the Dallas Cowboys, quite possibly an irrelevant fact but hard to avoid mentioning considering how perfectly Hill threw the ball. Earlier in the season, in the same game situation at Wake Forest, Hill had given Laettner a screwball that drove him out of bounds. But this time Hill's toss was perfect, straight, true, and high enough that the 6'11" Laettner, a decent jumper but no aerial acrobat, caught the ball.

It would be impossible to calculate how badly Kentuckians wanted Laettner to screw up the play. Earlier in the game, with Duke leading 73–68, Laettner and Kentucky's Aminu Timberlake had collided, Timberlake falling to the floor. Laettner promptly planted his right foot into Timberlake's stomach, not with a great deal of pressure but enough to make him feel it. As Alexander Wolff of *Sports Illustrated* later put it: "It was just a chippy, I'm-Christian-Laettner-and-you're-not thing to do."

Laettner, so often the villain, was not often the goat. He took one dribble, wheel-faked right, then spun left and unleashed a fallaway jumper, the twentieth shot that he had attempted that day. To that point, all nineteen—nine from the field, ten from the foul line—had gone in. Krzyzewski said later that, had he been aware of that fact, he might not have called Laettner's number, fearing the law of averages was against him. I doubt that, though.

Laettner's shot soared toward the basket, the rotation perfect, and those Kentucky fans who had started to head toward the exits stopped in their tracks, looks of horror beginning to take shape on their faces.

Bonnie Laettner admired Marlon Brando's performances in *Mutiny on the Bounty* and *The Young Lions* so much that she put "Christian," the name Brando had given to his son, on the birth certificate of her firstborn, even though she had unofficially named him Christopher. Laettner looked like what he was—a product of the Nichols School, a small, mostly white, coats-and-ties-mandatory preppy depot in his native Buffalo. Laettner loved to talk about Nichols, to the point that his Duke teammates grew sick of hearing about it.

He seemed tailor-made for Duke, a magnet for highly regarded Caucasian players who end up irritating the masses (Danny Ferry, Cherokee Parks, Chris Collins, Greg Paulus, Steve Wojciechowski, and J. J. Redick among them), but his mother, a strong influence in his life, loved the University of North Carolina and coach Dean Smith. She urged Christian to go to Chapel Hill, and he considered it. But, eventually, he was just too much a Dukie not to become a Dukie. And it is simply impossible to overestimate the hatred that, almost immediately, Laettner engendered in the opposition.

"Duke was like America's team and Christian Laettner was like God and I didn't like him," Juwan Howard said in the documentary *The Fab Five*, which chronicles the celebrated freshman class at the

University of Michigan that acted as a kind of cultural cross-reference to Duke back in the early 1990s.

"I thought Christian Laettner was soft," Jimmy King said.

"Overrated," Ray Jackson said.

"Pretty boy," Howard said.

Laettner was neither soft nor overrated, not as a college player. "Pretty boy" is right on. He looked (still looks) impossibly like a soap-opera star, with wavy hair, piercing blue eyes, and all that height. He would be cast either as the cad head surgeon who beds the OR nurses or, in a modern version, as the gay seducer of vulnerable young residents. Reports did surface that Laettner was gay, specifically that he was in a relationship with teammate Brian Davis. That was not surprising considering that the fan bases at rival schools, bent on out-crazying the Cameron Crazies who support Duke basketball, are brutal. What *was* surprising was how much Laettner defiantly encouraged those rumors, kissing Davis after he dunked in one game and, on other occasions, extending his arm and flopping his wrist while attempting a free throw, daring the crowd to insult him.

At the same time, Laettner was also, in the words of teammate Hill, a bully. "Christian was bigger than everybody and he could fight, and he always wanted to fight," says Hill. "He'd pick a fight with guys just to see if that guy had heart." Bobby Hurley, Duke's All-American point guard, was a favorite target. It drove Laettner nuts—still does—that Krzyzewski handed Hurley the ball and a starting job as soon as he hit campus, whereas Laettner was treated like the freshman he was.

He always played the role of alpha Dukie. One night in 1990, when he was a freshman, Hill answered a knock at his door around midnight. It was Laettner, who ordered him to get his coat. It was raining hard, but Laettner insisted they were going out and led him to his car. He drove through the night fast until he came to the empty parking lot of Duke Medical Center, at which point he began doing full-speed donuts by suddenly yanking on the emergency brake while traveling at a high rate of speed. Hill was afraid to say much because, well, he was only a freshman and Laettner was *Laettner*.

Hill says that the white-bread kid from Nichols School also wanted to be black. "One year Bobby [Hurley] got hurt and Tony Lang was starting for him and Christian's in the huddle clapping his hands and going, 'Okay, we got five brothers starting.' And it didn't seem like he was kidding."

By the time he was a senior, you could get a debate on whether Laettner was the best player in the country, but he was unquestionably the most-watched, the beloved idol of the Duke fans, the embodiment of frat-boy evil for the opponents. He was also a recognized archetype—the immortal collegian who would not be as good in the pros, everybody's All-American turned standard issue. Whereas Jordan was constrained by North Carolina's share-the-wealth-take-care-of-the-ball-philosophy, Laettner's talents were maximized in Krzyzewski's get-up-and-go system. Laettner, with talent all around him, could get off his perimeter shot with ease but was also able to post up and dominate with his size. He wouldn't be able to do that in the pros. He was a little soft, a little disinclined to improve, a little slow—a little of this and a little of that. It all adds up to a lot when you're talking about becoming an NBA star on the level of his Dream Team playmates.

But man, what a college player he was.

And so Laettner's shot settled into the basket, as it seemed destined to do, completing his 31-point perfect afternoon, one comparable to the near-perfect 44-point performance that UCLA's Bill Walton had famously inflicted on Memphis State in the 1973 NCAA championship game. At press row after the Laettner shot went in, veteran *Boston Globe* columnist Bob Ryan wrote out a question on a piece of notebook paper, "Greatest Game Ever?" and held it up. Many agreed, and Laettner was its unquestioned star.

Volumes have been written about that game, a predictable luncheon stop for anyone grazing through NCAA history. The late

Chris Farley, playing the role of Laettner, did an NCAA video promo about it. The shot has been replayed, by conservative estimate, a couple of thousand times since then. Laettner professes that he doesn't watch it, but Hill admits that he pauses each time it comes on—the perfect pass, the catch and graceful turn, the perfect shot, the orgiastic celebration. "That's the great thing about it," says Hill, "You get to relive it every year."

In the wake of that game, C. M. Newton, who was the athletic director at Kentucky as well as chairman of the Olympic selection committee, astonished the Kentucky seniors by retiring their jerseys even though they had been beaten. That's what kind of impact that game had.

So for the Olympic selection committee, it was an easy decision that Laettner would be the college guy, the lone concession to the old way of doing things. It would not be an easy task for anyone, far less for Laettner, the bully-boy antagonist with a lot of attitude.

*CHAPTER 18*

# THE GLIDE

· · · · · · · · · · · · · · · · · · · · · · · · · · · · · · · · · · · · · · · ·

### Clyde's on the Team, and Jordan Shrugs

On May 11, a few weeks before he was to meet Michael Jordan in a
Finals showdown that everyone was waiting for, Clyde Drexler was
named to the Olympic team along with Christian Laettner. The roster was now complete, and for all eternity Clyde would be the eleventh man, the add-on among the NBA players.

The main argument against adding Drexler to the team was
that he was too much like Jordan. At the same time, that was probably the best reason to add him, since being a lot like Jordan couldn't
be a bad thing. In truth, by this time, it didn't matter what style of
player or which position was to be added. Everything was set: ball-
handling with Magic, Stockton, Jordan, and Pippen; rebounding
with Robinson, Ewing, Barkley, and Malone; outside shooting with
Mullin, Jordan, and Bird; lockdown defending with Pippen and Jordan; scoring with everybody; high-level entertainment with Barkley. Coffee and donuts? The college kid could bring them. It was only

necessary to take the best available player, or, as the case might be, the best available player who wasn't Isiah.

For several years the Jordan-or-Clyde story line had been predictable chum for the sportswriter—I chomped on it from time to time—and Jordan invariably won in all places save the lovely city of Portland, Oregon, whose fans felt loyal to Clyde, ignored by three of the four time zones, and just plain sick and tired of hearing about Jordan. Plus, they *needed* Drexler to be as good since it was the presence of Drexler on the roster that prompted the Trail Blazers to bypass Jordan and go for a big man, Sam Bowie, in the 1984 draft. Portland-based broadcaster Steve "Snapper" Jones, a delightful man who loved to talk basketball and debate any question, was especially vocal about Drexler being the equal of Jordan. Rod Thorn, conjuring up his best West Virginia drawl, used to say to him: "Steve, d'y'all have TVs out there in Portland?"

For the most part, Drexler stayed away from the comparisons with Jordan, but he was just vain enough—a quality that does not distinguish him from most other high-achieving pro athletes—to stick one little toe into those dangerous waters every once in a while, to ask quietly, as he asked me from time to time off the record: *What can Michael do that I can't do?*

One answer was nothing. There was nothing that Jordan did that Drexler couldn't do.

The other answer was nothing . . . except that Jordan did everything *better*.

They played the same two-guard position with a similar athletic flair, but Jordan was a better pull-up shooter, a better driver, a better passer, a better defender, a better rebounder, and even a better dunker, though Drexler, whose running vertical was measured at forty-four inches, could probably outleap Jordan.

One can only imagine, then, the ghastliness of the waking nightmare in which Clyde found himself in Game 1 of the 1992 NBA Finals. His Trail Blazers had gotten off to a quick start against Jordan's Bulls in Chicago. But then came the second period and Jordan started draining three-point shots, one, two, three, four, five . . .

What the hell was going on? Neither Jordan nor Drexler was ever considered a drop-dead long-distance man. Drexler's career percentage on threes was 31 percent, and Jordan's was only one percentage point better. However, Drexler's long-range shooting sank to about 28 percent in the postseason, while Jordan's rose to 33 percent. That is well on its way to being an appreciable difference. Still, going into these Finals, Drexler was generally considered a better long-distance shooter than Jordan, or as Jordan pointedly put it before the series began, "Clyde is a better three-point shooter than I *choose* to be."

And then in this strange Game 1 Jordan hit his sixth three-pointer and . . . what was he doing? He was *shrugging*? Who the hell ever saw him *shrug*? But, yes, after the final one went in, Jordan glanced over at courtside commentator Magic Johnson and shrugged, as if to say, *I don't know what's going on myself.*

Drexler knew exactly what was going on. In the endless war of comparison between him and Jordan, he was getting torched again. And what did Clyde the Glide say to Jordan during all of this? Spicy comments such as "Aren't you going to miss?" "Nice shot," and "Good play." I wrote in *SI* the following week that Drexler "had set the art of trash-talking back about 30 years."

For a long time Drexler was said to have the highest score ever recorded on the psychological profile test that the Trail Blazers give rookies. Assistant coach John Wetzel used to talk about Drexler having "a gentleness to his soul." Clyde was also unfailingly polite and cordial, even to the media. All of those things sound good if you're running for student council president, but they're not necessarily barometers of NBA success.

As for basketball, Drexler played a lot of small forward at the University of Houston and a lot of center at Ross Sterling High School in Houston, so he did have an adjustment when he became an NBA shooting guard. He had some strange habits for a great player. He brought his hands down to his waist before he raised them to shoot, and he dribbled with his head down and almost exclusively with his right hand, habits that didn't change much as he matured. But neither did they seem to slow him down all that much. (Jerry West almost always went right and Lenny Wilkens almost always went left, and no one could stop them, either.)

Then, too, while Drexler didn't exactly feud with his coaches, he did spar with two of them—the respected Jack Ramsey and the less-respected Mike Schuler. Drexler's rep for showing up "just in time" for practice was widely known, especially since Drexler owned up to it. Whereas Jordan was picking fights and busting on his teammates during intrasquad scrimmages, Drexler put himself in the practice-kind-of-counts-but-not-really camp.

In 1990 Don Nelson called Drexler the most overrated player in the league and added a few other poisonous comments. "He chips away at what an organization is trying to do," said Nelson. "He is the worst of all kinds because he comes off as polite. He is religious, devoted to family. Yet in the context of a team, he is destructive." Drexler always figured that Nelson was in fact speaking the mind of his assistant, Schuler, who had been fired by the Blazers midway through the 1988–89 season and ended up with the Warriors. Whatever their source, those were inexcusable comments—indicative of why Nelson would've been the wrong man to coach the Dream Team—and Nelson later apologized for making them.

But by 1992, Drexler was considered by many to be the best non-Jordan player in the league. There was wide consensus that he had "toned down" his game, was playing with more consistency, and had enough playmaking skills to overcome Portland's rep as a dumb team, a criticism that nagged at Drexler. He insisted that he had always played with consistency and that his game had never needed toning down because it was never toned up. Of all the African American athletes I ever met who were sensitive to the stereotype that blacks make it on pure athleticism and whites make it on discipline and smarts, Drexler was at the top of the list, along with Isiah Thomas. As for the "dumb" tag, he and his Trail Blazer teammates used to joke about it during practice, scratching their heads and saying "Duh" after coach Rick Adelman called for a certain set.

But it was one of those clenched-smile jokes because, indeed, they had been out-thought by Chuck Daly's wily Pistons in the Finals the year before. And here came Jordan and the Bulls to face them in what they all knew was their last best chance to win it all.

It wasn't to be. Drexler was playing on a bum right knee, and in truth, though the Trail Blazers were a match for the Bulls on paper, they weren't as basketball-savvy and they didn't have Jordan, who remembered that, eight years earlier, he had been passed over because Portland was sure it had its two-guard in Drexler.

When Jordan made his sixth and final three-pointer, Drexler was not on him. Cliff Robinson closed out too late to defend it, and it was Robinson who was left shaking his head as Jordan shrugged.

But make no mistake about it: it was Clyde who got shrugged. That's how it always was. Another player might've searched for some rationalization—*I wasn't really on him when he made most of those threes*—or at least stared down a reporter when asked about Jordan's three-point orgy. But here's what Drexler said. "I said before the series that he had two thousand moves. I was wrong. He has three thousand. I can tell you this, I'm glad I'm going to Barcelona on *his* team."

# THE GLIDE

. . . . . . . . . . . . . . . . . . . . . . . . . . . . . . . . . . . . . . . . . . .

### "Jordan Was Damn Good—But Was He Better Than Me?"

*Houston, Texas*

Clyde Drexler insists that he will make me lunch. We are in the kitchen of his roomy house, which lies off the seventh fairway (a long par-4) of a beautiful suburban golf course. Living under such trying circumstances has turned Drexler into a low-handicapper who plays from time to time with a neighbor, Jim Nantz, a buddy from the University of Houston.

Lunch is good—chicken salad and fruit; Clyde is a careful eater who has always taken care of himself—and we talk of many things, including kids, the aggravation of aging knee joints (he has a little, I have a lot), and our mutual butchering past (both of our fathers were meat cutters). But being the eleventh man on the Dream Team nags at him, and I open up that conversational box. He does not close it.

"I learned I was on the team from [Trail Blazers general manager] Harry Glickman," says Drexler. "Harry was all excited about it, but I was . . . melancholy." I thought that a strange and interesting word to use. "I should've been on there with the first batch of players. You can only control what you can control, right?

"But it bothered me. How can you leave off Worthy, Dominique, and Isiah? And leave me off, too? I was runner-up for the MVP that season. I should've been on the team right away and so should they have."

Okay, I say, but who would he have left off? There were only twelve spots.

"You look at production that year," he answers. "What did Bird do that year? What did Magic do?"

Well, I say, we all know why they were there. It was a Dream Team. They'd saved the league.

He doesn't say much about Bird. Drexler remembers a night in Barcelona when he came out of his room and there was Bird sipping a beer. He fetched one for Clyde, and they stood there for a long while and talked. Years later Drexler treasures that memory. "Just standing there drinking beer and talking to Larry Bird," says Drexler with a big smile on his face.

(It's an example of that distant-legend mystique that Bird has, even with his fellow Dream Teamers. They knew him mostly as this mysterious, cold-blooded character, so he surprised them when he came across as loose and humorous off the court.)

But Magic, whom he knew better from years of Western Conference competition, was another story. "Magic was always . . ." And Drexler goes into a decent Magic impression: "'Come on, Clyde, come on, Clyde, get with me, get with me,' and making all that noise. And, really, he couldn't play much by that time. He couldn't guard his shadow.

"But you have to understand what was going on then. Everybody kept waiting for Magic to die. Every time he'd run up the court everybody would feel sorry for the guy, and he'd get all that benefit of the doubt. Magic came across like, 'All this is my stuff.' Really? Get outta here, dude. He was on the declining end of his career."

Drexler had played exquisitely in the 1992 All-Star Game in Orlando, although the MVP award eventually went to Magic, who had been added by Commissioner Stern as a special thirteenth player to the Western Conference roster (Chapter 20). "If we all knew Magic was going to live this long, I would've gotten the MVP of that game, and Magic probably wouldn't have made the Olympic team."

If those words sound harsh, or at best impolitic, keep in mind that later, when Magic drew criticism from many other players (especially Karl Malone) for returning to the NBA even though he had HIV, Drexler was one of his staunchest defenders.

Anyway, I tell Drexler, Magic would've still made the Olympic team, All-Star Game or not. Whom else would he have left off?

"Well," says Drexler, "Mullins was added." (Drexler was not the only Dream Teamer to call Mullin "Mullins.") "You going to tell me there weren't other guys on that team who could break a zone?"

Drexler is now laughing. This is the disarming tone he uses when bitching about something.

"If you took Isiah and Mullins and had them shoot shots, who do you think would hit more?"

"In that situation, Clyde, my guess is Mullin," I say. "And that's not to say that Isiah wasn't a great player. It's Mull-*in,* by the way."

"Yeah, Mullin was a great shooter," Drexler says. "But Isiah was better, especially when it counted. We geared our whole team to stopping Isiah. It's a whole different level of play with him. You never wanted Isiah to take a shot *ever.*"

Keep in mind that Drexler had a bond with Thomas that he did not with Mullin—the Glide and Isiah were opponents in the '90 Finals, when Drexler got a close-up view of Isiah's skills.

So why does he think Isiah wasn't on the team?

"I don't think Jordan wanted to play with Isiah," Drexler answers. "Two championships in a row, always an All-Star. And Isiah can't make it?

"I didn't like that. It's not the players' choice. It's who's *supposed* to be there. If you don't like me, I don't give a fuck. We're competitors. You're not supposed to like me. But when one player has the ability to leave another player off, we've lost control of the system.

"The one thing in sports that's been important to me is integrity. If someone is good, no matter what, I am never going to say he's not. If you're good, you're good.

"I came real close to being MVP of the All-Star Game, MVP of the Finals, and MVP of the season. You think I think I'm going to be inferior to these guys because I was named late? And two of the previous three years our team is in the Finals? I mean, I'm trying to show some humility here but . . . please. I feared no one. I didn't think there was any better than me."

Well, this is another conversational box that needs opening. So I ask: even Jordan?

"Are you kidding? In my mind? Jordan was damn good, but was he better than me?" Drexler ponders that for a moment and answers this way: "The question is not really is he better. The question is, do you think you can win against him? And the answer is absolutely. I had a lot of success against Jordan. I beat him often. At his game. Which is also my game. I was bigger, faster. I did everything he could do." Drexler stops and smiles. "Except shoot more."

# 2

## The Dream Unfolds

# CHAPTER 19

# THE WRITER

. . . . . . . . . . . . . . . . . . . . . . . . . . . . . . . . . . . . . . . . . . . . . . . . .

## And So It Begins . . . at a Cattle Call in San Diego

It is moments like this, such as the first Dream Team practice session on June 22, 1992, when I most hate journalism. The Bulls had completed their six-game victory over the Blazers in the NBA Finals only a week earlier, and it was clearly time to decompress and take a vacation from pro basketball. But there we were, the nation's, and some of the world's, sporting press—maybe five hundred of us—on the steps of the University of California at San Diego, shuffling around with equal parts anticipation and exasperation, waiting for the doors of the holy temple to open, at which point we would prostrate ourselves at the feet of the Dream Team and grovel, like face-down chickens pecking in a field, for any casually tossed-out nuggets they might deign to cast our way.

Okay, that's off my chest.

I wish I'd had a digital camera to record one moment that almost made it all worthwhile. There among our unwashed multitude, an outside-looking-in pariah like all of us, was Michael Jordan's best buddy, Ahmad Rashad.

"Don't they know I'm not a regular reporter?" an exasperated Ahmad was asking, apparently without irony.

In the normal scheme of things, Ahmad, then with NBC, went anywhere he damn well pleased, owing to his status as Michael's guy. The fact that he was not allowed into practice was one of the first signs that this Dream Team thing was going to be something entirely different from what everyone was accustomed to. (To be fair, Ahmad did eventually claim his place at the table alongside Jordan. They hung together all the time in Barcelona.)

The operation was now under the aegis of both the NBA and USA Basketball, the latter an organization that liked nothing better than to throw around a little protocol from time to time. The Dream Team was also, both figuratively and literally, an Olympian operation. The combined celebrity of the team seemed to warrant extra levels of security—how true that would prove to be—and the Games themselves, to which this team would be heading in about a month, are always a nightmare of restricted access for the media.

In this locked-down atmosphere, nuggets of information would be hard to find. I had gone over to the team hotel, the Sheraton Grande Torrey Pines in lovely La Jolla, the day before, and there was Barkley—then in marital interregnum and feeling even more liberated since he had been traded from Philadelphia to the Phoenix Suns and was looking forward to playing the 1992–93 season for a contender—chatting up two women in the lobby.

"Jack, you want to help out here?" he asked, before immediately reconsidering. "Never mind. You're too lame anyway."

Magic Johnson's people complained that he did not have a suite, and there was a moment of threat that he would boycott the practices. Magic didn't even know about it. But then it was made clear that only Coach Daly would have a suite and everything was smoothed over.

Christian Laettner had already made an impact, not in a positive way. Brian McIntyre, the NBA's head of public relations and a man universally respected around the league, was arranging a live TV hookup when he spotted Laettner, who was wearing shorts and a USA Basketball T-shirt, in the lobby.

"Just so you know, Christian," McIntyre said to him, "all the other players are wearing suits, sport coats, and ties." And Laettner responded, with a kind of fuck-you tone, "I don't give a shit."

That exchange confirmed what most journalists discovered during the weeks that they followed the Dream Team: Laettner, the one player who had never played a single minute of an NBA game, succeeded in being the biggest jerk.

Now, there is a distinction that must be made clear. Laettner was not a jerk in the presence of his teammates. Years later he describes the adjustment he had to make to being twelfth man as "fun and easy, just like going back to my freshman year at Duke when guys like Danny Ferry and Quin Snyder are way up here and you're way down there."

Well, I remind him, Ferry and Snyder aren't Michael/Magic/Larry.

"But it was still the same transition," Laettner insists. "I tell people that my favorite year at Duke was my freshman year, and they don't believe me because we won two championships later. But it's true. Everything was new and exciting and different and your head is spinning all over the place.

"See, people see only the cocky, arrogant Christian Laettner"— the one, for example, who refers to himself in the third person. "But if I'm not at that upper-echelon level as a player, I'm just a good kid with a good personality who knows his place. And my place on that team was very low on the totem pole."

All that is true, but it doesn't speak to his personality at the time and the situation he was in. It was hard enough being the twelfth man, but remember, too, that he was caught in the crosshairs of Shaquille O'Neal, who was telling anyone and everyone that he, not Laettner, should've been the collegian of choice. (Let me reiterate my opinion that while O'Neal would've been more fun, a genial giant of a target for the good-natured slings and arrows released from the quivers of Jordan and Barkley, Laettner was the right choice for the body of work that he had shown in four years.)

The quite unambiguous presence of Bonnie Laettner didn't help matters, either. She was present at the press conference her son held in San Diego related to the 1992 NBA draft, where he had been chosen as the third overall pick by the lowly Minnesota Timberwolves, and couldn't hold back when Laettner was asked about the boos that accompanied the announcement of his selection during the proceedings in Portland's Memorial Coliseum.

"That was the fifty family and friends he [Shaquille] took with him to Portland," Bonnie Laettner blurted out.

Christian was embarrassed and glared at his mother.

To reiterate, one cannot overestimate what a tough spot Laettner was in. He was like a kid fresh out of a high school play asked to join a repertory company with a dozen Oliviers, while his mother stands offstage shouting addled stage directions. Laettner may have been arrogant, but he was an intelligent young man who clearly realized he was the twelfth wheel, the one about whom everyone wondered: *What the hell is he doing here?* It was a tough spot for any twenty-two-year-old, never mind one who had spent the last four years as an exalted BMOC at a university where BMOCs are quite B. It's one thing to say that you're fine with being the butt of jokes, that it doesn't matter when Barkley mentions that you should run to 7-Eleven to pick up a deck of playing cards (which is what happened in San Diego), quite another to actually be fine with it.

And as I see it, twenty years later it's *still* tough to be Christian Laettner. After near canonization at Duke, Laettner has pretty much been consigned to the status of mere mortal over the last two decades. He never found a true NBA home, having played with five teams over thirteen seasons. He was never popular with the fans and media in any of those stops. He was a good player and probably would've retired as a very good one if not for an Achilles tendon injury he suffered in the 1998 off-season. But he was no NBA immortal, as were all of the eleven others on the Dream Team. He is involved in a real-estate business with former Duke teammate Brian

Davis, but it has been beset with financial problems, and one of the lawsuits filed against it, by NFL linebacker Shawne Merriman, drew a lot of media attention.

He has had some rocky moments with his former Duke teammates, one of them being Grant Hill, who angered Laettner by referring to him as "a jerk." That requires some context. Hill genuinely likes Laettner and referred more to Laettner's proclivity to act like a jerk, if such a distinction is possible.

But I think Laettner can become something else, something better. When I interviewed him, we met at a benefit golf tournament organized as a fund-raiser to help St. Anthony's, the high school where Bob Hurley Sr. coaches. It was an inclement morning and I was wet and shivering, and here came Laettner to my cart with an extra umbrella and parka. Laettner was sometimes distant and unengaged when we talked—that's the Laettner you know—but I did sense that he is a man trying to outrun his past. He doesn't want to be That Guy anymore, the unpleasant preppie, the pampered underachiever. When I asked about his business problems, he didn't exactly give chapter and verse, but he didn't pretend they weren't real, either. "The way the economy has been for the last three, four years, any money we made had to go back into our projects to keep them afloat," Laettner said. "Yes, I have fallen behind. But I will pay the Shawne Merrimans and those other people back. It would've happened by now if not for the economy." (Perhaps that has already happened, perhaps it has not.)

He spoke about wanting to get back into coaching, and though at this writing he didn't have a job, he has been giving individual clinic instruction, some of it to Hill, who wanted to improve his low-post game as his career winds down.

And so as I look back on the portrait of Laettner that emerges in these pages, I worry that it is too negative. Yes, back then he *did* act like a jerk, and his teammates, as Jordan will confirm, *did* go at him in scrimmages. I didn't make stuff up. Then again, sports tends to freeze its characters in time. They are, and continue to be, what we saw back then. But they can change—they can become the guy who brings you an umbrella in the rain instead of the one who laughs at you getting wet.

Cattle call notwithstanding, there was going to be something special about the first glance of these guys together. At All-Star Weekends I had seen almost all of the Dream Teamers in one place at one time, but this was different. They would be wearing the same uniform and going for the same goal.

You have to remember that the big question at this time was: how were they all going to play together? The rock star analogy that has been made ad nauseam about the Dream Team eventually came to fit, but it wasn't apt in the beginning. These guys, unlike the Rolling Stones, had never played together. They didn't know when to trade leads or let someone go off on a solo.

And as the days wore on, I came to realize that the truly remarkable aspect of all this was that the players bought into its remarkability. Experts at seizing the moment on their own teams, they saw right away that *this* was the moment. They weren't students of history, but they sure as hell heard the distant thunder and could sense the super-sized storm front that was moving toward them. "Normally you don't talk about the past when you're in it," Mullin told me recently. "But that wasn't the case here. We talked about how it was all going to look later. We were aware it was special even as it was going on."

They exchanged souvenirs like middle schoolers. I remember Barkley interrupting an interview to ask Bird for a pair of sneakers and adding, "I wouldn't mind a jersey, either." He said he was starting a "Dream Team museum" in his den. Twenty years later, any number of them would show me mementos from that time in their lives.

Yes, Jordan, Magic, and Bird all expected to be there and, needless to say, felt like they belonged. If I were guessing, I'd say that Barkley, Malone, and Ewing were next on the list of feeling they deserved it. But this was big stuff to all of them.

Here's Pippen talking to me about it years later: "I was astounded to have been invited. Yeah, we had won a championship by that time, and another one by the time we got ready for Barcelona, but I never saw myself as one of those in-crowd guys. I was overwhelmed when I was asked."

And John Stockton: "To be honest, the first time I ever thought about it was when Rod Thorn called me and invited me to be on the team. I never thought I would be considered. I was floored."

Years later, when I told Mullin that he had been one of the committee's first targets, he smiled like a fifth grader who had just won the spelling bee. "Well, I heard that, too," he said shyly.

So the gates to the gym swung open, and there they were, doing much the same thing as any team does after formal practice has concluded, some idly shooting free throws, some chatting, some just standing around. The only difference was that these guys represented what could become the best team ever.

There is something jarring about seeing a basketball team in the full blush of summer, when their gym-rat pallid complexions have changed hue. There was Bird, whose season had ended six weeks earlier, looking like he had just stepped off the beach. Bird, as was his wont, was shooting around with Mullin in what would become a post- and pre-practice pas de deux throughout their days together. Jordan and Barkley were jawing at each other as Ewing leaned in and smiled. Chuck Daly was chatting with NBA and USA Basketball officials, being briefed, no doubt, about his endless promotional and media responsibilities.

And there, in one corner, filibustering the masses, was Magic Johnson. By dint of all that had happened to him, this was Magic's Dream Team and it would be Magic's Olympics.

He was, after all, the only one of them who was playing with a death sentence.

# CHAPTER 20

# THE MAGIC MAN

. . . . . . . . . . . . . . . . . . . . . . . . . . . . . . . . . . . . . . . . . . .

## For a Man Who's Dying, He Sure Looks Pretty Alive

A couple of weeks before perhaps the most dramatic press conference in sports history, the one at which Magic Johnson announced
to the world that he had "attained" the AIDS virus, he was in Paris
with the Lakers for the McDonald's Open. The bloom had clearly
gone off the Stern-Stankovic rose by that time. It is impossible to
overestimate the low esteem in which most high-level athletes hold
international travel, augmenting cross-cultural IQ rarely being a
priority for them. We need only conjure up the example of a young
Shaquille O'Neal, who upon being asked if he had visited the Par-
thenon during a college basketball trip to Greece, responded, "I
can't remember the names of all the clubs we went to."

But Magic, being Magic, gamely put himself out front, the point
man at press conferences, hospital visits, and promotional stops.
Besides, there was a lot to talk about, Barcelona being one of those
subjects, and he made it clear that he had appointed himself Dream
Team captain.

"Ma-jeek, what will you do in Barcelona, if somebody on your team gets out of line?" a French journalist asked him during a press conference at the McDonald's Open in Paris.

"I won't *let* any somebodies get out of line," he answered. "If any players get out of line, I'll take care of it. That's my job, and I'm going to do it."

That was a classic Magic response. Had Bird been asked the same question, he might've said: "Hell, I ain't no damn babysitter. Those guys can take care of themselves." Jordan? He might've said: "We'll all take care of each other." But Magic was emphatic: *It's* my *job.* That's what some of his teammates loved about Magic—the fact that he would shoulder responsibility. That's also what some of his teammates hated about Magic—the fact that it was always *his* team.

It was at that tournament in Paris that I realized the extent to which Magic had wedged one foot in the business world. He had been talking about becoming a mogul for a long time—he'd owned a radio station in suburban Denver when he was a rookie; hell, he'd had his own lawn mowing business in Lansing, Michigan, when he was ten—but I never much pursued the subject because it didn't interest me. And I doubt if anyone knew then how far he was going to take it. Whenever a microphone was around he spoke of the philosophy behind his company, Magic Johnson T's, and how the Olympics "are going to put a whole new light on things in the business world for NBA stars. Michael and myself are really going to be able to cash in on it." What do you do with a guy like that? Praise his candor? Or condemn his capitalistic soul?

Magic Johnson T's was actually an official licensee of NBA Properties, Inc., empowered to sell NBA products. That meant that Magic was making money off the sale of T-shirts bearing the likenesses of Jordan, Bird, and the other Dream Team players. Magic even admitted, with a broad smile, that Jordan tees outsold Magic tees.

Magic was savant-like in his grasp of business. Ask him to sign an autograph to "Jim," and there would be a chance he would spell it "G-y-m"; he was even known to misspell Johnson as "Jonson." In later years he said he was dyslexic. But ask him the contract specifics of any player in the league and he could give you dollar figures and length of deal. His head worked in figures and numbers, not letters and words.

When Magic got back to L.A. from Paris, his doctor informed him that he had the AIDS virus, the shocking revelation from a physical Magic had taken weeks earlier. It was confirmed by a retest. Among the first calls Magic made were to Bird, Jordan, and Isiah. His doctors decided that he should retire from the game to work on fighting the disease. Then, with startling speed, came Magic's press conference, his tour of the talk shows, and his clear pronouncements that he had contracted the disease through heterosexual contact.

To describe Magic's sexual adventures as "conquests" is to vastly overrate the difficulty with which they came about. Women threw themselves at him, and Magic was a discerning fielder, catching the ones he wanted, letting the others sail by. Remember, too, that he had been a bachelor until the autumn of 1991, though only the woman who was then his fiancée and is now his wife, Cookie, knows what pain his lifestyle caused her during their relationship before they married. But at least his sexual adventures were not technically adulterous.

I never considered an athlete's extracurricular sexual activity to be my business—these days it's practically a beat—and Magic was reasonably discreet. Though there were later revelations that he would sometimes indulge in quickie postgame dalliances in the locker room's private sauna before presenting himself to soliloquize about, say, the efficiency of the Celtics' half-court offense, he rarely brought anyone to team functions except Cookie, whom he had been dating for a number of years. His most frequent date was Lakers PR man Josh Rosenfeld. "Magic used to tell me, 'Josh, you can't get a date, and I can't bring anybody else except Cookie because of all the other wives,'" Rosenfeld says.

I have an extremely reliable account of Magic, on one occasion in the late 1980s, arranging multiple trysts at the same time. "You go with me tonight, I'll see you next week in L.A., and when I get back a month from now you and I will get together," he said, directing each comment to a different woman. That's somewhat paraphrased but close to the truth. He handled it like a true point guard, getting this one the ball on a fast break, promising to set up this one next time down the floor, pledging goodies in a future game to a third.

(It seems necessary to mention that Magic and his generation didn't invent philandering. Lakers general manager Jerry West, for example, was celebrated for getting around. One day in the late 1980s, as I interviewed West at a Lakers practice session, he shook his head when he came upon a story in that morning's *Los Angeles Times* about NBA star Roy Tarpley getting suspended for drugs. "Whatever happened to pussy?" West said, almost to himself, not trying to draw a laugh, just one man ruefully pondering how strange this modern world had become.)

After the announcement that he was HIV positive, Magic's crusade began with riotous incongruity. He created a foundation to fight AIDS without including a single gay man or woman. He tossed off corny lines like "Keep your cap on," a reference to condom use. He urged sexual restraint but his wink-wink proclamations about the number and variety of his affairs seemed to send a different message. Any slings and arrows tossed by the vox populi seemingly bounced off him. "If it had happened to a heterosexual woman who had been with a hundred or two hundred men," complained tennis star Martina Navratilova, "they'd call her a whore and a slut and the corporations would drop her like a lead balloon." And what if it had happened to Navratilova, who had paid a heavy price for her bisexual lifestyle? "They'd say I had it coming," said Navratilova—accurately, it must be added.

At *Sports Illustrated*, meanwhile, plans were under way at that time to make Magic the magazine's first male swimsuit model. He was scheduled to be in the 1992 edition of the annual cash cow/ journalistic enterprise. It was the idea of editor John Papanek to feature the upcoming Barcelona Games with the usual cluster of scantily clad women and one superstar Olympian. Magic, whom Papanek had covered in his days on the NBA beat, was his first choice, and Magic had been enthusiastic about it. They would be shooting it soon.

After Papanek heard the HIV news, his first thought was that the Magic shoot, of course, was history. So he was surprised when he got a call almost immediately from Lon Rosen, Magic's representative, who said, "Magic wants you to confirm, John, that he's still going to be in the swimsuit issue. He's been looking forward to it and doesn't think this development should change things." Papanek had the idea that Rosen was presenting it as a condition for future interviews with Magic, including one that my colleague, Roy Johnson, was en route to Los Angeles at that moment to accomplish. Papanek told Rosen that it was a nonstarter and wrote years later in *ESPN The Magazine*: "I had to give it to Rosen straight." He told Rosen that Magic was admitting to unprotected sex with lots of women and said, "I don't think he, or anyone connected with him, will feel good seeing a picture of him in February cavorting in his underwear with bikini-clad women."

It took chutzpah for Magic to believe that *SI* would still want to do the shoot. But, then, it took a particular kind of grace for Magic to not only accept the decision and go ahead with the interview but also, upon seeing Papanek some weeks later, say, "Hey, John, next year can I be in the swimsuit issue?" (It never happened, by the way.) And Magic never brought it up to me in succeeding years, either.

Eventually, Magic began to pay attention to the drumbeat of criticism. In his defense, remember that this was new ground. He dialed down the cutesy sayings and reached out to the gay community, all seemingly without missing a beat. The man even backpedaled with irrepressibility. Perhaps inevitably, Magic proclaimed: "The further I go with this, the more I believe God picked me. If I didn't believe that, I'm not sure how I could go on the way I have."

I wouldn't be honest if I didn't cop to sometimes finding it difficult to buy into the whole Magic rap. One could say that Jordan was overly political, but it was more that he was apolitical. I never got the idea that Jordan was anyone else but Jordan. That goes double for Bird. Magic seemed to be a bit contrived, as if he had an on switch that he activated every time a camera was in his radar range. He came close to admitting it himself, stressing that "Magic and Earvin are two different people."

But it was hard not to like him. And the world? The world loved him, and when he got the virus the impact was something like that of an earthquake—widespread and devastating, with frequent aftershocks. The Spanish daily *El Pais* devoted two pages to "The Magic Man: A Living Legend and a Myth in World Sport." It mentioned the promotional visit that Johnson had made to Barcelona in the summer of 1991—in a setup for photographers, Magic made the "first basket" at the Palau Municipal d'Esports de Badalona, the new Olympic basketball venue—and rued the apparent fact that he would not be playing in the Olympics. All six major television networks in Japan, where basketball was not even a major sport, carried the news. Papers in Sydney, Milan, Oslo, London, and Munich also splashed the story on page one, as did, needless to say, virtually every newspaper in America. All of the stories, including those written by people like me, had the gloomy tone of a pre-obituary.

Only twenty-four hours after his announcement, the Los Angeles City Hall steps, where Magic had stood as an honored NBA champion five times since 1980, were renamed the Magic Johnson Plaza of Champions; it required a unanimous emergency vote of the city council. Many, like scholastic coaching legend Morgan Wootten of Demetha High School in Maryland, compared Magic's revelation to the day that President Kennedy was assassinated. UCLA's John Wooden, the Obi-Wan Kenobi of sports, conjured up the day that Lou Gehrig announced he was dying of a disease that was later named for him.

As for Magic, well, he did retire, but he never acted like a dying man. He continued to work out at Sports Club L.A., playing full-court basketball and steadily upping his aerobic activity. He gave up red meat and fried foods and loaded up on unsweetened juices (carrot was a favorite), fruits, vegetables, and grilled and broiled chicken and fish. He found an L.A. bakery that specialized in muffins made with honey instead of butter and another place where he bought sugar-free pies. Other HIV victims might've gone into seclusion, but Magic filled our lives with the details of his.

So when it came time for All-Star Weekend in February in Orlando, Magic had been given clearance to play by his doctors and special dispensation from NBA commissioner David Stern. Beyond that, it was clearly a trial balloon for Barcelona, and not everyone was happy. An official from the Australian Olympic Federation recommended that players from his country boycott games against the United States if Magic was on the team. The senior medical director of the federation's basketball program said that Johnson presented a "realistic threat" of passing on the AIDS virus. At least one Australian player, center Ray Borner, said that he would accept a silver medal rather than play against Johnson for the gold. (Like that was going to happen. Chuck Daly's response to Borner's comment was: "That's one less team we have to beat.")

Cleveland Cavaliers guard Mark Price, an Eastern Conference All-Star who would be playing against Johnson, said: "I think it's in the back of every player's mind. We still don't know much about the virus." Houston Rockets coach Don Chaney said that Magic shouldn't play. "If there's a risk at all," said Chaney, "I don't feel that risk should be taken." Price's statements were criticized by some because he was a conservative Christian, but how to explain Chaney, an open-minded African American? Or the skepticism about Magic's playing that was expressed by the Yale-educated Chris Dudley of the New Jersey Nets? Or that of citizen-of-the-world Sarunas Marciulionis, who would be playing against Magic in Barcelona? "When I'm driving to the hoop, I'm bleeding all the time," said Golden State's Marciulionis. "I don't know how AIDS can spread, how fast, how soon."

Even some of his Lakers teammates and good friends, Byron Scott and A. C. Green, had expressed their opinion that he should not be allowed to play in the exhibition. (To be clear, it was for different reasons. Scott wanted him to rest and take care of himself; Green, an intensely religious man who was famously saving himself for marriage, argued that the game was for active players.)

More to the point, as late as mid-January I had quoted an anonymous Dream Teamer in *Sports Illustrated* as saying: "I don't see how any of us could feel we were completely safe if he got injured and started bleeding." So it wasn't only people outside the United States who didn't want to go up against Magic in Barcelona—he had at least one on his own team.

Like many reporters, I did the due diligence, trying to find the truth about a disease that still perplexes us two decades later. Had the Internet been in existence then, one can only imagine the multitude of daily reports that would've seen the light of day—Magic's T-cell count would've been as widely reported as the weather.

In the end, of course, Magic, being Magic, shut his ears to "all the negativity." He wanted to play in the All-Star Game and there was never a doubt that he would not accept Stern's invitation that a thirteenth player be added to the Western roster. He got a two-minute standing ovation from the crowd, hugs from teammates and opponents. It was Isiah Thomas who motioned that everyone should come forward, and that included a game Mark Price. Perhaps some of the players felt more at ease since they had been tested for AIDS and had come up negative. Of the twenty-five All-Stars present on that afternoon, only Houston's Otis Thorpe and Detroit's Dennis Rodman said they had not been tested, while only Isiah and James Worthy would not comment.

Naturally, Magic put on a legendary performance, scoring 25 points to go with 9 assists, 5 rebounds, and 2 steals to win the MVP award in a 153–113 Western Conference rout. The afternoon included a long three-pointer with time running out, and here's what I wrote the following week in *Sports Illustrated*:

There he stood, twenty-four feet from the basket, a ball in one hand, a sprinkle of magic dust in the other. As the game clock wound down, Magic Johnson wound up and let fly. "I figured the shot was in," said the San Antonio Spurs' David Robinson, his Western Conference teammate. "He's been writing this script for years." Of course it went in, a three-pointer no less. And thus ended, in impossibly emotional and dramatic fashion, Sunday's 42nd NBA All-Star Game, better known as The Earvin Johnson Consciousness-Raising Love-In. Bank on this: You'll never see anything like it again.

That was laying it on a bit thick, but it was a moment for thickness. The defense, as in most All-Star Games, was less than assiduous, and that went double for defending Magic, either because players were giving him a break, didn't want to get near him, or a little bit of both. On his final three-pointer, he was "guarded" by his good buddy at the time, Isiah, who gave him all the space, in effect, encouraging him to launch the shot.

When the evening was over and Magic had talked to his last reporter, smiled for his last photographer, and signed the last autograph for the last fan, it became clear what single aspect of Earvin Johnson was irreplaceable. It was his capacity for giving everything to the game. Bird couldn't do it—he never liked the media attention as much as Magic and didn't deal well with cloying fans. Jordan couldn't do it—he treasured his free time and had become more and more zealous about guarding it. It was impossible not to contrast the way Jordan and Magic approached All-Star Weekend, the former renting a condo outside the Walt Disney World complex so that he could more easily get to the golf course, Magic at the designated NBA hotel, where he signed autographs for maids and busboys. And while Magic met with the press for three hours at the media sessions, Jordan skipped the mandatory gathering to play golf.

Once Magic played in the All-Star Game and neither he nor anyone on the court collapsed and died in spectacularly operatic fashion, we began to assume that Magic would be in Barcelona, Australians be damned. In retrospect, what is astounding was the degree to which Magic controlled the story. He was going to play; it was his decision, and who the hell was going to stop him? The NBA and USA Basketball had quietly done their homework after his announcement, enlisting a blue-ribbon panel of AIDS specialists, and could find no one who recommended that Magic be benched. The decision on whether Magic could play was never even put to an official vote within the committee. Magic was selected, Magic said he was playing, and no doctor said he couldn't. So Magic was playing.

Hard upon the heels of the All-Star Game followed what was surely the weirdest ceremony in NBA history—Magic's retirement gala at which he kinda, sorta hinted that he wasn't retiring. During his speech, Magic, the coy lover, told the crowd: "If I decide to come back, I hope you won't be upset and we have to do this all over again." The fans went crazy. Later he mused about what the comeback scenario could be, perhaps not playing back-to-back games, perhaps not playing as many minutes, perhaps skipping some road trips.

I was absolutely convinced at that point that Magic was coming back full-time, barring some rule from the NBA that would keep him from doing so. He said all this in his breezy happy-ringmaster tone, sobering only when he was asked if he was leading the Lakers on. "That's what they've got, so they can take it or leave it," he answered.

Now, that is a man with chutzpah.

So by the time the Dream Teamers gathered in San Diego, Magic was, for all intents and purposes, back. Whatever fears his fellow Dream Teamers had about playing with him, they didn't mention them when they got together in San Diego. Such was the fantasyland atmosphere of the Dream Team. Magic was here, and when Magic is around, it's his world and his team.

# THE MAGIC MAN

. . . . . . . . . . . . . . . . . . . . . . . . . . . . . . . . . . . . . . . . . . . . . . . . . . . . . . . . . . . . . . .

## "It's My Mind-Set That's Kept Me Alive"

*Dallas, Texas*

"I guess I was the blessing," says Magic Johnson, "and then I was the curse."

The subject is HIV. We are sitting in the lobby of a Dallas hotel during the NBA Finals, which Magic is working as an analyst for ABC. His broadcast work gets mixed reviews; his corporeal presence does not. Everybody likes him. Everybody always has. Over the course of a two-hour conversation, a dozen people approach him, most expressing some kind of connection to him, tacit or otherwise. He is the sports world's six-degrees-of-separation guy. *I used to be in business with Quincy Jones and I know you and Quincy are close. . . . Do you remember? I had a physical therapy business in L.A. . . . We have a friend in common, a hedge fund guy named . . .* And Magic Johnson will nod and say he remembers even if he doesn't remember, because that's his MO.

"The blessing was that I came out and announced and everybody started talking about AIDS openly, maybe for the first time," Magic says. "Then the curse came because kids started saying, 'Oh, I can get it and still be like Magic. He's all over the place. He's doing fine.'"

Magic feels obligated, as he should, to set the medical record straight.

"You can't look at the example of one person and say, 'I'll be like that,'" he says. "The virus acts differently in everybody. Hopefully the meds work and there's early detection. But you can't be sure. Early detection is the key because full-blown AIDS is still a death sentence. It's important that people get checked."

Over the years, as Magic remained in the spotlight, broadcasting and expanding his business empire, his weight went up and down with the regularity of Oprah's. He looked big, then he looked normal, then he looked *real* big, then he looked okay. At this writing, he looks great, having shed twenty-five pounds. "The road used to kill me," he says, "because I snacked a lot. And sweets are a weakness. That will never change. But I've cut back. Protein shake in the morning, maybe oatmeal." Whenever possible, he arises at 4:30 a.m. to stretch. Then he goes to the gym and runs outside or on the treadmill. The regimen he learned as an athlete helps him with the regimen he needs as someone living with HIV. "Thank God my knees and hips are okay," he says.

Like millions of people around the world living with the virus, he says that he has no manifest medical repercussions. He takes his cocktail of three drugs in the morning. "I forget once in a while, like everybody does," he says, "but never two days in a row. Anyway, the drugs are still working in your body even if you forget."

I suppose that I should dwell on Magic's business empire, the fact that he has an equity fund with $550 million in cash and a billion-dollar real-estate fund and that he wants to help bring an NFL team back to Los Angeles and that he's now a global player who gets Warren Buffett with one ring of the cell. That's what's going on now, anyway. But that doesn't interest me much except to juxtapose what Magic has accomplished with an anecdote from

Scott Price's excellent *Sports Illustrated* story about Scottie Pippen in 1999. Price describes Pippen, by then a Portland Trail Blazer, musing about franchise owner Paul Allen.

What does he have? Forty billion? I want to know: How can I make a billion? I just want one of them! What do I need to do? But I don't want to approach him like that. I don't want people coming up to me just for what I do, and I'm sure he doesn't. So I have to let that relationship grow a little bit. Like, win a championship and then I can say, "Tell me how I can make a billion dollars. Tell me how I can become a billionaire."

From the earliest moments of his career, Magic *did* approach people like Paul Allen, he *did* listen and take notes, and then he went out and did it, combining those lessons with the power of an inner drive and a thousand-megawatt personality. Pippen talked about it, dreamed about it. Magic did it.

What interests me most about the man, though, is that all this began to take place with a seeming death sentence hanging over his head. His sunny disposition was frequently the first thing anyone wrote about him from his rookie year, and that continues even now. I keep looking for the holes, wondering if it's real.

"I've been working with Earvin for four years," says Michael Wilbon, the ESPN commentator, "and during the playoffs that means I see him just about every day. And I've never seen him in a bad mood. I mean, *never*. How is that possible?"

Johnson's disastrous eight-week stint in 1998 as host of *The Magic Hour*, a monument to grimace-inducing, nervous, obsequious television hosting? The man ripped right through it like it never happened, learning experience and all that, on to the next thing, onward, ever upward. I ask him if having HIV had anything to do with his later success and whether or not, early on, he encountered some prejudice about it and fought even harder to put his stamp on the business world.

"I never felt that anybody, you know, *forgot* to shake my hand or something like that," he says. "The business world seemed pretty open about accepting me. But I guess HIV did launch my career faster in business. For one thing, I retired earlier than I would have. The disease brought a spotlight on me and what I was doing with business. And it probably made me a more disciplined business-man because it made me a more disciplined person."

Pat Riley, Magic's old coach with the Lakers and now the guid-ing force of the Miami Heat, comes over to join us. It feels like old times, almost makes me feel sentimental.

"You guys were tough to cover sometimes," I say, "but man, I do miss those days. There was nothing like them—the Lakers, the Celtics, the Pistons, the Bulls."

Magic and Riley agree, and for a moment we're just three old geezers lost in the past.

"I always remember something Pat told me then," says Magic. "He'd say, 'Look, this is a special time and a special place. You will never forget these moments.' But I didn't realize it at the time. You're too busy because—"

"You're in the heat of battle," says Riley. "You're in the trenches."

"Right," says Magic. "And you can't really enjoy it. But then, when it's over, man, you realize, 'Okay, that was special.'"

Riley and Magic embrace, and his old coach leaves.

"You know, when I look back on the Dream Team," I say to Magic, "the one astounding thing is that everybody thought at the time that you were going to . . ."

"Die?" he says.

"Yeah," I say. "Did you ever think that?"

"No," he answers immediately. "All right, there was one time, about a month after I learned that I had HIV, that I had to deal with death. I took a long walk on the beach with Lon [Rosen, his agent at the time], and we had to talk about getting all these things in order in case something happened.

"But other than that . . . never. And I have to believe that my mind-set is the thing that has really kept me alive, along with medicine and diet. But you have to be good with your status. You're living with HIV. You have to realize that. A lot of people aren't happy with it and that means they're stressing, so they compound everything. You have to realize it's a disease, and stress and depression will compound the problems of any disease."

We can be clear on one thing: few people have ever been as good with their status as Magic Johnson.

# CHAPTER 21

# THE COACH

- - - - - - - - - - - - - - - - - - - - - - - - - - - - - - - - - - - - - - - - - -

## Chuck Has a Message for His Assistants: Make Sure to Ignore

Chuck Daly carried himself like a guy who didn't have a care in the world, but for much of his adult life he was a restless insomniac who usually read himself to sleep, historical nonfiction and detective fiction being his favorites. During the 2005 Finals a bunch of us were driving home late from a party in San Antonio, and Matt Dobek, who was the Detroit Pistons' PR man and extremely close to Chuck, suggested we call him.

I reminded Matt that it was two hours after midnight.

"Trust me," said Matt. "He'll be awake."

Chuck was in bed but answered on the first ring. He was reading, as I recall, a Michael Connelly novel. We passed the phone around, and I asked him if he owed me any money, beating him to the punch.

As his time to coach the Dream Team drew near, Daly was coming off a trying 1991–92 season, which ended with him resigning in May. He wasn't pushed—his contract was up—but maybe he was nudged a little. One of the best attributes an NBA veteran can have is the ability to realize when the gig is up.

To understand that the Dream Team job was a tough one, at least in the beginning, one must remember, again, that this began as a chemical mystery. Jordan was popular in his own way, but he was so competitive that it was difficult to assess whom he might rub the wrong way. Barkley was everybody's friend, but would his unpredictability turn off his teammates when they got it in large doses? Bird, Malone, Stockton, Ewing . . . none was ever considered Mr. Congeniality. Mullin and Robinson weren't part of the NBA's in-crowd. Would it work? Or would it be a disaster? And what the hell to do with Laettner?

Daly knew that one of the keys was Magic. He and Bird were the natural choices to be co-captains, but Daly knew that that honor would be important only to Magic. Bird would be a leader just by dint of being Bird, but Magic would, to say the least, embrace the role, gather it in his arms, and hug it until he smothered it.

But it wasn't Magic and Larry's league anymore. It was Michael's, and no one knew that more than the coach. Daly's respect for Jordan as a player knew no bounds, stemming as it did from the years when Jordan came up on the losing end. No one knew better than Daly how hard his team had to play to beat this guy, and no one knew better how close he had come to losing to a one-man team. "This guy is so good," Daly said once, "he's an embarrassment to the league."

So soon after Daly checked into suite 4117 at the Sheraton Grande, the one with the view of the Torrey Pines golf course and the Pacific beyond, he called on Jordan.

"Magic and Larry are obvious choices to be captains, but so are you," said Daly. "I just want to know if you'd be interested in a leadership triumvirate." It sounded almost Roman.

"No way," Jordan told him. "It should be Magic and Larry. I have too much respect for those guys. I'll hang back."

If that sounds at odds with Jordan's competitive personality, it's not. Saying that Jordan knew his place sounds a bit plantation-like, so that's not what I mean. But he was (is) a smart man, wise in the ways of basketball tradition, more astute than most of his peers (faint praise acknowledged) at realizing how things should be. Mike Krzyzewski found that out at the first practice the next day. He didn't know Jordan well and wondered how he, a mere college coach, would be treated by the best player on the planet, especially one who wore his hatred of Duke on his sleeve and his Carolina blue skivvies under his uniform. But Jordan, his better angels prevailing, approached Krzyzewski and said, "Coach K, you got time? There's some stuff I want to work on."

When I talked to Krzyzewski about it not long ago, he teared up at the memory. "Michael didn't have to do that," the coach said. "It was his way of saying, 'You're important and none of that other bullshit means anything. We're all on the same team.'"

Anyway, by Dream Team time, Jordan was weary of endless responsibility. For two consecutive seasons he had dragged teams to the championship finish line, and he didn't need the tri-captainship. Everybody knew that, from a players' aspect, this would be Jordan's team, and if he wasn't captain, he'd be freer to make that point clear . . . which on many occasions in the upcoming weeks he did.

As time went on, Magic and Jordan made the team decisions together. As Magic remembers it: "Chuck would say, 'Okay, do we want to practice tomorrow?' and Michael and I would look at each other, and if he didn't want to, we'd tell Chuck no. Or Chuck would say, 'What time you want to go tomorrow?' and Michael would say, 'Early because I want to play golf,' then that's what we did. Michael had the things that were important to him, and that's when he made himself clear. We played off each other very well."

And the team knew the score. Magic was the sun, but Jordan was the North Star.

"So far as leading the team out, talking to the press, representing us, all that stuff, it was Magic," Mullin told me years later. "But once we got in the gym? It was all Michael."

In the weeks leading up to his Dream Team assignment, the Prince of Pessimism was especially nervous, grateful for the opportunity, of course, but keenly aware of the historical weight. What would his spurned peers such as Larry Brown and Don Nelson have to say if he couldn't take back the gold with these guys?

As he surveyed the immortal bunch that sat in front of him at the first Dream Team meeting at the hotel, Daly needed to strike a tone. Serious but not too serious. Light but not too light. Give the players a structure but give them room, too. It was tricky.

So Daly told them of two Spanish-owned Mediterranean islands: Majorca, a much-desired destination, the kind of place Dream Teamers would take their wives and girlfriends, and Minorca, which Daly described as a dark and dismal place with a high suicide rate. (Note to the Spanish Tourism Commission: I have no idea if this is true. I'm telling a story about a coach.)

"If we lose in Barcelona," says Daly, "we won't get beyond Minorca."

I have no idea if Daly came up with that himself. But it wasn't bad. Who knows, though, if it had any effect on a basketball team, which is fairly metaphor-proof. Anyway, Barkley had something to say. "Coach, we ain't going to no motherfuckin' Minorca," he said.

Daly brought up the next subject a little more gingerly. A history buff, he read Cold War literature and espionage/thriller fiction, and, as he put it more than once, "Our next six weeks is a Tom Clancy novel waiting to happen." He had read stories about the massacre of eleven Israeli athletes by Black September terrorists at the 1972 Munich Games. He knew about the Basque separatists in Spain. And his biggest nightmare—in a literal sense, since he confessed to dreaming about it—was a terrorist attack of some kind, with his team as the target.

His message was absorbed. This was a group of men used to the sight of mobs, benign though they might usually be.

Finally, Daly approached the most delicate subject, one even more frightening than terrorism since it was well within the realm of possibility.

"Look, there are twelve of you, and you're all All-Stars and future Hall of Famers," Daly said, "and there is no way I can get all of you the minutes you're used to having on—"

Magic and Jordan interrupted him.

"That isn't going to be a problem," Jordan said.

"We're here to win, and nobody is going to care about playing time, Chuck," Magic said.

Such problems, particularly the knotty one of minutes, are rarely solved that easily. This one was. Magic and Jordan said there would not be a problem, and that was that.

The meeting, by all accounts, was a success. Everybody loved Chuck. Everybody would play hard for Chuck. He is gone now—dead of cancer at age seventy-eight—so perhaps I would've gone light on the criticism in any case. But believe this: I never heard one negative word about Chuck Daly in all my years of covering the NBA. Mullin told me this years later, and it's the key to why Daly was so successful: "Before the Dream Team, I looked at Chuck as kind of a Pat Riley–type figure, you know, a big-timer who was able to beat the Lakers, won two straight championships, dressed like out of *GQ*. But after being with him from the first moment, man, I find out he's from my neighborhood."

After the dinner, it was time for Daly to meet with his three assistants: Lenny Wilkens, an old NBA hand; Krzyzewski, fresh off two straight NCAA championships at Duke; and P. J. Carlesimo, a fast-talking Jersey guy who had lifted a nondescript Seton Hall program into national prominence. Krzyzewski and Carlesimo felt like college freshmen entering their first lecture. In later years, Krzyzewski would talk about the holy-shit moment of stepping onto the court and seeing Magic, Jordan, and Bird shooting around.

"Look, for me it was a step up, not a step sideways," says Krzyzewski. "I was a peon in this whole process. I was suddenly with basketball royalty. Not the best players in college; the best players *anywhere*. And I'm also with guys like Chuck, who had won two championships, and Lenny, who had won a million games."

Krzyzewski and Carlesimo were wearing their USA Basketball regalia but otherwise looked like college coaches, notebook open, pen poised, ears wide open to hear what the coach of the world's greatest team was going to say. Here's how Krzyzewski describes it: "Chuck says, 'Listen, the very first thing I want you guys to do is . . .' and P.J. and I are all, 'Yes, yes, what is it, Coach?' and Chuck says, 'The first thing I want you to do is learn to . . . *ignore*.'"

Daly was giving them another version of one of his favorite sayings: "It's good to be hard of hearing." Over time, Daly had learned that teams grumble about coaches, argue about women, engage in petty squabbles and even fistfights over shooting games, and fall in and out of relationships like love-struck teens. The only thing that truly mattered, as he saw it, was that they came together most of the time when they were playing basketball.

"We have the best players in the world, and, as college coaches, you guys are going to look at every little thing like you have to do back with your own teams," Daly told them. "I understand that. But at this level most of it is not that important. Follow my lead, and don't go nuts about little things. We're going to need you to work the guys out because you're the young legs. But you have to ignore stuff within that. If there's something important, I'll know it. Keep your eyes open and tell me anything you want and bring any suggestions to me. Treat them not just like professionals but the *professionals* of professionals."

Krzyzewski left that meeting with one thought: Chuck Daly understood the superstar intellect better than anyone.

Daly was true to his word. Years later, when I talked to Drexler about Daly, he actually used the word *ignore*. "As time went on, we'd try to get under Chuck's skin at practice just to see if we could do it," said Drexler. "We'd always pretend to whine, 'Chuck, man, you're killing us. We want to get out of here.' And he ignored everything."

Daly then divvied up the coaching assignments. Wilkens, wise in the ways of the NBA, would be his general overseer. Krzyzewski would have more responsibility for the defense, particularly transition defense, while Carlesimo would be more of an offensive specialist and have the yeoman's job of breaking down tape. Krzyzewski said that he made a key strategic decision by volunteering to run the drills and leave the intrasquad refereeing to Carlesimo. "P.J. got immense crap when he had that whistle around his neck," says Krzyzewski. "And I mean *immense.*"

Krzyzewski and Carlesimo left the meeting in awe of Daly's command of the situation. "The feeling now is, anyone could've coached that team to the gold medal," says Carlesimo, "In fact, I'm not sure anyone but Chuck could've done it."

# CHAPTER 22

# THE ONE-DAY WONDERS

. . . . . . . . . . . . . . . . . . . . . . . . . . . . . . . . . . . . . . . . . . . .

**These Were the Best Days of His Life. . . .**
**Surely Grant Hill's Wife Understands**

To prepare the Dream Team for competition, USA Basketball lined up nine college players. Other pros would've been better, but asking an NBA player to volunteer his time at a party to which he was not invited was a nonstarter. Still, the mind is free to wonder how hard Isiah Thomas would've played in those scrimmages.

The college kids arrived in La Jolla a couple of days before the Dream Teamers, and one day, as they were returning from practice and boarding the elevator, Bird was just completing his check-in. They held the door for him.

"I hope you young boys are ready," Bird said, flashing his smile, which was somewhere between simple smirk and outright contemptuousness. "We're coming at you hard." Bird also told them he couldn't wait until they got to the NBA, "so I can bust all your asses." Then he got off.

The collegians were tongue-tied. "At that time," says Grant Hill, "none of us knew that Larry was a notorious trash-talker." The collegians managed a couple of mumbled responses, but as soon as Bird got off, they started chattering among themselves, in awe of what had just transpired: *Larry Bird is talking trash. To us!*

For the next few days the college kids lived the dream. The pros treated them with respect, Pippen being the one, as most remember, who went out of his way to play tour guide. Perhaps Scottie remembered what it had been like for him as a rookie playing next to an ascendant Jordan, that feeling of alienation upon entering someone else's magic kingdom.

The collegians knew that their big day was coming—June 24, the first scrimmage against the Dream Team. When they arrived at the UC San Diego gym that day, feeling very much, as Hill puts it, "like sacrificial lambs," the Dream Team was going through its paces. Laettner looked up and saw them and felt how strange it was that Duke teammates Hill and Bobby Hurley were up there and he was down here.

"As they were coming in, Barkley, at that moment, turned and dunked on Karl Malone," remembers Laettner. "The power of it was amazing, and I looked up at them and saw that amazed expression on their faces."

By then the college kids had their instructions from coach Roy Williams, who had gotten his instructions from Chuck Daly and USA Basketball. Hurley was to dribble-penetrate every time he could. The idea was not to finish at the rim—which Hurley couldn't do anyway and would not be able to do when he subsequently reached the pros—but to kick to jump shooters such as Alan Houston and Jamal Mashburn. The big men, Chris Webber, Eric Montross, and Rodney Rogers, were to battle underneath with ferocity, pretend that they were mature players such as Lithuania's Arvydas Sabonis. And the athletic all-arounders, Hill and Penny Hardaway, were to be relentless on offense and play at a pace to which the Dream Teamers were not accustomed. "Play like the Europeans," Williams instructed them.

As the collegians gathered at the sideline, Hill still remembers the chilling words from Williams: "Grant, you got M.J." *Oh, crap*, thought Hill. *I'm guarding Michael Jordan!* And Hill's heart skipped a beat when Magic Johnson ambled out to center court. He was the player after whom Hill tried to pattern his style, "and I do mean *try*," says Hill.

The Dream Teamers were at this early stage trying to figure each other out, over-passing and trying not to step on one another's game. The collegians, by contrast, were tuned-up high-performing automobiles impatiently waiting for the starter's flag.

Hurley was the key. He was an unusual player, a pallid six-footer with no discernible athleticism. But he had been schooled by two of the world's best coaches—his father, Bob Hurley Sr., at St. Anthony's in Jersey City, New Jersey, and Krzyzewski at Duke—so his basic chops were in order. And he wasn't a robot designed according to some instructional manual. There was a lot of street in Hurley. What he had was the best point-guard quality, albeit an ineffable one: he could get where he wanted to go.

And where he wanted to go was by Magic Johnson, who guarded him much of the time. The collegians won the game 88–80, Hurley its star. When the media were allowed in, I distinctly remember that the Dream Teamers looked a bit down in the mouth. When word filtered out that they had been beaten by the college kids, there was a certain and predictable it-was-only-practice tone to their comments. But it went deeper than that.

Now, let's keep this in perspective. There's no reason to believe that without the loss to the collegians, the Dream Team would've been in trouble in Barcelona. As Hill says, "I don't think they were alarmed or anything like that. It was more a wake-up call." Krzyzewski says that Daly "orchestrated" the loss, pulling Jordan out at crucial times and deliberately letting the action continue even though there were obvious times to stop it and make corrections.

I watched a tape of the game and can confirm that that is the case. It sounds like a fascinating historical document—as the intrasquad scrimmage in Monte Carlo would prove to be (Chapter 28)—but it isn't. It has too much the feel of a loose practice session.

"Chuck just wanted for one day to plant the idea that we could *conceivably* lose," says Krzyzewski.

Still, even though Magic was the one telling the team, "This is bullshit. We gotta get together," he was the focus of minor concern behind the scenes. Magic was never good at staying in front of small, quick guards, preferring to lurk in the passing lanes and use his wits and experience to make steals. Hurley had exposed him, and at that night's meeting the decision was made that Jordan and Pippen would defend quick point guards who might present problems.

Which didn't surprise Pippen. "I knew why I was on that team," Pippen told me years later. "I knew I was there more to defend than anything else. And that was fine with me."

That policy was enacted in the following day's practice. Jordan played Hurley some of the time, and the Duke quarterback struggled to even get the ball to midcourt. Then Daly put Pippen on Hurley and it was just as bad. Without a penetrating offense, the Dream Team drilled the collegians. I never saw a videotape of that game, but the rumored margin of victory was about 40 points, not that anyone remembers exactly. "We beat 'em like they stole something," said Barkley.

From that point on the Dream Team became a *team*, finding its own identity, cutting the corners that could be cut, discovering those little important details (*Robinson likes to post up here; Jordan will be available as a bailout there; Barkley likes to get the ball right away in transition but wait until Malone gets moving to give it to him*), adding the grace notes that give a team its harmony.

Years later, one of the best explanations of the Dream Team's level of play came from Laettner, to whom it was newest.

"The first thing I remember was how unbelievable their transition was from defense to offense," Laettner told me in 2011. "It was instantaneous, at least three steps faster than in college. That was a huge adjustment, even for a player who was used to running. It was the anticipation along with the quickness.

"And then what I remember is that, suddenly, all I had to do was move around and catch the ball. It was like I was a fourteen-year-old kid again playing with my dad's thirty-five-year-old men's league team. You're young and quick, so you do all the cutting and you run through with your hands up, and they're old and good and they will always find you. You don't have to do any one-on-one moves. You just move, put your hands up and the ball is there."

Most fun of all for the Dream Teamers, though, was finding a teammate's weak spot and grinding him into pulp. Ewing took grief for shooting outside too much. Barkley was derided for fading during scrimmages. Drexler would be torched for his proclivity to dribble with his head down and always to his right, after which he would try to go left, get fouled up, and then get verbally ground up again.

One way to put that college week in perspective, to gauge what it takes to become a truly great player—the sacrifices, the hard work, the good fortune—is to consider what happened in the NBA to those collegians who at that time represented the best and the brightest.

Hill was a terrific pro, still going strong at age thirty-nine at this writing. But his potential Hall of Fame, Dream Teamer type of career was derailed by injuries. Ditto for Hardaway, a splendid talent who made four All-Star teams but proved also to be a petulant locker-room lawyer. (Plus I, like so many others, wanted to terminate with extreme prejudice that damn Lil' Penny doll, a Nike marketing idea.) Like so many in the post-Jordan era, Hardaway's game never matched his hype. Houston was limited by a knee injury and by the stigma of being vastly overpaid, having gotten about $20 million per year from the New York Knicks before the 2001–02 season, one of the worst NBA contracts ever and representative of what the Knicks would do throughout the first decade of the twenty-first century.

Hurley never recovered from injuries suffered in a near-fatal car crash in his rookie season with the Sacramento Kings, 1993–94.

It's anyone's guess if he would've made himself into a great NBA player. My guess is no, but he would've been dependable and productive.

Webber had a fine NBA career with averages of 20.7 points and 9.8 rebounds, but he never pushed himself like Malone to be a truly dominant player, never developed a jump shot like Ewing, never glided around the court to block shots like Robinson, never got within sniffing distance of the Hall of Fame. Mashburn turned out to be a volume shooter who made only one All-Star team. Montross was a stiff, Erector-set-style center who never made an impact. Rodney Rogers was an okay pro who, sad to say, was paralyzed from the shoulders down in a post-retirement dirt bike accident in 2008.

So much promise. So much went wrong.

When the collegians got back to their rooms on that golden day after beating the Dream Team, they talked excitedly among themselves, theorizing that, with a few more good players, they could probably go out and win the gold medal. Only later would the realistic among them realize that that was not the case. But they still have the memories of mingling with the immortals and the distinction of being the only team in the world to get the best of the Dream Team, however briefly.

"It was unbelievable," says Hill, who shared his memories of San Diego with me for a solid hour. "I mean, with all due respect to the birth of my children and my marriage, it was the best week of my life." He smiled. "Make sure you go easy on that."

# CHAPTER 23

# THE WRITER

. . . . . . . . . . . . . . . . . . . . . . . . . . . . . . . . . . . . . . . . . . . . . .

## The Action Begins in Portland
## and Everyone Wants a Piece

For much of June and early July, Portland, Oregon, turned out to be the basketball capital of the world. The City of Roses had outbid Seattle, Hartford, and Indianapolis to host the Tournament of the Americas, through which the United States had to qualify for the Olympics, and by chance the Trail Blazers had also hosted Games 3, 4, and 5 of the NBA Finals, winning two of those but ultimately losing the decisive Game 6 to the Jordan and Pippen Bulls in Chicago.

So to those of us covering the playoffs and then the Dream Team, Portland had become a second home, and it couldn't have been more perfect. Portland was (still is) a fantastic city, hard by the Willamette River, funky and not overly gentrified, clean and comfortable, a city for your grandmother, your budding punk rocker, your underachieving intellectual driving hack. The citizenry took its Blazers extremely seriously but not itself. The city had great restaurants, an iconic local treasure called Powell's Books where one could lose himself for an afternoon, and an immortal bar on First Avenue called the Veritable Quandary (still there), where they had a lot on tap and a lot on tape. You wanted Stevie Ray Vaughan one night, you got it; you wanted the Clash the next night, you got that, too.

The tournament wasn't originally called the Tournament of the Americas and in fact wasn't even supposed to be in the United States. The FIBA schedule had called for the North and South American Zone Qualifying Tournament to be held in Brazil in March 1992, right around the time that NBA teams would be jockeying for playoff position and the NCAA was in full tournament mode. Had someone—be it the International Olympic Committee, FIBA, or the other qualifying teams—won a power struggle to keep that tournament in that place at that date, not only would there have been no Michael, Magic, or Larry, but there wouldn't even have been Hill, Hurley, or Webber.

But that was never going to happen. A little not-so-gentle arm-twisting by the NBA, Dave Gavitt, and the Inspector of Meat was all that was needed to move this clambake to friendly soil.

The broadcast rights belonged to COPABA, a corporate entity owned by a wealthy Brazilian named Jorge Ramos. Gavitt had been hanging around the NBA folks long enough by now to know what he had to do—put up some cold cash, a language Ramos could understand. It was between $3 million and $4 million and was supplied by the United States Olympic Committee, which had a surplus from the 1984 Games in Los Angeles. USA Basketball then bought television time from both NBC and TNT, the latter having recently come aboard as a broadcast partner, and handed the whole thing over to NBA Properties.

It was in Portland that one first realized the far-reaching scope of the Dream Team. La Jolla/San Diego had been crawling with American reporters, but at the Tournament of the Americas it turned international. The opposing teams were Argentina, Brazil, Canada, Cuba, Mexico, Panama, Puerto Rico, Uruguay, and Venezuela, each of which brought with it a local hero, most notably Brazil, whose high-scoring Oscar Schmidt was a legend overseas. At last the United States had a couple of flesh-and-blood targets.

"Ooh, Oscar Schmidt!" said Barkley. "I'm shaking in my boots." When Barkley would pause for a moment to actually offer a serious comment, it would go something like this. "I guard Larry Bird and James Worthy and Kevin McHale and Dominique Wilkins and a dozen other guys during the season," he'd say. "Why the fuck would I be worried about Oscar Schmidt?" As for Oscar Schmidt, who once had been talked about as being a draftable NBA player, (my own feeling is that he could've played in the league in his prime, which was between 1980 and 1988), here was his goal for the tournament: "I want all the American team's autographs if possible," said Schmidt. "Larry Bird is my idol. If I could play against him, it would be a great satisfaction." Now there was a real "Beat the USA!" battle cry. (Schmidt didn't get his wish in Portland, where he received only an autographed copy of *Drive*, an early autobiography Bird wrote with Bob Ryan, but he did in Barcelona.)

A small army of team officials, federation executives, entourages, and press contingents were there, too. International teams are notorious homers, but there was a different feeling about these visitors, who, like almost everyone else in Portland, were de facto Dream Team groupies.

Also in evidence were members of the United States Olympic Committee, who were close to getting their claws into the Dream Team. Until the United States officially qualified for Barcelona, the Dream Team was under the aegis of USA Basketball, but an Olympic team answers to the USOC, which was sick and tired of hearing about these millionaires who wanted to make their own rules.

The most obvious additions to this ever-expanding universe were the sponsors that had glommed onto the Dream Team. Behind closed doors they had been fighting pitched battles for months, trying to maximize their brand by association with this gang of all-star pitchmen. It was serious business with serious business consequences, but there was also a ludicrous territoriality to the whole thing that would culminate on the gold medal podium in Barcelona, where Nike god Michael Jordan would be forced to don a jacket made by Reebok. (Another topic for later.)

To those fighting the battles inside the NBA, USA Basketball, and the USOC, parsing out the conflicting contracts and relationships was a daily rat's nest. These weren't junior varsity sponsors that had come aboard; there were sixteen of them, and they were companies such as AT&T, Coca-Cola, McDonald's, Gatorade, and Visa USA, all of which had paid seven figures for the privilege of association with USA Basketball, but really with Michael, Magic, Larry, et al.

A dizzying number of retailers, twenty-four of them, had also signed on with NBA Properties, which was now in full control of marketing and turning out all kinds of red-white-and-blue fiddle-faddle. NBA Properties hadn't even existed a decade earlier, but by 1992 it had grown into one of the most sophisticated marketing juggernauts in the world. (David Stern would even suggest to Billy Payne, who was in charge of the 1996 Games in Atlanta, that NBA Properties assume all control of Olympic marketing; Payne, unwisely, said no.) In Portland, you couldn't swing a cat without knocking over a USA Basketball cup or a USA Basketball calendar. My sons, who were fifteen and twelve at the time, had their instructions: they could buy anything they wanted with their own money, but we weren't buying extra luggage to lug home a cache of Christian Laettner place mats. Then we took a trip to the Nike outlet store in Beaverton, Oregon, a requisite consumer journey, and had to buy an extra suitcase anyway.

The real intrigue came from the scrimmages about whose likeness could be put on what. Remember that the players had all sorts of endorsement deals of their own with companies that were not necessarily a part of Olympic marketing. And remember that no one can be a bigger pain in the ass than (a) agents who feel that their guy is getting screwed and (b) company execs who feel that they are not getting ultimate leverage out of their deals.

The earliest battles were fought over the feet. Converse was an official sponsor of USA Basketball, not to mention a longtime supporter of the amateur basketball program and America's de facto historical basketball shoe. Which made not a scintilla of difference to Jordan and Nike. Months before the team got together, Jordan's agent, David Falk, had told USA Basketball officials that his client's likeness was not to appear on Olympic apparel that was not sponsored by Nike. Some saber-rattling and tort-threatening ensued before a tentative compromise was worked out, one that, to echo once again the words of William Goldman, was set, just not *set* set, and would erupt in Barcelona.

The players were due some monies from the fast-flowing revenue stream that came from sponsorship and merchandise sales. Charles Grantham, a member of the USA Basketball committee but also president of the National Basketball Players Association, had insisted early on that the Dream Teamers get 33 percent of the pie, a figure that was unpopular both with his fellow committee members (who preferred something more like 0 percent) and other agents (who preferred something more like 50 percent). "As politically sensitive as all this was," Grantham says today, "I didn't want players to appear greedy. But neither did I want them to be exploited. So I thought one-third was fair."

However, by that point Dave Gavitt—the political marvel—had already intervened, having buttonholed his Celtics captain, Bird, about giving the money back. "USA Basketball needs it, Larry," Gavitt told him. "You're the first guy I'm coming to." Nobody was exactly sure what the sum would turn out to be, but Bird remembers it as somewhere between $600,000 and $800,000. "You're crazy, Dave," Bird told him. "But go ahead and ask." Gavitt went to selected guys. Magic, of course, who said he would do what Bird did. Jordan, of course, who said he would give it back. Eventually, Gavitt secured enough pledges, and the deal was done. A couple of players may have kept the money. But not many. "That's how smooth Dave Gavitt was," Bird says today. "He got a bunch of basketball players to give up money."

Still, there was much understandable cynicism attached to, say,

Jordan's Olympic participation. *You mean to tell me he's not doing this for the money?* Well, he wasn't. In fact, the bigger the star, the *less* he prospered from Barcelona. The Olympics needed Jordan; Jordan didn't need the Olympics. "Did it make Michael more international and give him a broader stage?" says David Falk. "Of course. But Michael already had that and we didn't do any new deals because of the Olympics. From purely a commercial standpoint, the Dream Team didn't have nearly as much impact on Michael, or, for that matter, on Patrick, as the 1984 Olympics." Lon Rosen, Magic's representative, says much the same thing: "The value of bigger stars, like Earvin and Michael, is always as individuals, and most of the Olympic marketing was as a group."

But all that was backroom stuff, background noise. When I look back at Portland, I still feel it represented the last pure moment of the Dream Team experience, the last time you could feel that, despite the growing vastness of the thing, you could get your hands around it, caress it, enjoy it. You had partial ownership of it; you were *invested*.

The press was invited to an opening-night party at the Nike campus, and I cadged tickets for my family. Dutifully I trotted my sons over to meet the gods, interrupting the players in mid-bite or mid-sip. Jordan, sporting a Fu Manchu that he said was a favorite of his wife, Juanita, was polite and slapped the boys on the back. Barkley put an arm around each of them and said, mock seriously, "I know you can overcome the disadvantages of having a father like that." There were fireworks and fresh seafood and booze, and while I made comments to my wife about the cultish, overly Nike-y aspects of the whole thing, I also thoroughly enjoyed it, wearing my half-price Jordans, the happy hypocrite, fortunate that I was walking this journalistic trail at this moment.

It was indeed a triumph of timing for all who were there. By then I was familiar with Art Kane's famous black-and-white photo of jazz musicians that was taken in 1957 on the corner of Fifth and

Madison in Harlem: Count Basie, Art Blakey, Dizzy Gillespie, Coleman Hawkins, Gene Krupa, Charlie Mingus, Thelonious Monk,
Gerry Mulligan, Sonny Rollins, et al. Later, in Ronald W. Clark's terrific biography *Einstein: The Life and Times*, I came across an iconic
photo of a physics symposium attended by the great minds of the
time—Einstein, Marie Curie, Hendrik Lorentz, Max Planck, and the
famous French mathematician Henri Poincaré, whom Einstein
considered his lone intellectual equal. I used to stare at it, fascinated
that all those visionary thinkers were gathered there together at
one time, a fortuitous accident of history.

The musicians and the scientists constituted Dream Teams in
other universes. And while the '92 Dream Team members weren't
as creative as jazz musicians or as brainy as physicists, they were, in
their own world, the resident geniuses of their time, and most of
them have endured as such. When you tunneled in and got closer,
yes, they were at root a bunch of guys on a basketball team, the
guys I covered from October to June. Ask Barkley about Jordan's
greatness, and you'd be liable to get, "Man, all I know is that he is
the *blackest* sumbitch I ever saw." Ask Bird to comment on Magic's
passing ability, and you'd be liable to get, "I don't know. He hasn't
passed me the ball yet." Maybe it was like that for the scientists, too;
maybe if you got close, you'd hear, *Hey, Curie. Your last theorem? My
Chihuahua figured it out in five minutes.*

But from afar it had a kind of majesty to it. It was a secret kingdom to which I had one of the keys, at least to a side door.

Others felt the same way. Not long ago I asked Dick Ebersol, who
as president of NBC Sports had by that time presided over a hundred dramatic events, what he felt as he sat courtside in Portland
with David Stern and Boris Stankovic, the Inspector of Meat, when
the team ran out together for the first time. Up to that point, Ebersol
had not been using the Dream Team for much of his Olympic promotion. "Prime time was still going to be about the cute little wom-
en's gymnastic team, and the swimmers, people like Matt Biondi,
Pablo Morales, Summer Sanders, and Janet Evans," said Ebersol,
who in May 2011 resigned as NBC sports chief. But then the doors

Dave Gavitt (left) with Boris Stankovic, the real force behind NBA players being eligible for the Olympics.

*Nathaniel S. Butler/Getty Images*

The *Sports Illustrated* photo that launched the name "Dream Team."

*Theo Westenberger/ Getty Images*

Chuck Daly (second from right) had some advice for his assistants (from left) P. J. Carlesimo, Mike Krzyzewski, and Lenny Wilkens: "Learn to ignore."

*John W. McDonough/Getty Images*

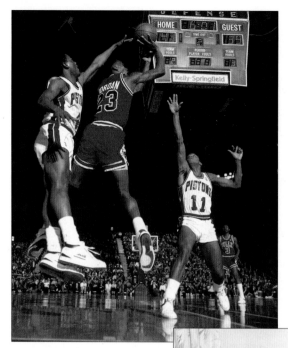

Michael Jordan—attempting a shot as Isiah Thomas (11) defends—had always claimed that he had nothing to do with Thomas's exclusion. But he says now that he made it clear he wouldn't play if the Pistons captain, a bitter rival, was on the team.

*Walter Iooss Jr./Getty Images*

Jordan sometimes resented Magic's refusal to cede the position of lead dog, but together they commanded the Dream Team.

*Andrew D. Bernstein/Getty Images*

At a dinner in Monte Carlo, Prince Rainier is flanked by the Dream Team princes.

*Andrew D. Bernstein/Getty Images*

Johnson and Bird became so linked as icons that it is often forgotten they were bitter oncourt rivals, particularly early in their careers.

*Manny Millan/Getty Images*

The saviors of the league, Larry and Magic, will forever be bound together.

*Andrew D. Bernstein/Getty Images*

The Dream Teamers stole the show at the opening ceremonies, and the USOC wasn't happy about it.

*Bill Frakes/Getty Images*

The games were blowouts, but Charles Barkley's competitiveness never waned.

*Andrew D. Bernstein/ Getty Images*

Quite often, there wasn't much to say during time-outs, but the team never tuned out Daly.

*Manny Millan/Getty Images*

Barkley's unique inside game made him Coach Daly's go-to guy, to the extent that the Dream Team needed one.

*Andrew D. Bernstein/Getty Images*

"Harry" (Patrick Ewing) and Larry comprised the Dream Team's Odd Couple.

*Andrew D. Bernstein/ Getty Images*

Karl Malone befriended boxer Oscar de la Hoya during the Games.

*Andrew D. Bernstein/Getty Images*

After struggling with alcohol early in his career, Chris Mullin worked as hard as anyone to become a Dream Teamer.

*Nathaniel S. Butler/ Getty Images*

Alone of the Dream Teamers, John Stockton could go virtually unrecognized on the streets of Barcelona.

*Nathaniel S. Butler/Getty Images*

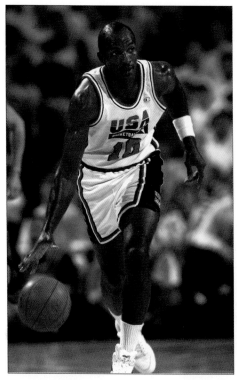

Not surprisingly, Clyde "The Glide" Drexler resented being a Dream Team add-on.

*John W. McDonough/Getty Images*

No matter how much he claimed that it wasn't difficult, college-kid Christian Laettner had a hard time being one of the boys.

*Andrew D. Bernstein/Getty Images*

Jordan felt that David Robinson (shown here jamming with Branford Marsalis in Barcelona) loved music more than he did basketball.

*Nathaniel S. Butler/Getty Images*

The ferocious manner in which Scottie Pippen and Jordan went after Croatia's Toni Kukoc (7) is a vivid Olympic memory for all the Dream Teamers.

*Richard Mackson/Getty Images*

Daly's love of golf was a big reason that Jordan signed on.

*Andrew D. Bernstein/Getty Images*

Jordan and stogie were frequent companions.

*Andrew D. Bernstein/Getty Images*

As Bird reclines in the background, Jordan furiously pursues another table-tennis victory.

*Andrew D. Bernstein/ Getty Images*

Wherever Magic went, the world's most famous HIV carrier drew a crowd.

*Andrew D. Bernstein/ Getty Images*

Barkley was at once the team's public relations nightmare and its greatest ambassador.

*Andrew D. Bernstein/ Getty Images*

Barkley and the author on Las Ramblas. In case you aren't sure, Charles is the one in purple.

*Nathaniel S. Butler/Getty Images*

The casually draped American flag enabled Jordan to obscure the Reebok logo at the medal ceremony.

*Richard Mackson/Getty Images*

to the kingdom swung open, the Dream Team came out, and Ebersol was transfixed. "It was like nothing I had ever experienced before," said Ebersol. "I had chills."

Magic Johnson was leading the way. It had been decided moments earlier, back in the tunnel, that one of the co-captains was going to carry the American flag, and you knew how that was going to go. Taking the advice of NBA PR man Josh Rosenfeld, whom he had worked with for several years in Los Angeles, Magic had already selected jersey number 15, ensuring that he would always be announced last, since the numbers ran from 4 to 15.

"You carry the flag," Bird said to Magic. By then Bird had ceded most of his captaincy duties to Magic. If he couldn't play at full strength, he was not going to act like a full-strength captain.

"Okay," said Magic, needing no convincing.

That was the best moment for me, watching the team jog out for the first time before the actual competition, a giant metaphorical jolt of electricity coursing through the arena. Terry Lyons, who headed up international public relations for the NBA, feels the same way. "It's still in my mind watching them run out and peel off to begin their warm-ups," said Lyons. "I was thinking to myself, *Ho-lee hell. It's actually happening.*"

I looked up from the press section to where my sons were sitting, taking it all in, not processing what it all meant but knowing it was something special, and said to myself, *Man, I'm lucky to be here, a moment in time that won't—can't—be repeated.* Thousands of flashbulbs exploded, thousands of fans rose to their feet, and the Cubans sank to theirs, stopping their warm-up to pay homage like pilgrims to Mecca. But all of us, each in our own way—weren't we pilgrims, too?

# CHAPTER 24

# THE LEGEND

. . . . . . . . . . . . . . . . . . . . . . . . . . . . . . . . . . . . . . . . . . . . . .

## Larry Shoots and Scores . . . and at Night Lies Awake in Pain

Before the first game, representatives of the Cuban basketball team had sought out Kim Bohuny, the NBA's point person on matters related to the international teams.

"We would like to take photos of the Dream Team," one of them asked her.

"I'm sure we can arrange that after the game," Kim said.

"No, we want to do it before," the man said. "So we make sure there is no problem with it."

Kim shrugged, then sought out Chuck Daly and bounced it off him. "Whatever," said Daly, upon hearing about the thousandth weird request put before him since he signed on. Terry Lyons nearly went apoplectic until Bohuny said that she had cleared it with Chuck. Had someone else—Pat Riley or Larry Brown—been in charge, perhaps the pregame photos never would have happened, and they became an irresistible part of the Dream Team lore.

And so the Cubans grabbed their cameras, waved posing instructions to their heroes, and snapped as many photos as they could, like doomed men demanding favors from their hooded executioners. I marveled at the absurdity of it, but in retrospect, I'm glad it happened. The Cubans were just a bunch of guys who recognized that this was their moment, guys who would never play in the NBA or even in Europe, but who could one day walk into their living room, point to a photo on the wall, and tell their grandchildren, *Mire, es tu abuelo. Con Michael Jordan!*

The United States won 136–57, suggesting that this whole pros-in-the-Olympics might be a tad more unbalanced than anyone had thought. As I gazed at the Inspector of Meat in his courtside seat, I wondered if an Oscar Wilde quote had passed through his mind: *When the gods wish to punish us, they answer our prayers.*

What would become the boilerplate reaction of the vanquished was provided by Miguel Calderón Gómez, coach of the overwhelmed victims: "For us it was an elegant game, a historic game. We can take back to Cuba a beautiful photograph of us with them." He sounded like a cruise director making the best of a shipwide epidemic of dysentery: *Be sure to take with you that wonderful portrait of Captain & Tennille from Karaoke Night!*

The loudest applause in the pregame introductions went not to Jordan, Magic, or Bird but to the hometown kid, Clyde Drexler. His smile was wide, and there was, perhaps, a tear in his eye. It was a great moment. Later, the Glide would walk over to Rod Thorn and say thank you for adding him to the roster. In later years, Drexler wouldn't be happy about having been the add-on, but in this first flush of Dream Team competitive excitement there was nothing like it.

Daly could've made the hometown play and started Drexler. But he didn't. The coach would later say—and the Dream Teamers to a man would insist—that starting lineups did not matter. Which came to be true. By the time this squad got to Barcelona, it could've started any five guys and won the day, and Daly did indeed institute a kind of mixed starting-lineup bag. But this was the *first* starting lineup and it meant something. It was not assembled capriciously. "You better believe I wanted to start that first game," Bird says today.

Magic and Bird had to start because they were . . . Magic and Bird, the men who had saved the league. Jordan had to start because . . . he was Jordan, the best player in the world. If Daly fretted at all about whom to start at center, a dislocated thumb suffered by Ewing during drills in San Diego had taken care of that; David Robinson walked to center circle. My own guess is that Daly would've started Robinson anyway. The coach had grown to respect Ewing's ferocity and accurate jump shot, but at that stage he was still more enamored of Robinson's jaw-dropping athleticism.

The final starting position went to Barkley, a guy who was not among the first players chosen for this Dream Team. To that point, he had been the team's best performer in practices, and that would continue in games, his springboard jumping and single-minded ability to attack the basket giving him a clear edge over his foil, Karl Malone. Daly started Barkley because, simply, he deserved it.

The ball went up, flashbulbs went off like a thousand small suns, and David Robinson tapped it back to Magic, who dribbled quickly over the midcourt line. Magic was looking in only one direction. He passed to Bird on the right wing, which is what he had dreamed about doing. Bird caught it and took two aggressive dribbles into the lane with his left hand, then another that forced his defender backward. Then, looking amazingly spry, Bird fell away and released a soft jumper from just inside the free throw line that spun, rotation perfect, toward the basket. . . .

We tend to think of a superstar's career as one long march into immortality, but in fact, near the end, it's usually characterized by a slow and sometimes painful slog toward the finish line. Rare is the athlete who goes out at full throttle; Jordan would've been that rarity had he not come back to play for two seasons with the Washington Wizards in 2001.

You have to understand how long Bird had been in pain. His

slog, albeit well-disguised, had started as far back as 1986, and throughout the Olympic competition, in San Diego/La Jolla, Portland, Monte Carlo, and Barcelona, Bird would float in and float out, depending on his mood, which depended on his level of pain. Few people knew how hard he had worked to get ready. Once he decided to be a Dream Teamer, he called up one of his old Celtics workout buddies, Rick Carlisle, and asked him to come out to the Indiana homestead to help him get in shape.

"Everything in French Lick was based on getting up at five in the morning," Carlisle, the coach of the 2011 NBA champion Dallas Mavericks, told me. "Things start early there. Our workouts were done by 9:00 a.m. We'd have something to eat, then go play golf or go fishing."

By that point, Bird's back had degenerated badly. There were times he couldn't drive his car without frequently stopping to stretch. In lieu of running, Bird and Carlisle rode bikes. They stretched, lifted, and did resistance work in the pool, all of it low to medium impact. Then they shot on Bird's outdoor full court, sometimes for an hour or more. With Bird, it was always about shooting, keeping the rhythm, keeping the stroke. If he did that, he believed, he could always be effective no matter how badly his body had betrayed him.

(There's a terrific anecdote in *Those Guys Have All the Fun*, an oral history of ESPN, about Mickey Mantle catching Bird in one of his pregame shooting rituals at a deserted Boston Garden. As Bird makes shot after shot after shot, the baseball immortal watches entranced on an internal feed at a TV studio. "This boy doesn't miss," Mantle says. And then there is Florida coach Billy Donovan, once a New York Knicks backup guard, who tells of arriving early at Madison Square Garden one evening for a game against the Celtics. Workers were still assembling the floor, and Donovan stood transfixed as he watched Bird "standing on a piece of wood shooting shots." Bird once estimated that when in rhythm, he could make as many as ninety-five out of a hundred shots moving around the floor in practice.)

During their French Lick workouts, Bird's physiotherapist, Dan Dyrek, was, as Carlisle put it, "on speed dial." The goal was to hold things together and maintain conditioning, just so Bird could get through the Dream Team games. Once in a while Bird would wonder if some magical surgical remedy would come along to extend his career, but he didn't talk much about his long-range future. In the short term, he just wanted to be fit enough and pain-free enough to make some contribution in Barcelona.

The summer workouts had helped, but throughout the Dream Team's time together Bird was in agony some of the time and just in plain pain some of the time. A fiberglass body brace gradually became full-time raiment, the armor that reminded him of his vulnerability.

Within the team structure, however, Bird was consistent in his role as the cantankerous but plain-speaking leader, the needler, the homespun humorist. When talking about Bird, one must be careful not to carry those midwestern attributes too far because you run the risk of making him sound dumb, which—trust me—he is not. I always regretted that in my book about the 1990–91 Celtics I used Bird's Hoosier vernacular when I quoted him directly, throwing in "kin" for "can" and "jest" for "just" and clipping off most of his *g*'s. It was a kind of reverse racism. I didn't dare quote Robert Parish's distinctive Louisiana patois because I would've come across as a racist making fun of the way a black man talks. But I could do it with Bird because we're both white. The rule here is: be sparing in your use of idiomatic language. Faulkner made it work; you probably won't.

In any case, there was no one who was more fun to be around than Bird when he was feeling good, as I had discovered during that '90–'91 season. Bird's target that year, besides eternal target Danny Ainge, was Michael Smith, a handsome and athletically gifted forward who had about 2 percent of Bird's heart and guts and consequently about 1 percent of his career. On a bus ride to a game around the NBA trading deadline, Smith related to Bird a trade that would send Milwaukee's Ricky Pierce to Seattle for Dale Ellis. Smith said that his agent had gotten the news of the deal on his speakerphone.

"I can't believe that," said Bird.

"The trade?" said Smith. "I can't believe it, either."

"No," said Bird. "I can't believe *your* agent has a speakerphone."

On the Dream Team, Magic was the public voice and Bird did the private things that set a tone. One day he had left his practice gear in the wrong place, and a team manager, Jay Price, now an assistant coach at Illinois, couldn't find it.

"I'll go get it, Larry," said Price.

"It was my mistake, Jay," said Bird. "I'll get it." And before Price could move, Bird was off. He doesn't deserve the Medal of Honor for that, but it's a telling little nugget that helps explain how the Dream Team operated. Ed Lacerte, the Celtics and Dream Team trainer, watched this and said to Price: "That's why he is who he is."

Throughout this Olympic journey, no story line recurred as much as the one about the unlikely friendship that grew between Bird and Ewing. They hung around so much together and hurled insults at each other with such ardor that Bird took to calling Ewing "Harry," so together they would be known as Harry and Larry. It seemed to be a play on the ongoing series of Dan-and-Dave Reebok commercials that featured U.S. decathlete rivals Dan O'Brien and Dave Johnson. But in Jackie MacMullan's *When the Game Was Ours*, Bird said that he picked Harry both because it rhymed with Larry and because he'd had a teammate at Indiana State named Harry Morgan.

Years later, virtually every Dream Teamer brings up Harry and Larry and starts chuckling about it even though no one can explain exactly why. It was just the goofy name of "Harry" and the sight of two head-bashing bitter rivals who never cared a whit about tailoring themselves for public consumption yukking it up, riffing on each other like a couple of high school lettermen. "They were just two unlikely guys to be close, I guess," said Jordan, "but there they were, hanging out, every night."

I can only remember one classic line that came out of it. Ewing, searching for something to say, told the cameras one day that he wanted to "pick Larry's mind," to which Bird responded, "I already picked Patrick's, and it only took about three minutes." Other than that, Bird's recurring theme was to insist to Ewing that he really wasn't a center "because you're always hanging around outside trying to shoot jump shots," to which Ewing might add, "Come inside and we'll find out who's a center." Not legendary comedic material, but it said a lot about the bond that the team members had formed with one another.

As I watched Bird throughout this competition, my mind kept going back to the regular season and how unlikely it was to see him on this team. The Celtics went a more-than-respectable 51–31, but Bird played in only forty-five games because of his back. It was excruciatingly painful for him, and not just on a literal level. He had desperately wanted to perform well during the season to prove that his Olympic inclusion had not been merely ceremonial, as some were writing. True, he got spirited defenses along the way from players such as Jordan. "You tell me this," Jordan said one night. "What other forward in the league can shoot from the outside, pass the basketball, rebound, get the break started, play team defense, and has been as much of a winner as Larry Bird? I don't care how many injuries he's had and how old he is. Tell me who's as good all-around as Larry Bird from the forward position."

Good question. In 1988, NBA Entertainment mortared into place a marvelous capsulization of Bird's career, a panoply of highlights that ran with John Cougar Mellencamp's "Small Town." NBA Entertainment debuted the video during All-Star Weekend in Chicago. As the lights went down, Bird slipped into the back of the room, accompanied by Dyrek. (Dyrek was a good guy and good company—I consulted with him for my own back problems—but it does say something when you pal around with the guy whose job it is to keep you upright.)

The video began. There is Bird anticipating the direction of one of his own misses, running to the spot, rebounding and left-handing in a layup, the video's money shot. There is Bird with a two-handed, over-the-head feed to a trailing Robert Parish for a dunk. There is Bird making precision passes from a sitting position on the floor, and there is Bird making two back-to-the-basket moves on the same play, finally knifing between two defenders for an underhand scoop shot.

We kept stealing glances back at Bird, to see his reaction, but his face was a blank.

There is Bird dribbling between two defenders and finally tapping a pass, à la Pete Maravich, back to McHale. There is Bird looking one way, then wrapping an entry pass around an opponent from the other direction. There is Bird, far under the basket, battling Milwaukee's Jack Sikma for a rebound, somehow corralling it, and, almost in one motion, somehow left-handing an outlet under James Worthy's outstretched arms to start a fast break.

Nobody makes those plays. Those plays are impossible. But Bird made them. And, finally, there is Bird stealing that fateful pass from Isiah in the '87 playoffs.

The lights come on. Someone starts applauding and we look back at Bird. He smiles ever so slightly, raises his hand ever so slightly, and leaves the room.

In its own way, Bird's career offers up more of a highlight reel than Magic's. That is no slight to Magic. The success of the Lakers guard was built on flash, yes, but more on straight dash. With the ball, he got from point A to point B as quickly as anyone and, once there, could usually get where he wanted to go, often with that killer spin. He was an unstoppable combination of size, strength, and speed, a running back hitting the hole hard and then having enough open-field chops to find the end zone.

But Bird, not Magic, was the earthbound, 180-degree version of Jordan's aerial artistry. Bird's gems were the product of some kind of extraordinary muscle memory, strength, and vision. They often occurred in the midst of armed combat, when he suddenly emerged with the ball and, not content merely to have it, went on to make a play out of it, turn a positive into a positive-positive. In his own way, Bird, the fundamental master, made more spectacular plays than Magic, the architect of Showtime.

And then there was his mind. In one of the *SI* polls I did during the 1991–92 season, the question was: who is the league's smartest player? Though Bird was in and out of the lineup, he won the voting over Stockton 10–8. Since we're on the subject, Mullin and Utah Jazz guard Jeff Hornacek got the next highest numbers of votes. That's four white players. Isiah Thomas got 1.5 votes. Racist? I can't say that. But I never saw any evidence that Thomas was not as smart a player as, say, Stockton, and that's a compliment to both of them. One caveat: several GMs and coaches say that they would've voted for Magic, an African American, had he been active during the season. But then, I never saw any evidence that Thomas was not as smart a player as Magic, either.

The most conclusive case that I can offer that Bird may stand alone at the top of the list of heady players comes from former Pistons player Laimbeer. Laimbeer does not like Bird and the feeling is mutual. But not long ago Laimbeer told me: "Let's face it, it would be hard to find a smarter player than Bird."

In the months before the Dream Team got together, the sometimes hobbled Bird probably drew the most attention during the strange and sometimes surreal circumstances surrounding the maybe-I-am-and-maybe-I'm-not retirement of Magic Johnson.

Magic had picked the date of his ceremony as February 16 because the Celtics and Bird would be in Los Angeles. That was one of the times when Bird was sidelined, and he would not have flown cross-country had Magic not been hanging up his sneakers . . . or whatever the hell he was doing. Gamely and uncomfortably, Bird stood on the podium during the forty-five-minute ceremony. He wore a double-breasted suit and looked for all the world like an Indiana undertaker. (Later, after he had returned to his more comfortable sweats, he uttered the obligatory line: "I rented it out, now I gotta take it back." It sounded funny coming from him because a lot of stuff sounded funny coming from him.)

Bird's introduction drew such loud and sustained applause that he was prompted to say, "I'm not the one retiring here, but thank you very much." Magic, standing a few feet away, asked with a smile: "Soon?" To which Bird replied: "Very soon." (Nobody but Bird knew how soon.) Bird then presented Magic with a piece of the Boston Garden parquet floor, the same memento the navel-gazing Celtics had given Kareem Abdul-Jabbar during his retirement tour in the 1988–89 season.

My best guess is that Bird honestly thought that Magic was retiring, because he was emotional during his brief remarks, promising, "We're gonna go to Barcelona and bring back the gold"—quite an enthusiastic turnaround for one who had initially seemed so disinclined to play.

And Bird had by this time, with the reality of his basketball mortality settling in, begun to appreciate his relationship with Magic and understand their dual impact upon the NBA. This is not exactly new ground, having been covered in the outstanding HBO documentary *Magic and Bird: A Courtship of Rivals* and in *When the Game Was Ours*. Some players, most notably Michael Jordan, were dismissive of the "shared legacy" story line, believing it to be mostly a Magic creation. (See Jordan interlude.) But it's worth another brief look.

Never in the history of sport has there been such a clear delineation of an era than the one that began when Magic and Bird came into the league, forever bound by blessed timing. Their rookie season, 1979–80, coincided with the coming of a new decade that would begin a new age in the NBA. They had been the two most-watched athletes in college basketball the previous season. They were dispatched not only to teams with contrasting styles but also to cities with a contrasting ethos—Magic's Los Angeles, the glitzy and showy entertainment center, and Bird's Boston, the conservative, traditional pride of the workingman.

The easy thing was to typecast the principals as reflections of their environment, the fast-breaking Magic as metaphor for fast-breaking Hollywood, the fundamentally sound Bird as metaphor for fundamentally sound Beantown. It worked at a certain surface level, but to draw such contrasts was to ignore the basic and all-important similarity between them: stylistic contrasts aside, they played the game unselfishly and democratically, and, not coincidentally, their teams won championships. Magic and Bird were, to an extent, *the same person*, midwestern children of the working class, blue-collared, nothing handed to them on a platter. That's what came out when they laced up their sneakers.

"What happened with Larry and Magic was they set a precedent of how the game should be approached, physically and mentally," Chris Mullin said during that 1991–92 season. "They taught everybody to not just focus on the money they were making or not making, but to play every single game like it's important. And when you have the best guys doing that, it rubs off. I think back to before I was playing, when the league had a bad name, there were only certain guys who would do that, a few on each team and maybe not even that. But just as bad habits are contagious on a team, so are good habits. And a lot of them started with Larry and Magic."

Both later said that when the NBA schedule was released each year they would circle the games they were to play against each other. Between December 28, 1979, and February 16, 1992, that happened thirty-seven times, the Lakers winning twenty-two of those games, further evidence that Magic had the better career. Each Magic-goes-against-Bird game was a red-letter date not just for them and the NBA but also for the sports world at large. By the time they had finished hammering away at each other, the league had been fundamentally transformed by their construction work. Teams were truly better, so good that an immortal like Bill Walton was a sixth man on the Celtics and a legendary scoring machine named Bob McAdoo was the eighth man on the Lakers.

Early in his career, Bird never thought much about those legacies and shared contributions, or at least never wanted to speak of them. He was too busy trying to beat Magic rather than philosophize about him. Since Magic's Michigan State team had defeated Bird's Indiana State team in that 1979 NCAA final, and then Magic's Lakers won the title in his rookie year, 1980, Bird felt like he was playing catch-up. When they finally got to spend extended off-court time together, during the filming of a Converse commercial in 1985, they enjoyed each other's company.

On or off the record, background or deep background, I never heard one say a bad word about the other. And they treasured their competition. Steve Bulpett, the veteran Celtics reporter for the *Boston Herald,* told about encountering Bird, dressing alone, in the nearly deserted visitors' locker room in the old Forum, home of the Lakers. "We're playin' the Lakers," he sang almost to himself. "We're playin' the Lakers."

And so there they were, in the same starting lineup on the day of that first game in Portland, soon-to-be-departed icons, so much history behind them. Magic got the tip and looked only for Larry. "I was only going one place," Magic said years later, "and that was to him."

And Larry looked only to the basket. "I knew I was going to shoot it," Bird would joke later, "because I didn't know if I'd get another chance to score." Today he says: "I had a smaller man on me, and I was open. That's all I ever needed."

He rose and shot, somehow young again, backpedaling while the ball was still in the air, secure of its destination, just as he had been in all those three-point contests.

The Legend wouldn't play in the next game because his back was stiff, and in fact he participated in only one more of the five remaining games in Portland. It was at the postgame interview session, in fact, when Bird felt such a severe stab of pain that he thought he'd be going home. But in those opening minutes he felt great, as if he had somehow gotten a cosmic reprieve just so he could catch that first pass from Magic and launch that shot.

For sure, the ball settled into the net, the first basket scored by the Best Team That Ever Played and also, in some way, the most glorious. "I'll never forget that flash of joy on his face when he made that shot," said Magic years later. "I can still see it today. I can still *feel* it today."

# CHAPTER 25

# THE KID FROM SPOKANE

. . . . . . . . . . . . . . . . . . . . . . . . . . . . . . . . . . . . . . . . . . . .

**Daly Had a Pistons Phone Number in His
Hand . . . and It Wasn't Isiah's**

The day after the United States opened the Tournament of the
Americas with the rout of photo-snapping Cuba, it played Canada,
a team that brought its elbows and knees, not its cameras. What
else could a hockey nation do but try to hard-check the Dream Team
into the boards? The result was a rough, shoddy game, and in the
first half, on a defensive switch, John Stockton knocked knees with
Jordan and went down. It didn't look bad at first and Stockton
started to walk it off, which is what Jordan did. But then Stockton
collapsed. It was bad, a spiral fracture of the right leg that would
take between six and eight weeks to heal.

In this first incarnation of pros in the Olympics, there was too
much of the old red-white-and-blue bonhomie in the ether for anyone to have raised much of a fuss about the specter of injuries. But
as much as the fans back home might've been rooting for their respective Dream Teamers, general managers and coaches were wor-

ried, and, as time wore on, owners such as Mark Cuban of the Dallas Mavericks began to complain about the injury risk to their assets. Frankly, it's hard not to see their point. After Stockton went down, Malone said he was worried about communicating with Jazz coach Jerry Sloan. "I was afraid he'd tell me to come home," said the Mailman.

(As time goes on, the prediction here is that owners will be less and less inclined to allow their best players to participate in the Olympic Games. That represents the principal threat to the continuance of the best pros playing for their national teams.)

On one level, Stockton's injury was a nonstory. Magic was playing well and either Jordan or Pippen could move to the point if necessary; it wasn't like exact positions were mandated anyway. But behind closed doors the injury did make for a lot of intrigue and, once again, brought Isiah into the conversation.

Daly's mind was all but made up. He looked in on Stockton in the training room after the game and told him, "We're going to need to replace you." Stockton protested that he should sleep on it, wait a day. Daly said okay. The coach went to dinner at Jake's, a Portland seafood institution popular with NBA types, and considered his options. Matt Dobek, who was rather like a son to Daly, was there, as were assistant Dream Team coach P. J. Carlesimo and USA Basketball committee member Rod Thorn, who was as inside as any executive.

Daly knew that Stockton didn't want to give up his spot. Though he went about his business more quietly than, say, Barkley—need we note that this is an immortal understatement?—Stockton was exquisitely happy as a Dream Teamer. He had blended in perfectly with everyone. He was, like Mullin, a student of angles, a player who knew the precise moment to slip a teammate a pass so that the recipient was in perfect position to shoot. He knew when to take his own shot, having become a master at going off the wrong foot and shooting a driving layup quicker than the defense thought he would, a stratagem employed by Steve Nash these days. Stockton was the first player I noticed, too, who split a high double-team *im-*

*mediately* upon its formation, rendering it useless. When I suggested that to him not long ago, Stockton said: "Well, I don't think I was, but I'll be glad to take credit for it."

The one thing that drove Stockton to distraction on the court was when a teammate would tell him, "Hey, I was open but you didn't give it to me."

And Stockton would say: "No, you *weren't* open. Just because no one seemed to be guarding you, that doesn't mean you were open, because you couldn't do anything with the ball if you got it." For the record, that sometimes happened early with Malone but almost never as time went on.

Stockton would get kidded now and again about his relationship with Malone. "Hey, don't bother running if Karl's in the other lane," Barkley used to shout at practice, "because John's only going to throw it to him."

And Stockton would come right back: "Charles, I throw it to Karl because, unlike some guys, he actually catches it."

"Playing with these guys on the Dream Team was basketball heaven," Stockton remembers. "It was like someone would run to the spot and, upon getting there, the ball would be there. Guys made reciprocal moves. It was basketball poetry. There was no place you could throw the ball that was wrong."

Stockton told me all that in a small locker room in the gymnasium that he owns in Spokane. I never heard him, or too many others, speak so eloquently about the game in a short burst. It stuck with me.

At any rate, Daly was honestly worried about the point guard position, as ridiculous as it might seem today. Matt Dobek had two phone numbers out, ready to call, those of Isiah and Joe Dumars, Detroit's championship backcourt from 1989 and 1990. Thorn, a realist, laughed as he watched Daly squirm. Thorn knew that Stockton didn't really need to be replaced, and he knew how tough this was on Chuck.

"Let's wait," Daly said finally.

Meanwhile, back in his room, Stockton was sad. Patsy-Clineon-the-jukebox sad. More than anything, he wanted the noise about his being selected over Isiah Thomas to go away. He had a fierce pride—Stockton never forgot the booing that accompanied the announcement that the Utah Jazz had taken him with the sixteenth pick of the 1984 draft—and he didn't think for a minute that he didn't belong with the Dream Team. With an eight-season resumé behind him that included four All-Star Games, he was no token. But he also knew that Isiah could've just as easily been there in his stead.

(It wasn't just Isiah who thought that. In a poll question I had raised in *Sports Illustrated* several months earlier, I asked NBA coaches and GMs whom they would rather have between Stockton and lightning-fast Kevin Johnson of the Phoenix Suns. I used K.J. instead of Isiah because he was more like Stockton. Isiah probably would've won the poll had he been in it. I was surprised at the result: Of those who answered, Johnson got sixteen votes and Stockton got only five. To be clear, Stockton's best days were in front of him.)

As Stockton stewed, Barkley and Malone paid the disconsolate point guard a visit. "Don't give up your spot," they told Stockton. "We want you here." That made Stockton feel better, but he was still uneasy. He desperately wanted to stay. As clearly as anyone, Stockton realized the dimension of being a Dream Teamer, how much it would mean to him later. Back in February, when there was some noise about agents holding out their players because of corporate complications—read: Jordan and Nike—Stockton had personally called Dave Gavitt and said, "Don't worry about it. That is not going to happen."

Back home after Stockton's injury, newspapers took temperatures and ran polls, eager to have something newsworthy to write about this Dream Team besides how badly they would kick the puppies in their next game. Of some ten thousand fans responding to a *USA Today* poll that asked who should take Stockton's place should the need arise, Isiah got 2,872 votes. Golden State's Tim Hardaway was second with 2,275, Cleveland's Mark Price third with 2,274 votes, Duke's Bobby Hurley fourth with 1,290 votes, and Kevin Johnson fifth with 1,201. Dumars got scant attention.

Daly and Stockton talked again. "Don't send me home, Chuck," said Stockton. "I'll be back for the Olympics. Heck, you can play with six if you have to."

Daly thought it over. "Okay, John," he said. "You're staying." If Daly were to speak truthfully, the injury actually helped him. With Stockton out and Bird on the shelf from time to time, it was much easier to divvy up minutes.

But had Daly come to a different conclusion, the call he was going to make was not to Isiah.

"I know for a fact that Chuck wanted Dumars," Jordan told me recently. (Remember that he and Daly played golf together almost every day.) "But Chuck just felt he couldn't because of how badly Isiah wanted to be on the Dream Team. He just couldn't do it. So he let John stay even with a broken leg."

I stand behind no one in my respect for Joe D., now the Pistons' general manager. But I'm glad that Stockton stayed and Daly never made that call to Dumars. However many potholes Isiah had dug for himself over the years, that would've been just too cruel.

# THE KID FROM SPOKANE

. . . . . . . . . . . . . . . . . . . . . . . . . . . . . . . . . . . . . . . . . . . .

## "You're Not Writing That Down, Are You?"

*Spokane, Washington*

When John Stockton picks me up in front of the hotel in his hometown, he is wearing a brace around his left knee.

"What happened?" I ask, and Stockton starts to tell me that in a recent pickup basketball game he had bumped knees with . . .

"Wait a minute," he asks suddenly, terror in his eyes. "You're not writing that down, are you?"

"Well, yeah," I answer.

And so begins a pleasant day of negotiation and secret note-taking. Stockton has taken quite literally that my visit is to talk about the Dream Team. In his view, that is the sole reason that I have flown three thousand miles to Spokane. It is part of Stockton's worldview that not only does he consider himself not interesting but also he is uninterested in revealing any part of his life that can be construed as personal.

That includes, evidently, his knee, which was injured when he bumped knees with—get this—the son (Parker Kelly) of the guy (Terry Kelly) whom he grew up idolizing.

"See, that's interesting stuff, John," I tell him.

"No, it isn't," he insists. "Why would anyone care about that?"

"Because they do," I say. "I find it interesting."

Stockton adds that the collision was his fault ("I was slow to react"), accepting blame being a central part of his DNA.

In telling you this, I am running the risk of pissing off Stockton, an athlete for whom I have deep respect. This on-or-off-the-record stuff can get complicated, but never so much as when you're dealing with Stockton. I'm going to err on the side of revelation, concluding that nothing controversial came out during our five hours together. Stockton, I concede, may not see it that way. That doesn't mean that it isn't revelatory, going a long way to explain how and why this plain-speaking, plain-appearing citizen of Spokane ended up on the Dream Team and later in the Hall of Fame.

We start our tour at the spectacular Spokane Falls and end up at St. Aloysius, where Stockton went to grammar school. I ask if he was an altar boy, and—I'm not making this up—he grows as animated as if he's talking about the Dream Team.

"Sixth and seventh grade I was the top altar boy," Stockton says. "I'm not kidding about that." (Didn't infer that you were, John.) "I used to call up to ask to serve. I served more masses than any five kids put together. But then I got screwed over. I had a kid take over for me when I had another commitment. But he didn't show, so they suspended me for one service. Then they suspended me again for not serving when I was suspended and *couldn't* serve. Do you believe that? So that was the end of my time as an altar boy."

We were inside the school now, and John shows me the small wooden-floored gym where he learned to play ("We'd put on a 1-3-1 press and it was all over") and the small hallways they were ordered to run after practice ("Our coach was a psycho; he's one of my best friends today"). A teacher passes by and nods. "His aunt," says John, "was my first girlfriend." Those are the kind of connections you get when you stay home.

Stockton spends the next few minutes talking about how well various teachers and teammates have done in life. Then a young girl taps him on the shoulder. "That's my buddy right there," John says, hugging his daughter, who is dressed as Dracula. "We're doing Wax Museum," she explains. An older daughter once trick-or-treated as Pat Summitt. Yes, this is a basketball family.

We take a brief tour around Gonzaga Prep, his alma mater, where in 2011–12 he served as assistant coach, his daughter, Lindsay, the team's star guard. We pass by his parents' house ("You're not writing down the address, are you?"), hard by the one to which John moved his own family after his first season with the Jazz. We have lunch, at my request, at Jack and Dan's Bar and Grill on North Hamilton Street, where there is scant evidence that a Hall of Fame Dream Teamer is related to the former longtime owner. (Jack Stockton has sold his interest.) "It's always been a tough wall for me to make," Stockton says.

We finish up at "the warehouse," the *Hoosiers*-evoking gymnasium that Stockton bought a few years ago. It includes the floor from the old Salt Palace, which was given to him by Larry Miller, the late owner of the Jazz. Stockton rents out the facility to various basketball, indoor soccer, and volleyball leagues. I remark at how content he seems.

"My family is around me and my kids are doing well, and my life is just busy enough following them around," he says. "For right now, I don't need anything else."

It just seems perfect, the idea that the Spokane Kid—who kept his head down and his oars in the water, always working, always listening, always improving—now holds the literal keys to the kingdom, handing out gym-rat time to the succeeding generations, the circle unbroken.

# CHAPTER 26

# THE CHOSEN ONE

• • • • • • • • • • • • • • • • • • • • • • • • • • • • • • • • • • • • • • •

### So Many Balls to Sign . . . and Jordan Almost Reaches His Breaking Point

As the Tournament of the Americas wore on, the Dream Team began to get bored with the blowouts—the average margin of victory for the six games would be 51.5 points. Before the Argentina game, even ever-smiling team leader Magic got annoyed because guard Marcelo Milanesio kept pestering him for his jersey, which he didn't want to give up and didn't. After the 41-point defeat, Milanesio said, "I am so overwhelmed by joy."

The U.S. players were not. You have to remember that competition was their lifeblood, and this was not competition. As the tournament neared its end, the players just wanted to get the hell out of Portland and get a few weeks of downtime before the Olympic grind.

Plus, all was not going well behind the scenes. Always there were balls to sign. Balls for sponsors. Balls for charities. Balls for auction. Balls for presidents, politicians, pencil pushers, pashas, and pals from every principality on earth. Balls for friends, friends of friends, and friends of friends' friends.

"I remember walking down this hallway and all I saw was balls that were waiting there for us to sign," Jordan told me in the summer of 2011. "All right, I get it. We have to sign. But hundreds and hundreds of balls? That's not fair.

"I had told Russ and Rod and Dave Gavitt from the beginning that it bothered me that business was wrapped around everything. Sure, I was in business, but these were long-standing relationships I had with companies. They were contracts. All of a sudden I'm being asked to do a lot of stuff I wasn't comfortable with."

Doing a lot of the asking were two members of the United States Olympic Committee, LeRoy Walker and Mary T. Meagher. They gave Jordan the standard lecture, intent on sending the message that the Dream Team was nothing special, that it had its Olympic responsibilities, that revenue produced by the Dream Team was being used to support other athletes who weren't staying in luxury hotels and who weren't highly compensated, and . . . on and on.

"They went at Michael with the attitude of 'Don't be an asshole,'" says Barkley. "So you know how well that shit went over with Michael."

Not well at all. "I'm outta here," said Jordan, throwing down his Sharpie one day and giving the impression that he meant to leave the team, not just the room.

Had Jordan really meant it, had he upped and left, Magic would've been next. Then Barkley would've exited stage left, and after him Pippen, and next thing you know there would've been, in the immortal words of Bob Dylan, mutiny from stern to bow. (Or from Stern to bow.)

But Jordan didn't mean it.

"Of course I never came close to quitting," Jordan says today. "I wasn't going to disgrace the Olympic team and walk out. And I wasn't going to look like the only idiot who didn't have my name on a ball. But I wanted everyone to know that they promised one thing and did something else."

(The ball issue would surface again in Barcelona, when suddenly there was a need for players to sign at least a hundred more balls. There might've been a revolt except for the intercession of respected NBA PR chief Brian McIntyre, who kept the balls in his room and had the players stop by whenever it was convenient to get it done. When it was Bird's turn, he said to McIntyre, "What's the quickest it's taken anyone to do this?" McIntyre said between fifteen and twenty minutes. Bird said, "Time me," finished in about six minutes, tossed the pen to McIntyre, and said, "Won another one, didn't I?" Stockton, on the other hand, was the most careful signer, the Dream Team's Hancock. "I want people a hundred years from now to know that I was on this team," he told McIntyre.)

Indeed, while all ran rather smoothly within the Dream Team's incestuous fraternity, the responsibilities of fame—as dictated to them by the USOC and sometimes by USA Basketball—got to the players, as did criticism from the outside world that filtered through the walls of the castle from time to time. *You're just a bunch of spoiled millionaires. Why are you bothering to beat up on teams like Panama (112–52), Argentina (128–87), Puerto Rico (119–81), and Venezuela (127–80)?*

In some quarters there continued to be residual resentment that the great honor of representing one's country had been taken away from the amateurs. Plus it was hard to muster up empathy for rich men who were being treated like royalty and, in between the beatdowns they were hanging on the Third World, were spending most of their spare time at Pumpkin Ridge, the exquisite Portland-area golf course that lies at the base of the Tualatin Mountains. (A team joke was that P. J. Carlesimo's main duty was setting up tee times. In point of fact, Carlesimo logged hundreds of hours editing videotape of opponents. But yes, the tee times were important, too.)

The players' position was: *You came to us. You begged us to play. We're getting you all this revenue and all this attention, but every time we turn around there's something else to sign, somebody else to shake hands with.*

The players felt that they had allies at USA Basketball, men such as Steve Mills, who had a basketball background and was a close friend of Magic Johnson's. Plus they genuinely liked Rod Thorn and respected both Russ Granik and Dave Gavitt. The USOC, by contrast, was distant and imperious.

"Everybody understood the issues," Mills told me recently, "but it was the *way* they were presented that the players clearly took as offensive. It was sort of, 'You're just another athlete. You're just like everyone else and this is what you're going to do.' Except that they *weren't* like everyone else, not in terms of fame and the revenue they generate."

No one felt the pressure more forcefully than Jordan, who was at the apex of his fame and who, as he saw it, had compromised more than a few of his business relationships by joining the Olympic team. At this point in his life he was a human ATM: people pushed the Jordan button and out came money. He had been selling out arenas for years. I remember being at back-to-back Washington Bullets games in the mid-1980s even before the Bulls were good. The first game drew about five thousand; the Bulls and Jordan came to town two nights later, and it was a sellout, about seventeen thousand. That's twelve thousand additional people on one isolated night in one isolated arena in one isolated season. Get out your calculator to see how much money Jordan generated just in terms of attendance.

As for Jordan's own franchise, Chicago Bulls chairman Jerry Reinsdorf had bought the team for less than $20 million midway through Jordan's rookie season. It was valued at five times that by the time that Jordan won his first championship and, until a full-scale renaissance led by Derrick Rose in the 2010–11 season, had increased its value mainly because it was, eternally, Michael Jordan's team.

Sure, Nike helped make Jordan, but the reverse was true, too. In his first full season under the Swoosh, the Air Jordan line produced more than $153 million in revenue.

By Dream Team time, Jordan believed that the seesaw was unbalanced, that he was the one with legs swinging uncomfortably in midair and no one would allow him to come down.

A few months earlier, before the Dream Team got together, I sat down with Jordan in his suite in a Berkeley, California, hotel for a long interview related to his having been chosen *Sports Illustrated's* Sportsman of the Year, an honor he singularly deserved and deeply appreciated. There were no distractions, as there had been months before at the *Saturday Night Live* set, and I continued to see a changed Jordan, a man who, at twenty-eight, was realizing the perils of fame. He had . . . hardened. That's the best way I can put it.

There was anti-Jordan backlash about his White House snub, about the revelations in Sam Smith's *The Jordan Rules*, about his role in keeping Isiah off the team, about his refusal to involve himself with the black community and speak out on issues. Jordan had by this time made his famous comment that "Republicans buy sneakers, too," when he refused to endorse Harvey Gantt, the former mayor of Charlotte, North Carolina, who had mounted a Senate challenge to unseat Jesse Helms.

(My own opinion about the Gantt issue is this: the degree to which an African American athlete—or any athlete—is obligated to involve himself in politics is a long and complicated subject, but Jordan was absolutely wrong in this case. Helms was an anachronistic racist hypocrite, and Gantt deserved more than a dismissive comment about footwear. On the other hand, when Charles Barkley made his oft-quoted statements about being a rich Republican, he got a pass.)

"Sooner or later, I knew things were going to turn around," Jordan told me. "Five, six, seven years at the pinnacle of success and it's going to happen. Signs are starting to show that people are tired of hearing about 'Michael Jordan's positive influence' and 'Michael Jordan's positive image.' I've seen it in letters to the editor, magazines, newspapers. That feeling of 'God, quit talking about Michael Jordan. I'm tired of hearing about him.'"

I thought that showed an unusual degree of self-awareness, as did his subsequent comments about the way the tornado of fame had swept him up unexpectedly.

"What everybody has to understand is that my success caught me completely by surprise," said Jordan. "If you told me in college that soon, within a year, my face, my image, would be all over the country and the world, I would've said you were crazy. What I was trying to do was project everything positive, and maybe that was wrong. Maybe people wanted to see some negative with the positives, so that they'd have more of a sense of you as a human being. I accept that.

"The real problem with what happened to me was that it happened so early. That's the difference between me and some of the other superstars, like Julius Erving. And so my longevity was bound to produce overkill. It had to. The negative stuff, the backlash, is coming down on me, and heck, I'm at the peak of my career."

That was unequivocally true. He was recognized by anyone with half a brain as the best player on the planet, and his earning power seemingly had no limit. Estimates of Jordan's endorsement earnings for the 1991–92 season were between $16 million and $20 million, a figure that would eventually rise to about $35 million; even more astonishing was the money he routinely left on the table. His philosophy back then, as it is now, was to refuse most appearances outside of those associated with his corporate obligations. Mark Vancil, who covered the Bulls for the *Chicago Sun-Times* and later got into business with Jordan as president of Rare Air Media, wrote about some of them. For example, Jordan turned down $250,000 for a three-day appearance for a Canadian company in Toronto and spurned a cool $1 million for what would've been a one-day commitment to promote tourism in Jordan, the country. As Jordan saw it, that was chump change compared to a free day to play golf.

Jordan had the sense to know that he had been lucky as well as good, and he brought up Magic to make that point.

"Magic should've had what I had," he told me. "The way I was presented out there from a PR standpoint, marketing-wise, he was never portrayed like I was away from basketball. With fewer credentials, at least of basketball championships, I got more than he did. Is that fair? No. But I didn't have control of it. He should've had the Wheaties, the big deals before me, but he didn't."

Magic was in Chicago on December 17, 1991, when Jordan was presented with his Sportsman of the Year award, to publicize the Magic Johnson Foundation, a charitable organization he had set up (with much alacrity, since his shocking announcement had only been made a month earlier) to support AIDS education, research, and awareness. Magic, like Jordan, was dealing with his own backlash at the time. If he had heard it once, he had heard it a thousand times since his November 7 press conference: *Why are you treating this guy like a hero?*

In short, everything in Magic's life was in turmoil—his health, his public image, his career with the Lakers, his Olympic participation. And yet, after both Jordan and Johnson had finished their press duties on that December evening, one was left with the head-shaking feeling that it was Jordan's life coming apart at the seams and that Magic's principal duty in Chicago was to provide succor for the healthiest, wealthiest, and most successful athlete on the planet. Jordan, on the podium, said all the right things about the honor, but his defensiveness came through. "I went from un-American, to tyrant [a reference to some of the anecdotes in *The Jordan Rules*], to Sportsman of the Year."

Then Magic stepped up and the sun came out. "First off, I can't tell you how excited I am to come in second as Sportsman of the Year," he began. "I lost to him again." It was a terrific opening line. Johnson then patiently answered questions for thirty minutes about his foundation, his health, his family, and his views on mandatory AIDS testing (he opposed it) before finally turning the subject back to Jordan and scolding the press, in his gentle way, for making it tough on the world's best player.

"It seems like this has been Michael's hardest year," said Magic, as if it had not also been his own. "It's too bad that nothing he can do makes it better, and I'm sure my retirement made it worse. Now Michael has it all on him. I wish I could come back and take the pressure off." (Magic was again demonstrating his extraordinary ability to be humble and self-aggrandizing in the same monologue.)

But remember this, too: Jordan would stay in the backseat for only so long. In both the Dream Team pre-Olympic practice in Monte Carlo and the Games in Barcelona, Jordan rose up from time to time and, in the strongest thus-spake-Zarathustra terms, made sure that everyone—*especially* Magic—knew who really ruled the basketball world.

# CHAPTER 27

# THE WRITER, THE JESTER, AND THE CHRISTIAN SOLDIER

. . . . . . . . . . . . . . . . . . . . . . . . . . . . . . . . . . . . . . . . . . . . .

## Monsieur Barkley Will Indeed Take a Hit on 19

My late father-in-law was a straight-shooting kind of guy—he kept the trains running on schedule at a plant that manufactured condensers and pumps, good old-fashioned American stuff like that—so he understandably had trouble getting his mind around the Dream Team's decision to hold pre-Olympic training in Monte Carlo.

"You don't go to Monte Carlo to play basketball," he said. "You go there to gamble and horse around. It's like Las Vegas, only more expensive, and, you know, dressy."

"They have gyms there," I said, not altogether convincingly. "At least I think they do."

"Anyway, why are *you* going?" he asked. "If they're only practicing—and I even doubt that—what are you going to write about?"

"I'm a journalist," I answered. "I follow the story. Something will come up."

The negotiating for the team to train in the world's most exclusive gambling enclave started, believe it or not, with Commissioner David Stern, who at the time was understood to be fervently anti-gambling and terrified of betting lines; he was born in New Jersey but raised in New York and had grown up with the unsavory memory of the college point-shaving scandals that all but killed city basketball for years in the 1950s. But he was also the league's guardian and recognized that a training camp in, say, Fort Wayne, Indiana, was not the inducement he needed to get players such as Jordan and Magic to buy in. So he began talking to a friend, New York Giants owner Bob Tisch, who also owned the Loews Hotels, including a showpiece property in Monaco. From there, Russ Granik and Loews chairman Robert Hausman negotiated the deal with the principality.

Players, coaches, and schlubs like me said bravo to the decision. The Dream Team did get in some work—and from its stay emerged some of the legendary basketball moments from 1992, those detailed in the next chapter—but on balance it was more like a mini-vacation. The team's daily schedule called for two hours of basketball followed by twenty-two hours of golf, gambling, and gaping at the sights, nude beaches and models always a three-point shot away, sometimes closer. "I'm not putting in a curfew because I'd have to adhere to it," said Chuck Daly, "and Jimmy Z's [a noted Monte Carlo nightclub where Jordan, Barkley, Magic, and Pippen spent many hours] doesn't open until midnight."

Speaking for myself, I suffered two of the least sympathetic injuries in sportswriter travel history—a sprained thumb and a chafed thigh, both incurred while riding a Jet Ski in the warm waters of the Mediterranean.

"They both really hurt," I told my wife in a phone call.

"Shut up," she explained.

In truth, the Monte Carlo visit wasn't nearly as sybaritic as it might sound since most of the players brought along wives, children, and babysitters, the whole caravan en route to the Olympics immediately following the days and nights in Monaco.

The Dream Team had flown into Nice at midnight, greeted by the usual throng, and made a literal crash landing at the Loews, Jet Set Central. During a security meeting before the team arrived, Henri Lorenzi, the legendary hotel manager, had complained about the sheer numbers and aggressiveness of the NBA's security forces, which were already roaming through the hotel.

"Do you realize who is gambling in my casino right now?" Lorenzi said to the NBA's Kim Bohuny. He ticked off the names of politicians, movie stars, and even tennis immortal Bjorn Borg. "No one will care that much about this team," he said.

"Well, we'll see," said Bohuny.

When the team bus pulled up, there was such a rush forward to see the players that someone crashed through the glass doors at the entrance.

"I get your point," said Lorenzi.

(A couple of days later, a deliveryman pulling up to the Loews caught sight of the Dream Team boarding a bus. He was so entranced that he got out to gape, forgot to set the emergency brake, and watched in horror as the truck began rolling down a hill and crashed into two cars, knocking them through the window of a fashionable shop.)

For once, though, there was a level of royalty above that of the Dream Team, namely, Prince Rainier, or, if you're scoring at home, Rainier Louis Henri Maxence Bertrand Grimaldi, Count of Polignac, His Serene Highness the Sovereign Prince of Monaco. What I liked best about Rainier was the fact that his mother, Princess Charlotte, had bedded down with René the Cane, a celebrated jewel thief.

Like everyone else, Rainier wanted to meet the Dream Team, so a dinner in a private room at the Loews was arranged for July 20, which also happened to be the sixty-second birthday of Chuck Daly. Daly, himself a prince, he of the sovereign state of Pessimism, was already antsy about prep time and quite irritable during the protocol meeting that preceded the event.

"You can't sit down until the prince sits down," the protocol chief told a delegation of the U.S. team that included Daly, Jordan, Bird, and Magic.

"What if I have to go to the bathroom?" asked Chuck. "I'm at that stage in life." They were also told that they couldn't lift fork to mouth until the prince was ready.

When the Dream Teamers assembled, they were kept waiting for a while, something to which they weren't accustomed. "The Pistons didn't have to wait this long at the White House," Chuck whispered, "and we won the championship."

But the prince, accompanied by his son, Prince Albert, a basketball fan, finally showed up, and positioned himself between Magic and Jordan. (Barkley said later, "They kept me far away from the royalty.") The dinner went well, and Magic, predictably, spoke for the team. "I always thought the closest I would get to royalty was playing with Michael Jordan," he said, "but this tops that." Typical Magic. Chuck's wife, Terry Daly, had arranged for a birthday cake to be wheeled out at the end, and everyone sang "Happy Birthday" to Chuck, and everyone went home—or back to the casino—happy.

(The crown prince later proved to be a down-to-earth guy. Upon encountering a group of American journalists at Stade Louis XV, he stuck out his hand and said, "I'm Al Grimaldi." To which the best response would've been: "Yeah? I'm Paulie Walnuts from Joisy." But we all showed the requisite obsequiousness, second nature to a journalist covering the Dream Team.)

The Loews casino was located in the middle of the hotel, thereby serving as a kind of theater-in-the-round when the Dream Teamers were there, the regulars being Jordan, Magic, Barkley, Pippen, and Ewing, the same group that had started playing a card game called tonk back in San Diego and would play right through the last night in Barcelona. Bird ventured down once, heard the price of a beer, which was $7 outside the casino and $18 inside, and rarely appeared again. (Barkley reported that the suds at Jimmy Z's went for $40.) On one occasion Barkley, feeling like the luckiest blackjack player in the world, asked for a card at 19; it would be a better ending to the story to say he drew a deuce, but he busted.

Even though the Dream Teamers were the main show, not every casino employee could tell them apart—when Magic went to cash in one night, he was asked to repay the markers for a Monsieur Jordan, which stood at about $50,000.

I traipsed around in a fashion, looking in on the blackjack tables and high-stakes crap games, but, frankly, I was nervous about taking notes, the chronicling of athletes' free time being an ongoing what-is-news-and-what-is-private? issue in my line of work. But I wasn't nearly as nervous as the NBA. Though it was Stern who had brought this whole circus to Monaco, the Dream Teamers' gambling was awkward for the NBA hierarchy since it was only a few months removed from an embarrassing issue that involved its marquee player.

Questions about Jordan's gambling and off-court associations had come to the surface when three of his checks totaling $108,000 were found in the briefcase of a murdered North Carolina bail bondsman named Eddie Dow. To be clear, there was never any association established between Jordan and Dow or the Dow murder. But Dow's lawyer said that at least some of that $108,000 was payment from Jordan for gambling debts incurred at golf and cards, and Jordan acknowledged having paid about $57,000 to one James "Slim" Bouler of North Carolina. Bouler had formerly done time for selling cocaine, was then under indictment on six counts of money laundering, and had a handle and a personality right out of an Elmore Leonard novel. He was an acquaintance not just of Jordan but also of other NBA players. Jordan said that the money was a loan to Bouler to help him build a driving range. But a U.S. attorney in Charlotte said that that money, too, was to pay off gambling debts.

The NBA investigated the issue for two weeks before releasing a statement that read in part: "There appears to be no reason for the NBA to take action against Michael." Saying that it would take no action and completely believing in his innocence are two different things, and privately, Stern and others were concerned about Jordan's choice of playmates and his penchant for heavy gambling. But there was Jordan in Monte Carlo, gambling the night away, Horace Balmer, the NBA's security man with him much of the time. (The players called Balmer "Bam" for the exclamation he uttered when he threw down his cards; this was before Emeril Lagasse.) From time to time Jordan even had his own blackjack table reserved and played all five hands. Jordan was breaking no laws, remember, although the casino couldn't have been thrilled that on some occasions a mysterious man stood behind him at the blackjack table. "Michael's personal card counter," someone in the Dream Team party described him.

Each afternoon, workout and lunch behind them, a gaggle of players trod through the foot-thick casino carpeting in golf shoes, sticks on their backs, bound for the Monte Carlo Golf Club, a twenty-five-minute ride outside the city. The course wasn't a jewel, but it was mountainous and commanded wonderful views of the sea and the French and Italian Rivieras. There were worse places on earth to spend an afternoon.

There was a golfing hierarchy: Jordan, Daly, Rod Thorn, P. J. Carlesimo, and whatever touring pro was around. Barkley worked his way into their group from time to time, but he wasn't at their level, and Jordan, as much as he would've enjoyed busting Charles, preferred the company of good players. Magic, who could've broken into any foursome simply by announcing that he was going to do so, was not a golfer. He had decided long ago that, given his competitive personality, he had better not start. "It would've become an obsession to me, just like it is with Michael," he told me, "and would've distracted from the other things I wanted to do." That was a man who always had his eye on the prize.

One day after practice *Newsday*'s Jan Hubbard arranged a foursome with Barkley, Drexler, and me. Barkley was at that time unencumbered by the as yet undiagnosed neuropathic/psychosomatic disorder that has come to plague his golf game, which at this writing remains a wretched smorgasbord of tics and stops and twists and turns. He hit the ball far and had a decent short game, though, need it be said, he was subject to lapses in concentration. Drexler, whom Barkley called "Long and Wrong," was just learning the game. With a full, aggressive coiled swing—he was at that time one of the best athletes in the world—he routinely hit 300-yard drives, usually 150 out and 150 to the left or right.

Hubbard and Drexler (who were both from Texas) played against Barkley and me (Philly guys), though it quickly became apparent that accurate scorekeeping might be an issue. Hubbard remembers that, for a while at least, Drexler and Barkley changed personalities, Clyde talking nonstop and Barkley quiet, the result of too much golf the day before and too much clubbing after that.

Hubbard and I pushed our rented clubs, while a single caddy, who weighed all of 140 pounds, lugged around the bags of both players. I can still see the poor guy, head down, heavy bags on his back, slinking across two fairways to retrieve a geographically challenged Drexler drive. Clyde was playing with clubs he'd borrowed from Jordan, adorned with the Jumpman logo, and after the round Hubbard stole all of the logo balls.

"Why did you do that?" a visibly irritated Jordan asked Hubbard later.

"Think about it," said Hubbard, who saw the long-range possibilities. Then Jordan quickly understood. "Twenty years later," Hubbard says now, "and I'm still telling the story."

Our merry group played nine, then picked up David Robinson at the turn. He was fairly new to the game and, in the fashion of a naval officer who had built televisions with his father, was working on it with consummate dedication.

"David," I said to him, "you hitting those irons with *impunity?*"

"Man, you never let me forget that, do you?" he said.

In the Spurs locker room after Robinson's first game as a rookie in 1989, I asked him about his ability to protect the basket. "Well," he answered, "I just can't let people come into the lane with impunity."

"That's the first recorded use of *impunity* in NBA history," I told him.

Robinson was as enthusiastic as anyone about being a Dreamer, this being a redemptive journey for him as the only member of the failed 1988 team with another chance. Everybody on the Dream Team liked and respected Robinson, and he had struck up a friendship with Drexler and also with Malone and Stockton, which surprised him since their Jazz and his Spurs were bitter rivals, mirror images of each other's hard-boiled, competitive style. "John's photo was on the Spurs' refrigerator as one of the most hated guys in the league," said Robinson.

(Years later I asked Robinson if, after the Dream Team experience, Malone was less likely to throw an elbow at him during skirmishes under the basket. "Probably not," he said, "but you didn't take it as personal.")

But Robinson was, to a large extent, a loner. I always thought he existed on a slightly different competitive plane than the other Dream Teamers. "Music was what was really in David's DNA," Jordan says. "He wasn't driven like myself and most of the other players were." He didn't mean it as an insult; it was merely fact. And years after Barcelona, as we talked about some of his teammates, Robinson still seemed unable to fully comprehend the thirst-for-blood style of his teammates.

"When I first got into the league, Karl tested me every time we played, knocking me down, trying to intimidate me," Robinson said. "I said, 'What the heck is going on with him?'" (Yes, he said *heck*.)

"And Larry? In my rookie year? I switched out on him near the three-point line, and I hear him say, 'This is in your eye, David.' I mean, who says stuff like that?"

Larry Bird, I answer. Then I ask if Bird made the shot.

"Of course," Robinson says. "It was Larry Bird."

Robinson continued with a Jordan story from the first time they met, which was in a 1988 exhibition game when Robinson was playing with the national team.

"I go back to meet Michael because, like everybody else, I'm a big fan, and you know the first thing he says to me? 'I'm going to dunk on you, big fella. I dunked on all the other big fellas and you're next.'

"And he said it almost every time we played. I'd go back at him: 'Don't even think about it. I will take you out of the air.'" (Even the tone of Robinson's threat sounds churchlike.) "And Michael would always promise to get me."

And did he?

"Eventually. It was a two-on-one with him and Scottie, and one of them was going to get me. Michael took the shot and I went up to block it because that's how I played. I went after shots. But I didn't get there and he dunked it and the crowd went crazy. It wasn't really a poster dunk, but he got me. And he remembered. 'Told you I was going to get you one day,' he said."

Robinson shakes his head. "Man, what a competitor. He never forgot anything, never let you get away with *anything*."

By Dream Team time, Robinson had, as he puts it, "been born again in Christ." He had gotten married six months earlier to a deeply religious woman named Valerie Hoggatt, who is still his wife. David didn't drink or swear and was finding it uncomfortable to be around those who did, just as some found it uncomfortable, at times, to be around him.

"I first got saved in 1991," he told me years later. "It was something that was really emerging in my life, and I was just trying to understand it myself. I probably did talk about it a little too much in the locker room. Larry Brown [the San Antonio coach at the time] and some other people didn't like it. Guys are like, 'Christians are soft. They're not going to cut your throat out when it's throat-cutting time.' That was the thinking.

"But my mentality was, I want to help my teammates. If I can stop someone from running around in circles in their private life, I want to do that. I just had to find the right way to go about it. I was struggling about when to say something and when to keep my mouth shut."

Robinson's overt faith was never an issue on the Dream Team, a mature group (you can point to Barkley as an exception to that, but by now you understand how he blended in) that was able to gather in all the individual foibles, expose them to some kind of cleansing process, and have it all come out okay. But a golf course—certainly one with Charles Barkley on it—is a very tough place for a true believer. Our fivesome went on, insults flying like molecules under heat, four-letter words our lingua franca, at least for Barkley, Drexler, Hubbard, and me. I could tell Robinson was getting squirmy with all the blue being thrown around, and at one point he complained to Hubbard about Drexler's cussing and also wanted Barkley to tone it down. Charles seemed to comply, but then at one point—I believe around the fourteenth hole—he let loose with another barrage, all of it in good humor, of course, but salty.

So Robinson shook his head, smiled beatifically, picked up his bag, and left.

On the way home, I drove the rental car, Drexler beside me, Barkley and Hubbard in the back. I felt compelled to challenge the mountain passes like a thief fleeing from a heist because, well, when in the Riviera . . . We later discovered that it was on that road in 1982 that Princess Grace had suffered a stroke, which caused her to crash her Rover P6. She died from injuries the next day at Monaco Hospital.

"At the top of the mountain, the four of us were talking/arguing but in between educating/correcting us all on every subject, Barkley noticed that you were driving faster and the curves on the mountain were getting sharper," remembers Hubbard.

"'Damn, Jack, slow down!' Barkley yelled. 'You're gonna get us all killed. Nobody will give a shit about you, but the NBA's gonna be pissed!'"

According to Hubbard's memory, I continued at the same pace, and a nervous Drexler actually raised his voice and implored me to slow down. He couldn't be heard, however, because Barkley was screaming louder and threatening me with bodily harm. "Charles, the guy behind me is on my ass," I said. "I can't slow down. He'll hit me."

202 · JACK MCCALLUM

As we got closer to the bottom of the mountain, we began rumi-
nating about the headlines that would ensue from a fatal crash.

"'Barkley, Drexler, Two Others Die in Monte Carlo!'" Hubbard
suggested.

"They'll probably just make it 'Two Dream Teamers Killed in
Crash' and leave us out entirely," I said.

"Shit, they won't even care about Clyde," Barkley offered.
"'Charles Barkley Dead!' That's what it would say."

"That is cold, Charles," Drexler said.


Later, in Barcelona, Robinson and Barkley would have a conversation about Christianity, Apollo sitting down with Dionysus.
They were lifting weights—"Well, I was lifting and Charles was
just sitting there," says Robinson—and Barkley said to him,
"David, you need to say what's on your mind. You need to be more
honest." Robinson responded this way: "What you mean to say is
not more *honest*. You mean more *controversial*. That's two different things."

And then Robinson opened up to him.

"Charles, I love the fact that you're not afraid to say what you
want to say even if it's going to get you in trouble. And that will be
an even better thing if you ever give your heart to the Lord. You're
going to need that quality of talking plain because people will not
necessarily want to hear what you're saying."

After Robinson told me that story, I said that while Charles had
not yet given his heart to the Lord, the Lord clearly had not yet smit-
ten him for all his wicked ways; indeed, the Lord might have been
laughing along with everyone else at Barkley's TNT act. "How do
you explain that?" I asked.

Robinson laughed. "I'm still praying about that," he said. "I love
Charles. I still love talking to him. It's not my job to make him do
something. All I can do is plant seeds."

In my mind's eye, I still see Robinson walking off the course on
that day. I didn't necessarily want to be like him, but I knew that it

took much personal commitment, inner strength, and conviction to do that. Most athletic teams and most athletic relationships are built on a foundation of sophomoric humor, insults, and dick jokes, all of it wrapped in testosterone. To stand with your team, yet somehow to have the guts to stand alone from time to time . . . now, that takes a particular kind of man.

# THE CHRISTIAN SOLDIER

. . . . . . . . . . . . . . . . . . . . . . . . . . . . . . . . . . . . . . . . . . .

## And What Shall a Man Do with All His Gifts?

*San Antonio, Texas*

I am in the quietest school I ever heard, talking to the tallest academic CEO in the world. Ten years ago, when David Robinson was still a productive starting center for the Spurs, he launched Carver Academy, a five-acre kindergarten-through-sixth-grade private school built on blocks of ugly urban blight in San Antonio. "There were crack houses, prostitutes, drugs all around," says Robinson, shaking his head at the memory before adding unnecessarily, "it was not a great neighborhood."

I remember when Robinson started talking of his dream for Carver—how animated he would get about the idea of offering a private-school-quality education to an underserved class of kids, how he had been reading up on George Washington Carver, the African American scientist, botanist, and educator after whom he would name his school. Red McCombs, who owned the Spurs at the time, would tell him, "David, you're underestimating how much time and money this is going to take." And though Robinson had been the exception to so many rules over the years, there was a lot of reason to doubt him. Lots of athletes—lots of anybodys—start out with grand plans only to see them fade in the harsh light of reality. When you've made enough money to live for a lifetime, it's easier to become a broadcaster, a real estate magnate, or a full-time recreational golfer.

But Robinson never lost sight of his goal. He put up $10 million in seed money—even for a highly compensated athlete, $10 million is walking the walk—started the school from scratch, and is still at it. After he retired in 2003, a year in which the Spurs won a championship, he bought a small interest (about 2 percent) in the franchise. But the vast majority of his time and money go to Carver. He and his wife, Valerie, have put in additional millions as the school has flourished, and Robinson continues to spend the majority of his waking hours keeping the school humming, raising money for scholarships and facility upgrades, supervising curriculum, hiring and firing, traveling to conferences—all those day-to-day things that define the lives of most of us, though generally not the lives of Hall of Fame athletes.

"I've been asked to franchise the idea," says Robinson, pursing his lips and shaking his head, "and I would really like to do it. But right now . . . I just don't know. There's too much to do here." He sounds vaguely guilty that he hasn't peppered the nation with other Carver Academies. "Man, Red was right," he says. "This is more work than I ever thought." On the day we talked, Robinson had just arrived back in San Antonio from New York, where he had toured an Abyssinian school in Harlem. "I'm always looking for other models, other ways to do things," said Robinson. "It's just what you need to do."

Hadn't it been tempting, I ask him, to just kick back after retirement? I know that might be hard for a navy man who used to build TVs from scratch, but . . .

"This is what my calling is," says Robinson. "I mean, what's your goal in life? Just to enjoy money? Is that fulfilling? If I do less than this, I've taken all those gifts I've been given and buried them under a rug. I want my own kids and the kids at Carver to understand about passion, that there is a calling in life and that you have to find it."

Carver is a faith-based school because Robinson, as you've already learned, is a faith-based person. At this writing, Robinson was leading, as he has for many years, a morning devotional group for men at Oak Hills Church, the home of superstar preacher Max Lucado. The crowd is usually around two hundred, many of whom originally came to see the pivot-man preacher but now just see him as a big man with a message.

"My faith is much stronger now than it was when I was playing," Robinson says, "because when I look back I see how little I had to do with it. Okay, God, you blessed my career ridiculously. Two championships as a player and two as a part owner. Two Olympics. The Dream Team. I have these three amazing boys. My wife is just the best. I'm still learning about her. You're going to nourish her and cherish her and encourage her. The Bible says to present her to God. You can't ever quit on that."

Being unsaved myself, as well as one whose wife rarely needs "encouragement," I never know exactly where to go when Robinson talks about his faith. Several years ago I had a friendly debate with Lucado himself (I was interviewing him because Robinson and teammate Tim Duncan shared *SI*'s Sportsman of the Year Award) about his church's fundamentalist position against homosexuality. Lucado is a far more skilled rhetorician than I, and I didn't get far.

"Well, the Bible is clear on its message about homosexuality," Robinson tells me when I broach the subject with him. "It's against it. But I think our role is the compassionate role, the same role I had when I went into the locker room, which is not to start preaching and say, 'Hey, you guys have to stop cheating on your wives,' but to love those guys and encourage those guys and lead them to want to live better lives."

I protest that that still sounds like double-talk, like you're fervently against someone who's different and telling him he's wrong

for living that way, but then making it sound like a benevolent position.

"It's not about making them feel bad," answers Robinson. "It's
not my job to run around making people feel like, 'Hey, you're a
freak of nature.' Look, *I'm* a freak of nature. All I'm saying is live in
a way that honors the word of God."

Still, no one is cudgeled with fundamentalism at Carver. Faith is
only one of the "six pillars" that form the bedrock philosophy of the
school, along with service, leadership, initiative, integrity, and discipline. "We keep the kids thinking about those pillars all the time,"
says Robinson. He makes a special point of this next comment,
sounding as earnest as a Sunday school teacher stressing perfect
attendance. "You learn the six pillars inside and out," he says, "and
you earn your Carver pin."

As he leads me around the school, I can see his deserved pride,
though to a man who follows the Word, pride goeth before a fall. So
Robinson keeps his pride in check. There are no more than fifteen
students in any classroom. Discipline problems are almost nonex-
istent, he says, and I believe it. The only sounds I hear in class-
rooms are a teacher's voice or the higher register of a student's
response. About 95 percent of Carver students, who pay $10,000
for tuition, get some kind of need-based aid, which comes from
fund-raising, an investment fund, and Robinson.

"Anyone, rich or poor, can come here," says Robinson. "But I
did want to particularly impact the kids in this neighborhood, offer
scholarship opportunities, build a real fire in the community."

He shows me the broadcast studio, the music room with fifteen
Casio keyboards (the man whose DNA is more about music than
basketball, as Jordan put it, still bangs out some chords for the
students from time to time), the library, and the reading center (do-
nated by the Spurs). He points to the signs, all quotations from
Carver, that dot the walls—no graffiti here: "There is no shortcut to
achievement." "Life requires thorough preparation." "Veneer isn't
worth anything."

There is nothing to indicate that the school's founder played fourteen NBA seasons and retired with career averages of 21.2 points and 10.6 rebounds and once scored 71 points in a single game, one of only five players to reach that absurd number.

"We look for excellence in sports here, too, but that's not what it's about," said Robinson. "It's not corny to be a good student here. Man, I always loved school. That's what I wanted to foster in these kids."

Hanging around Carver with Robinson makes a man ponder, if only for a moment, what he's done with his life, whether he's made a mark. As I look back on these pages, I see how comparatively little I've written about Robinson, at least in comparison to Michael/Magic/Larry and Charles. I get Google Alerts that mention Michael Jordan virtually every day, but when the name David Robinson shows up in those alerts, it more likely refers to a reporter for the *Morning Sentinel*, a business writer for the *Buffalo News*, the sheriff of Kings County in California, the biographer of Charlie Chaplin, a Tyne-class lifeboat, a climatologist for the state of New Jersey, the executive chairman of Australian Food and Fibre, or the bass player for the Cars. There is scant mention of Carver Academy.

As I write this, Robinson will not be aboard the Celebrity Love Train in Canton, Ohio, with Mike Tyson, Patti LaBelle, the O'Jays, and Mo'Nique, as Magic was in the summer of 2011. He will not command airtime all over the country to comment on the size of Brett Favre's penis, present his idea that mediocre teams should "throw games" to move up in the draft, quip that truTV is "the white BET," or discuss any of a dozen other subjects on which Barkley is called upon to comment in any given week.

Robinson was sometimes an afterthought, too, on that immortal team, whose members admired his athleticism, his grace, and his integrity but didn't know him particularly well, and who talked, as Jordan did, about how basketball wasn't his passion, how his success was due to the accident of his astounding genetic composition.

But twenty years later, as the greatness of the 1992 Olympic gold medalists becomes more and more a flickering light in history, I think that Robinson might be the truest Dream Teamer, a gentle and complex man from two worlds who lived the dream and, through the power of his own sweat and blood and faith, now gives a dream to others.

# CHAPTER 28

# THE GREATEST GAME THAT NOBODY EVER SAW

· · · · · · · · · · · · · · · · · · · · · · · · · · · · · · · · · · · · · · · · · ·

## "They Just Moved Chicago Stadium to Monte Carlo. That's All They Did"

The referee, a gentleman from Italy whose name no one seems to remember, dribbles to midcourt and looks to his colleague, Dream Team assistant coach P. J. Carlesimo, to see if he is ready. Carlesimo is ready, though *ready* is relative in this case, since P.J.'s participation over the next forty minutes will be limited, bringing new dimension to the phrase "swallowing the whistle."

If the gentleman from Italy had to do it all over again, I'm sure he would've tossed the ball to Carlesimo and proceeded rapidly to the nearest exit of Stade Louis II, the all-purpose arena in the Fontvieille section of Monte Carlo. For soon he would become the unluckiest person in town, including all those who were surrendering vast quantities of French francs at the tables.

He tosses the ball up between Patrick Ewing and David Robinson, and Robinson taps it—on the way up and illegally—toward his own basket. Robinson's teammate on the Blue team, Christian Laettner, races Scottie Pippen for the ball. Take note, for this is the first and last time in recorded history that this sentence will be written: *Laettner beats Pippen to the ball*. Laettner sweeps it behind his back to Blue teammate Charles Barkley, who catches it, takes a couple of gathering dribbles, and knifes between Michael Jordan and Larry Bird. Jordan grabs Barkley's wrist, the whistle blows, and Barkley makes the layup.

"Shoot the fouls, shoot the fouls," Chuck Daly yells, sounding like that character in *Goodfellas*, Jimmy Two Times. It's morning and almost no one is in the stands, and Daly is trying to install gamelike conditions because even the best of the best need a kick in the ass from time to time. As Jordan calls for a towel—it is extremely humid in the arena and almost everyone is sweating off a little alcohol—Barkley makes the free throw.

**Magic Johnson's Blue Team 3, Michael Jordan's White Team 0.**

And so the Greatest Game That Nobody Ever Saw gets under way.

About twelve hours earlier, the United States had finished an exhibition game against the French national team. Prince Rainier had requested that Daly, his birthday homeboy, sit with him to deconstruct any nuances of the game of which he might be unaware, such as, for example, the one about coaches sitting on the bench. After some explanation, Rainier accepted Dave Gavitt as a replacement.

The United States–France game looked exactly like one would think an exhibition game in Monte Carlo would look like. It was awful. The players were still getting used to conditions—meaning the hilly terrain at the Monte Carlo Country Club and the nocturnal bass-beat rhythms at Jimmy Z's—and even the seemingly inexhaustible Jordan was tired after walking eighteen holes and arriving back at the Loews not long before the 8:30 p.m. tip-off. One of his playing partners had been Daly, who proclaimed, "It's a two-Nuprin, three-Advil day." The Dream Team was sloppy and even allowed France leads of 8–2 and 16–13 before it woke up and went on to win 111–71.

It didn't matter to the fans, though, who had gobbled up the 3,500 available tickets in a fifteen-minute box office frenzy a few days earlier. As had been the case at the Tournament of the Americas in Portland, the opposing team's guys, at least a half dozen of whom had brought cameras to the bench, were deemed heroic by dint of being slain. And there was certainly no thought of fallen French pride among the royals—Rainier beamed like a schoolkid when Magic climbed into his box for a photo op.

Happiest of all was the French coach, a man named Francis Jordane. "He was very excited because he figured that his last name would give him special entrée to Michael," remembers the NBA's Terry Lyons. "We took a photo and, sure enough, there is Jordane right next to Jordan, with his arm around him."

After the game, Daly's pessimistic nature began to take over, and by breakfast the next morning he had decided that his team had better beat itself up a little bit. The Dream Team had scrimmaged several times before this fateful day, a couple of the games ending in a diplomatic tie as Daly refused to allow overtime. He normally tried to divvy up the teams by conference, but on this day Stockton was still on the shelf and Drexler was out with a minor injury. Lord only knows how this morning would've gone had Drexler been available. Jordan had already taken it upon himself to torture the Glide in scrimmages, conjuring up the just-completed Finals, taunting Drexler: "Stop me this time!"

(Jordan still describes Drexler as "a poor man's Michael Jordan." Honest, he said that. "I wanted to go against Clyde every chance I could back then," Jordan told me in the summer of 2011. "When we played them in the [1992] Finals, we were being compared, and I wanted to show there was a big difference between me and him. I knew how to *think* the game. I knew how to play different varieties of the game. Clyde plays one way—head down, drive straight to the hole. Big difference." We already know what Drexler thinks about that analysis.)

So with two fewer Western players than Eastern players, and only two true guards, Magic and Jordan, Daly went with Magic, Barkley, Robinson, Mullin, and Laettner on the Blue Team against Jordan, Malone, Ewing, Pippen, and Bird on the White.

Whatever the result, there would be few to bear witness. The gym was all but locked down. The media were allowed in for only the last part of practice. Officials from USA Basketball even kicked out the NBA PR people and videographers from NBA Entertainment. A single cameraman, Pete Skorich, who was Chuck Daly's guy with the Pistons, recorded the day. It was a closed universe, a secret little world, when ten of the best basketball players in the world began going at each other.

Before the game began, Daly had a message: "All you got now," he told them. "All you got."

The absence of Drexler means that Magic and Jordan are matched up, a fact that will turn out to give the morning scrimmage its noisy character. "Those two going against each other," Krzyzewski told me in 2011, "was the pimple being popped."

Jordan dribbles upcourt and Magic yells, "Let's go, Blue. Pick up now." This is what Magic has missed in the months that he has been retired. The juice he got from leading a team, being the conductor, the voice box, the man from whom all energy flows. A half hour earlier, during leisurely full-court layup drills, Magic had suddenly stopped and flung the ball into the empty seats. "We're here to *practice!*" he yelled. That was his signal that they had been half-assing it, and the day turned on that moment. Whether the players thought it was unnecessary is a matter of conjecture, but Magic had promised Daly back in San Diego that "I will see to it that there will be no bad practices." He took that pledge seriously.

Bird gets the ball on the right side, guarded by Laettner. With an exaggerated, almost theatrical flourish, Bird swings his torso as if to pass to Jordan in the corner. The man made better use of body fakes than anyone else who ever lived, his remedy for his relative lack of quickness. Laettner bites and Bird is free to drive left into the lane, where he passes to Malone on the left baseline. Malone misses a jumper, Ewing misses an easy tip, and Laettner grabs the rebound.

Magic dribbles upcourt and goes into his Toscanini act, waving both Laettner and Mullin away from the right side of the court and motioning for Barkley to isolate on the block. Bird has him on a switch. "Go to work, C.B.!" Magic instructs. "Go to work"! Barkley up-fakes Bird but air-balls a jumper. Laettner is there for the rebound and lays it in.

### Magic Johnson's Blue Team 5, Michael Jordan's White Team 0.

Playing tit-for-tat at the other end—this happens often in the NBA—Malone posts up Barkley on the left side. But the Mailman misses an easy jumper and Laettner—player of the game so far—gets the rebound. At the other end, Laettner drives baseline on Ewing, who shoulders him out of bounds. "Don't force it if we don't have it," says Magic, directing his comment to Laettner. Magic can be a scold to his teammates. He considers it part of his leadership duties.

After the inbounds pass, Magic dribbles into the lane and spins between Jordan and Pippen, a forced drive if there ever was one. (As with most leaders, it is incumbent upon the followers to do as he says, not as he does.) The gentleman from Italy blows his whistle and no one is sure what the call is, including the gentleman from Italy. Bird, a veteran pickup-game strategist, turns to go upcourt, figuring that will sell the call as a travel, but Magic is already demanding a foul. He wins.

"That's a foul?" Jordan asks in his deep baritone.

Years later, I would watch Magic in a pickup game at UCLA, this one without referees, and he would win the foul battle virtually every time, stand around incredulously until he was awarded the ball, and, on defense, pointedly play through his own fouls and act like a petulant child when one was called on him.

A minute later Barkley bats away Pippen's shovel pass to Ewing and storms off, pell-mell, to the other end. Bird is ahead of him but overruns the play—at this stage in his life he's hardly going to take a charge on a Mack truck—and Barkley puts in a layup.

### Magic Johnson's Blue Team 7, Michael Jordan's White Team 0.

Jordan is now getting serious and calls out, "One, one!" Pippen gets the ball on the right wing, fakes Mullin off his feet, and cans a jumper to break the drought for White.

**Magic Johnson's Blue Team 7, Michael Jordan's White Team 2.**

Mullin, always sneaky, taps the ball away from a driving Jordan, and Barkley again begins steamrolling downcourt, this time going between Malone and Ewing for another full-court layup, taking his two steps from just inside the foul line with that sixth sense all great players have about exactly when to pick up the dribble. "Foul! Foul!" Barkley hollers, but he doesn't get the call.

**Magic Johnson's Blue Team 9, Michael Jordan's White Team 2.**

Malone misses another open jumper; Magic rebounds, heads downcourt, and yells, "I see you, baby," to an open Mullin. Mullin misses but Barkley rebounds and finds a cutting Laettner, whose shot is swatted away by Ewing. Laettner spreads his arms, looking for a call, soon to be joined by his more influential teammate.

"That's good!" Magic yells, demanding a goaltending violation.

"He didn't call it," says Jordan.

"It's good," Magic says again.

"He didn't call it," says Jordan.

Magic wins again. Goaltending.

**Magic Johnson's Blue Team 11, Michael Jordan's White Team 2.**

Bird goes right by Laettner and takes an awkward left-handed shot in the lane that misses. It's obvious that his back is hurting and he would be sitting out had Stockton or Drexler been available. Laettner has a layup opportunity at the other end off a quick feed by Magic, but Ewing blocks it, a small moment that presages Laettner's NBA career. He wasn't springy enough to dunk, nor physical enough to draw a foul.

"Dunk that shit, Chris," Jordan says. "Dunk that shit."

(Years later Jordan told me, coldly and matter-of-factly, "Anybody who had Laettner on the team lost. He was the weak link and everybody went at him.")

Bird misses an open jumper and Magic clearly goes over Pippen's back and knocks it out of bounds; nevertheless, Magic still flashes a look of disbelief when the ball is awarded to White. Ewing swishes a jumper.

### Magic Johnson's Blue Team 11, Michael Jordan's White Team 4.

Magic drives, a foul is called on Ewing, and Malone, no fan of this Magic-dominated show, is starting to get irritated.

"*Sheet!*" he yells at the gentleman from Italy. "Everything ain't a foul!"

His mood is no better seconds later when he gets caught in a Barkley screen and Mullin is able to backdoor Pippen, get a perfect feed from Magic, and score a layup.

"Whoo!" Magic yells as he heads back upcourt. Things are going well for him.

### Magic Johnson's Blue Team 13, Michael Jordan's White Team 4.

(Years later Pippen goes on a nice little riff about Mullin's ability to read the game. "Mullie just killed me on backdoors," Pippen said, watching the tape with me. "He wasn't that fast, but he knew just when to make his cut.")

Jordan is now looking to score. He forces a switch off a Ewing screen, takes Robinson outside, and launches a three-pointer that bounces off the backboard and into the basket. A lucky shot. Magic calls for it immediately—you know what he's thinking, tit for tat—and Jordan retreats, fearing a Johnson drive. But Magic stops, launches a jump shot from just outside the three-point line, and yells, "Right back at you!" even before it reaches the basket. It goes in.

### Magic Johnson's Blue Team 16, Michael Jordan's White Team 7.

In the winter of 1989, a televised one-on-one game between Magic and Jordan, to take place in the off-season, was on the table. It sounded like a no-brainer, particularly if you had no brain. It would only reinforce the strongest stereotype about the NBA—that even its best players are selfish one-on-one carnival acts. Still, Magic was intrigued and even talked of having "developed strategies" to defeat Jordan.

His Airness was far more reticent, grasping that he had nothing to gain except pocket change. If he won, all it would do was cement his rep as the best one-on-one player in history; if he lost, it would've been to a guy who is recognized for being unselfish and team-oriented. Plus Jordan would've had to endure Magic's crowing until global warming melted the planet. The NBA was against the idea and then the Players Association jumped in and said it was not in the "best interests" of the game. The president of the group at that time happened to be Isiah Thomas, and for a moment Jordan's interest was piqued, simply as a way to get back at Thomas. But it never came to pass.

There is little doubt that Jordan would've drilled Magic, who simply had no way to defend him. Magic is bigger but not stronger, he can't jump as high, he's nowhere near as quick, and Jordan's predaceous instincts were unmatched in one-on-one challenges.

But this morning, in a near-deserted gym in Monte Carlo, was Magic's one-on-one game against Jordan. He hadn't been able to do it in an exhibition, and he hadn't been able to do it in the '91 Finals, when both Pippen and Jordan limited his effectiveness. Going one-on-one against Jordan, however, not only was flawed strategy but also went against Magic's basketball nature. Johnson was a conciliator. *I'll bring everybody together* was his mantra, just as it had been back at Everett High School in Lansing, where the principal used to call upon him to settle racial disputes among his fellow students. Jordan was the classic lead dog who did not speak with an ambassador's tongue. *You have to play at my level. You have to elevate your game to play with me.* "You understand the respect I have for Michael," Krzyzewski says many years later, "but one thing about him—he cannot be kind."

When Magic got out of his comfort zone and tried to *be* Jordan, as he did on this morning, he was doomed to failure.

Jordan, with the surety of an IRS accountant, is starting to get into it. He initiates the play from the point, goes through the lane and out to the left corner, gets a pass from Ewing, and hits a jumper as Magic arrives too late to stop him. At the other end, Magic waits until Barkley sets up on the left low block and gives him a pass. Barkley turns around and hits a jumper.

"Take him, Charles, all day," says Magic.

Jordan dribbles slowly downcourt and motions Malone to the right block. Jordan makes the entry pass and Malone turns and quick-shoots over Barkley. Good. Tit for tat.

## Magic Johnson's Blue Team 18, Michael Jordan's White Team 11.

Bird air-balls a wide-open jumper. He looks a hundred years old. White gets the ball back and Jordan signals that the left side should be cleared for Malone to go against Barkley. The entry pass comes in and Malone clears space by slapping away Barkley's hand. He turns toward the baseline and, legs splayed, releases a jumper. Good.

"Right back at *you*," Jordan yells, echoing Magic from a couple of minutes earlier.

## Magic Johnson's Blue Team 18, Michael Jordan's White Team 13.

After a couple of futile exchanges, Magic races downcourt and throws a pass ahead to David Robinson. "Keep going, David," he hollers, and Robinson obligingly drives to the basket, drawing a foul on Ewing.

"All day long," Magic hollers. "All day long." Then he gets personal: "The Jordanaires are down," he yells. That's what Jordan's "supporting cast" used to be called in Chicago before the Bulls started winning championships, a nickname that came about because the original Jordanaires were also Elvis Presley's backup band.

Jordan is not amused. And it is at that moment, about halfway through the Greatest Game That Nobody Ever Saw, that Magic may have sealed his own fate.

"Hold the clock!" Jordan hollers, now clearly irritated, making sure there is enough time to strike back. Robinson makes one of two.

## Magic Johnson's Blue Team 19, Michael Jordan's White Team 13.

A minute later Barkley spins away from Malone on the right

block and Malone is called for a foul. "Called this same shit last night," Malone says to the gentleman from Italy, referring to the game against France. "This is *bullshit!*" To add to Malone's frustration, Daly hollers that the White team is over the foul limit.

"One and one," says Daly.

"*Yeah!*" Magic yells. "I love it. I *love* it! We ain't in Chicago Stadium anymore," he adds, and punctuates the insult with loud clapping. It is a predictable jab but carries weight. Throughout his career Jordan heard the complaints that the referees favored him. During a Michael/Magic/Larry photo session in Portland, Magic had quipped, "Can't get too close to Michael. It'll be a foul." Jordan was tired of hearing about it, particularly from Magic. Barkley makes one of two.

**Magic Johnson's Blue Team 20, Michael Jordan's White Team 13.**

Now amped up, Jordan goes through four defenders for a flying layup, and then Pippen steals Mullin's inbounds pass. Jordan misses a jumper, but Pippen rebounds, draws a foul on Mullin, and gets an enthusiastic palm slap from Jordan. As Barkley towels himself off from head to toe—all that alcohol coming out—Pippen makes both. Perhaps they *are* in Chicago Stadium.

**Magic Johnson's Blue Team 20, Michael Jordan's White Team 17.**

Bird grabs the rebound off a missed Robinson shot and Jordan cans a jumper to bring White within one. Magic, determined to make this a one-on-one contest, spins into the lane and misses badly. Barkley is starting to get irritated at Magic's one-on-one play and will later complain to Jordan and Pippen about it. Jordan races downcourt with Pippen to the left and Ewing to the right. You know where this is headed. Pippen catches and throws down a ferocious left-handed dunk. (Dunking left-handed was something Pippen did better than Jordan, as even Jordan acknowledged.)

**Michael Jordan's White Team 21, Magic Johnson's Blue Team 20.**

First lead for White.

Mullin drives and draws a reach-in foul on Pippen. "Wasn't

that all ball?" says Jordan. Mullin makes one free throw, misses the next.

Jordan drives the lane and Magic, now visibly tired, gets picked off. Robinson, the help defender, is whistled for a foul. After Jordan misses the first, Magic knocks the ball high in the air—a technical in the NBA, but who cares?—and keeps jawing.

"Let's concentrate," hollers Daly, trying to keep everyone's mind on the business at hand.

Jordan makes the second.

**Michael Jordan's White Team 22, Magic Johnson's Blue Team 21.**

Malone comes down hard on his right ankle after making a layup off an assist from Jordan. His bad mood has grown worse. Malone walks it off—a normal man would've gone for ice—as Pippen and Bird come over to slap palms and Jordan yells, "Way to go, Karl."

**Michael Jordan's White Team 24, Magic Johnson's Blue Team 21.**

In March 1992, a few months before the Dream Team got together, I asked coaches and general managers around the league this question: *If you were starting a team and could take either Malone or Barkley, which one would you select?* It was a hot topic at the time, probably *the* topic, since there was no longer a question that Jordan was the best player in the world. It had the ingredients for a Magic-or-Larry?-type debate. Mr. Conservative vs. Mr. Volatile. The Muscleman vs. the Leaper. Mr. Olympia vs. the Round Mound of Rebound. Mr. Reliable vs. Mr. We Hope He Shows Up and Isn't in a Bar Sending a Drunk Through a Window.

Malone won the poll 15–7, and there were common threads in the voting. Malone's supporters invariably mentioned his loyal-soldier qualities and contrasted them with Barkley's penchant for controversy; Barkley's backers felt there was no substitute for talent and that Charles achieved more with less, having no John Stockton to deliver him the ball. This was from one typical Malone voter: "It's gotten so bad this year with the off-court distractions and his un-happiness with being on the Sixers that it finally has had an effect on Barkley's play. With the Mailman, you know he's going to play hard every night, and you don't have the worries of what might happen after the game." And this summarized the Barkley advo-cates: "I like Charles's heart, the way he overcomes the size disad-vantage, the way he takes over a game all by himself."

Malone won, I suspect, because the question was which you would choose to *start a team*, not which was the better player. Malone played nineteen seasons and in almost every one of them played in every game. Nobody—*nobody*—ever prepared himself better than the gym-ripped Stairmaster addict from Louisiana. Barkley, by contrast, played in eighty-two games in only his rookie year. He went like a madman during games but didn't take care of himself and something always broke down.

Years later, upon considering the full flush of their careers, it's still a difficult call by the numbers. Malone, the second-leading scorer in NBA history behind Abdul-Jabbar, averaged 25 points per game, compared to Barkley's 22.1. Barkley outrebounded Malone by 11.7 to 10.1. Both have been accused of folding under pressure—"The Mailman doesn't deliver on Sunday," Pippen fa-mously said to Malone, who then missed two crucial free throws during Game 1 (held on a Sunday) of the 1997 Finals—but that's more the result of both retiring titleless. The big picture reveals that both were outstanding postseason players with numbers almost identical to their regular-season metrics. Bill Simmons, in his ency-clopedic *The Book of Basketball*, has Malone (18th) and Barkley (19th) together in his pantheon, which seems fitting.

For the first two years of Malone's career he appeared headed on a Wilt Chamberlain–like course, a player who could be fouled late in the game because he would miss from the line. But as much as any player in NBA history, the Mailman made himself into a free-throw shooter by pure will and repetition, turning that early .548 percentage into a .742 lifetime mark. That is a monumental achievement that made his career, since he is still the all-time leader in made free throws. When the defense has a guy it can't stop and can't foul, it has a major problem.

But there is always the root question in sports: who was *better*? You have that moment when you can give only one person the bat, the club, or the ball, and who would you choose? It's not a media thing; it's a player thing. You can talk about how Jack Nicklaus dominated golf for two full decades and won a Masters at age forty-six and never tore up his knees with an overtorqued swing or his private life with an overtorqued libido. But if you had that moment when something had to get done, some miracle shot had to be pulled off, wouldn't most players say, *Tiger, you take the club?* Wouldn't they hand the ball to Jim Brown? Wouldn't they send Ted Williams up to hit?

In basketball, I'm sure that if players spoke honestly, Jordan would always get the ball over anyone. Magic or Bird? I have no basis on which to conclude this, but my guess is that the majority would say Bird, even though Magic had the greater career. The modern-day equivalent is Kobe Bryant or LeBron James, and I'm certain that most would say Bryant . . . unless they said Dwyane Wade, or now Dirk Nowitzki.

And I'm equally certain that this Barkley-or-Malone nod would go to Barkley. Charles had that ineffable something that Malone didn't have. He was just *better*. He wasn't more important to a franchise, he wasn't as dependable, and he wasn't as good over the long haul. He was just . . . *better*.

Drexler offered a simple but perceptive analysis of Barkley when we talked about it in 2011. "If Charles had worked out and done things like he was supposed to, the way that Karl did them, then he wouldn't have been Charles," said Drexler. "He was creative, and creative guys have to do it at their own pace and in their own way." It's another way of saying that we don't ask our poets to diagram sentences.

Of all the Dream Teamers, though, Laettner came closest to paying Barkley the ultimate compliment. When I made the casual comment that everyone believed that Jordan was the best, Laettner pursed his lips for a minute and considered. "I guess," he said. "But by a very, very small margin over Charles." That sentiment could be the result of his being much closer to Barkley than he was to Jordan during his Dream Team experience. Or it could be an honest opinion.

Jordan and Pippen walk up the court together. "He's tired," Jordan says of Barkley. How many times had they seen that with the Bulls, some little tell that an opponent was in oxygen debt and the Bulls were about to take over? As if to disprove Jordan, Barkley plows into the lane and Malone is called for a block. Taking a cue from Magic, the Mailman bats the ball high into the air. Seeing a profusely perspiring Barkley at the line, Jordan moves in for the kill.

"A man is tired, he usually misses free throws," says Jordan. This is a recurring theme for His Airness. "One and one now," says Jordan, wiggling two fingers at Barkley. Barkley makes the first—"Yeah, Charles, you gonna get your two anyway," sings Magic—but Ewing bats the second off the rim before it has a chance (maybe) to go in.

Bird misses another open jumper but decides to make something of this personal nightmare. As Magic yo-yo-dribbles on the left side, Bird suddenly comes off Laettner and steals the ball. He bumps Magic slightly, but even the gentleman from Italy is not going to call that one. As Magic tumbles to the ground, Bird takes off, Barkley in pursuit, *pursuit* used lightly in this case. (As a matter of fact, *takes off* is used lightly, too.) Bird fakes a behind-the-back pass to a trailing Jordan and Barkley takes a man-sized bite at it, his jock now somewhere inside the free-throw line. Bird makes the layup.

"Way to go, Larry!" Jordan yells. "Way to take him to the hole. I know you got some life in you."

(Years later I watched some of the game with Mullin. When we came to the part where Bird made this turn-back-the-clock play, Mullin called to his wife, Liz, "Honey, come here and watch this. Watch what Larry does here." And we run it back a couple of times, Mullin and his wife smiling, delighted by the sight of the Bird they both loved. A couple of months after that, I remind Jordan of the play. He grows animated. "That was the game-winner, right?" he says. Not exactly, I tell him. But Jordan is amped up, not even listening to me. "That's Larry, man, that's Larry," he says. "Making a great play like that. That's Larry Bird.")

### Michael Jordan's White Team 26, Magic Johnson's Blue Team 22.

Laettner makes two free throws, and at the other end Jordan feeds Malone for a jumper. Barkley misses a jumper, but Robinson, an aerial acrobat, a giant with a gymnast past, leaps high over Ewing and taps the ball in off the board.

### Michael Jordan's White Team 28, Magic Johnson's Blue Team 26.

Jordan launches a jumper from the top of the key, outside the three-point area, as Mullin flies out to guard him.

"Too late," Jordan yells while the ball is still in the air, like the queen (played by Judi Dench) in *Shakespeare in Love*, reacting disdainfully when a courier is tardy throwing his cloak over a puddle.

### Michael Jordan's White Team 31, Magic Johnson's Blue Team 26.

Now mostly what you hear is Jordan's voice, exhorting his team, sensing the kill. Magic backs into the lane, Malone guarding him on a switch. The gentleman from Italy blows his whistle . . . and the Mailman blows his top.

"Oh, come on, man," he yells. "Stop calling this fucking *bull-sheet*." Jordan comes over and steps between Malone and the ref.

"Forget it, Karl," says Jordan. "Don't scare him. We might need him."

"*Fuck him!*" yells Malone.

As Magic lines up at the foul line, the whistle in P. J. Carlesimo's mouth actually moves. That's because his face is twisted into a grin.

Magic shoots the first, which rolls around as Jordan, hands on shorts, yells to Ewing, "Knock it out!" Too late. Magic swishes the second.

### Michael Jordan's White Team 31, Magic Johnson's Blue Team 28.

Pippen pops out from behind a Ewing screen and swishes a jumper. At the other end, Mullin loses his grip on a Magic pass and Bird recovers. Jordan begins a break, motions Ewing to join him on the left side, and watches in delight as Patrick takes a few pitty-pat steps and makes a jumper.

"That's a walk!" a couple of voices yell. But no call is made.

**Michael Jordan's White Team 35, Magic Johnson's Blue Team 28.**

Ewing is whistled for a foul on Robinson, and Jordan says, "That's okay. Let's see if they can make free throws." The tip of the knife is in and he has begun to twist. Robinson makes both. At the other end, Jordan feeds Malone, who draws a foul on Barkley.

"One and one?" the Blue team asks.

"Two shots," says Jordan, who has clearly taken over the whistle from Magic. Malone misses both. Barkley grabs the second miss, steams downcourt, and passes ahead to Laettner, who goes up and fails to connect but is fouled by Jordan. *Dunk that shit, Chris.*

"Every time!" yells Magic from the backcourt, desperately trying to regain the verbal momentum. *"Every* time!"

Laettner, who has been and will remain silent throughout the game—one could only imagine how he would've dominated the conversation had this been an intrasquad romp back in Durham, North Carolina—makes both free throws.

**Michael Jordan's White Team 35, Magic Johnson's Blue Team 32.**

Magic is called for a reach-in and now he goes after the gentleman from Italy, trailing him across the lane. Magic lines up next to Ewing and pushes his arm away as Ewing leans in to box out on Jordan's free throws. Jordan makes both. Magic is steaming.

At the other end, the gentleman from Italy calls an inexplicable moving screen on Robinson, which delights Jordan.

"My man," he yells, clapping his hands. "My man, my man, my man." *We might need him.*

"Chicago Stadium," Magic yells. "Chicago Stadium." His fresh ammunition has run dry; all he has is the refrain.

Malone backs Barkley down and the whistle blows, and now it's

Barkley attacking the gentleman from Italy. "Come on, man!" he yells. "That was clean!" For a moment it appears as if Barkley might strike him. He does have a history, after all. . . .

Malone misses the first.

"Plenty of time," comes a voice from the sideline, probably that of Krzyzewski.

"There ain't no plenty of time!" yells Jordan. "*Fuck* plenty of time!" The clock says 1:21. Malone makes the second.

## Michael Jordan's White Team 38, Magic Johnson's Blue Team 32.

Laettner makes a weird twisting layup. Over on the sidelines, Daly is beginning to pace, hoping this thing will come to an end before a fistfight breaks out or one of his players assaults the gentleman from Italy.

As Robinson lines up to shoot a free throw, Jordan and Magic begin jawing again, and Magic changes up slightly.

"All they did was move Bulls Stadium right here," Magic says. "That's all they did. That's *all* they did."

"Hey, it is the nineties," Jordan says, reaching for a towel.

Robinson makes both.

## Michael Jordan's White Team 38, Magic Johnson's Blue Team 36.

Jordan yo-yo-dribbles out front, running down the shot clock, pissing off Magic all the while. Finally he drives left, goes up for a jumper, and draws a foul on Laettner. Before he shoots, Magic moves in for a few words. They are not altogether pleasant. Jordan makes the first. Magic keeps jawing. Jordan takes the ball from the gentleman from Italy, slaps him on the rump, and says, "Good man." He makes the second.

Chuck Daly watches in relief as the clock hits 0:00. He waves his hands in a shooting motion at both baskets, the sign for players to do their post-practice routine, and ending the Greatest Game That Nobody Ever Saw.

## Michael Jordan's White Team 40, Magic Johnson's Blue Team 36.

Except that it isn't over. Not really.

"Way to work, White," Jordan yells, rubbing it in. He paces up and down, wiping himself with a towel, emperor of all he sees, as Magic, Barkley, and Laettner disconsolately shoot free throws.

"It was all about Michael Jordan," says Magic. "That's all it was." It's no joke. Magic is angry.

Jordan continues to pace the sideline. He grabs a cup of Gatorade and sings, "Sometimes I dream . . ." Jordan had recently signed a multimillion-dollar deal (was there any other kind in his world?) to endorse Gatorade, which then needed an advertising hook, a task assigned to a creative genius named Bernie Pitzel. Inspired by "I Wan'na Be Like You," the Monkey Song in the animated film *The Jungle Book*, Pitzel wrote the lyrics to "Be Like Mike" on the tablecloth of Avanzare, his favorite Chicago restaurant.

Sometimes I dream
If I could be like Mike

And as Magic looks on in this sticky-hot gymnasium, sweat pouring off his body, a towel around his neck, there is Jordan, captain of the winning team, singing a song written just for him, drinking a drink that was raking in millions, just rubbing it in and rubbing it in, as only Jordan can do. And on the bus back to the hotel? Jordan kept singing and singing: *Be like Mike . . . Be like Mike . . .*

In the days that followed, the game would have reverberations in Barcelona, as Michael and Magic, equally relentless, continued to try to get the verbal edge on each other. And in the years that followed, this intrasquad game—more like a scrimmage, really, officiated by the stouthearted but vastly incompetent gentleman from Italy—took on a mystery, became part of basketball lore, "kind of like an urban legend," as Laettner described it years later. As such, the details got all scrambled, muddled with those of other scrimmages on other days. Even Magic didn't have the details correct when he talked about it in *When the Game Was Ours*.

And not everybody loved it. "You have to look at who relish that kind of thing," said Karl Malone. "As they say, it's their geeeg." By "their" he meant Jordan and Magic. (In the spring of 2011 I asked Malone if he wanted to watch a few minutes of the scrimmage video. "No," he says. "Doesn't interest me.")

But Krzyzewski, no fan of trash talk, looks back on it fondly, remembering almost every detail. And when I talked to him about it years later, we agreed that the basketball played on that morning was not an artistic triumph. But that isn't the point.

"Every once in a while, I'll be doing something, and a line from that game will just flash into my head," says Krzyzewski. "'They just moved Chicago Stadium to Monte Carlo.' It just makes me smile.

"A lot of players talk trash because the TV cameras are on. But the doors on that day were *closed*. This was just you against me. 'This is what I got—whatta you got?' It taught me a lot about accepting personal challenges.

"You know, if somebody could've taped the sound track of the game, not necessarily recorded the basketball but just the sounds, it would be priceless."

Well, I did get the original VHS tape, convert it to DVD, and even get a specialist to make a CD of the sound track. I didn't pick up everything, but I got most everything.

It was not about the hoops. It was about the passion that those guys put into the game, the importance they placed on winning and personal pride. At times it was childish in the strictest sense of that word. But they were playing a kid's game, after all, and pursued it with a childlike determination to come out on top.

Years later, in a conversation with Jordan, he brought up the game before I had a chance to ask him about it. "In many ways," said Jordan, "it was the best game I was ever in. Because the gym was locked and it was just about basketball. You saw a lot about players' DNA in games like that, how much some guys want to win. Magic was mad about it for two days."

Magic, for his part, estimates that his anger lasted only a few hours. "Michael understood that because that's how he was, too," said Johnson. "Let me tell you something—it would've been worse for everybody if he lost. Because I could let something go after a while. But Michael? He never let it go. He never let *anything* go."

So into the history book it goes.

## JULY 22, 1992, STADE LOUIS II, MONTE CARLO

OFFICIALS: Carlesimo, gentleman from Italy

### WHITE (40)

|  | FG | FGA | FT | FTA | Reb | Ast | PF | TO | Pts |
|---|---|---|---|---|---|---|---|---|---|
| Bird, f | 1 | 7 | 0 | 0 | 4 | 0 | 2 | 0 | 2 |
| Malone, f | 4 | 8 | 1 | 4 | 1 | 0 | 3 | 0 | 9 |
| Ewing, c | 2 | 5 | 0 | 0 | 4 | 1 | 6 | 0 | 4 |
| Pippen, g | 3 | 3 | 2 | 2 | 2 | 1 | 4 | 3 | 8 |
| Jordan, g | 5 | 7 | 5 | 6 | 2 | 8 | 2 | 1 | 17 |

Three-pointers: Jordan 2–3; Bird 0–1

Steals: Pippen 2; Bird 1

Blocked shots: Ewing 2

Insults: Jordan 7

Referee explosions: Malone 2; Bird ½; Jordan ½

### BLUE (36)

|  | FG | FGA | FT | FTA | Reb | Ast | PF | TO | Pts |
|---|---|---|---|---|---|---|---|---|---|
| Laettner, f | 3 | 4 | 4 | 5 | 4 | 0 | 3 | 0 | 10 |
| Barkley, f | 4 | 7 | 3 | 5 | 5 | 1 | 2 | 0 | 11 |
| Robinson, c | 1 | 2 | 5 | 8 | 3 | 0 | 4 | 0 | 7 |
| Mullin, g | 1 | 3 | 1 | 2 | 0 | 0 | 1 | 2 | 3 |
| Johnson, g | 1 | 3 | 2 | 2 | 0 | 2 | 2 | 5 | 5 |

Three-pointers: Johnson 1–1; Mullin 0–1

Steals: Mullin 1

Blocked shots: 0

Insults: Johnson 11

Referee explosions: Johnson 1; Barkley 1

# CHAPTER 29

# THE WRITER

. . . . . . . . . . . . . . . . . . . . . . . . . . . . . . . . . . . . . . . . . .

**"There's Helicopters Up There—
This Shit Is Serious!"**

By the time David Dupree and I arrived in Barcelona—having turned a six-and-a-half-hour drive from Nice into nine hours in that pre-GPS age—the Dream Team had already arrived, launching a nonstop, sixteen-day freak show. The accreditation process at the airport had been a zoo, as camera crews repeatedly broke through police lines to fire off shots of the gods. If you think American paparazzi are obnoxious, you haven't seen European photographers in action. One Italian cameraman, walking backward, stumbled and fell and others tripped over him, thousand-dollar lenses and scopes flying everywhere, and for a brief moment some in the American party thought they were about to witness the equivalent of a soccer riot:

**"17 Onlookers Crushed in Dream Team Debacle!
Stockton, Mullin Pick Up I.D. Badges!"**

My digs were a few subway stops from the Ambassador, the new hotel that had been almost completely taken over by the Dream Team and its attendant retinue—as the story went, only one of the $900-per-night rooms was occupied by someone not associated with the Dream Team. It was a small miracle that they were ensconced there at all, given the Spanish predilection for a casual approach to labor. Nine months before the Olympics, NBC's Dick Ebersol, who was in Barcelona on one of his frequent pre-Olympic visits, called David Stern. "You know that hotel you're planning to stay at?" Ebersol told the commissioner. "Well, I've over here at a hotel nearby, and I can tell you it's a hole in the ground." After much barking at the IOC, followed by the IOC's barking at the Spanish Olympic Committee, the Ambassador was finished just days before the Dream Team's arrival.

I decided to venture over there upon arriving, see if I could grab a beer with the PR guys, maybe get a couple of minutes with one of the players, Barkley, Malone, or Drexler, perhaps, and . . .

You might've thought that by this time I had fully grasped the Dream Team phenomenon, but I hadn't. For there, outside the hotel, lined up on Pintor Fortuny, the narrow street that fronted the hotel, were hundreds and hundreds of spectators, just waiting and watching, waiting and hoping for . . . what? A glimpse. That's all. Just a *glimpse*. When the team bus had rounded the corner a few hours earlier, fans began running after it, a phenomenon that Malone compared to the running of the bulls at Pamplona. "I don't know what they were going to do if they caught us," said Malone.

Anyone still demanding to know why the Dream Team had special accommodations needed only to glance at an aerial photo of this scene to realize how completely its presence would've wrecked the delicate ecosystem of the Olympic Village. Police holding bayoneted rifles were everywhere. It was midnight, remember, and the hotel was in lockdown. I couldn't get close to the front door, and, this being the pre-cellphone age, I had no one to call to let me in. It wouldn't have mattered, anyway, since a couple of days' advance notice was needed. Over the next two weeks I would worm my way into the inner sanctum of the Ambassador a couple of times, always requiring a badge and an escort from the NBA or USA Basketball, flashing my credential to the steely-eyed policemen like Wayne and Garth backstage at the Aerosmith gig in *Wayne's World*.

"Meester, get us pleez Ma-jeek's autograph," I'd hear on my way in.

Around town and in the arena, one achieved a certain celebrity just by being associated with the Dream Team. I gave a dozen interviews, not because anyone had the slightest interest in me or the clever way I had around an adjective, but because I could shed light on the Dreamers. It is impossible to overstate how invested most international reporters are in their respective teams. It's not like in the United States, where there is a distance (or supposed to be) between journalist and subject. I still have a vivid memory from the 2010 FIBA World Championships in Istanbul of a dozen Lithuanian reporters hugging, celebrating, and singing songs with the team members after they won the bronze medal.

Therefore, most of the international press assumed that since I covered the Dream Team I was a de facto member of it. One Japanese reporter even said that he wanted to follow me around on a day when the team wasn't playing.

"Why in the hell would you want to do that?" I asked.

"I will follow because you will probably see Michael Jordan or Magic Johnson, no?" he said.

"No," I said. "Actually I'm going to do an hour at the Picasso museum, then go watch the table tennis."

He wisely withdrew his request.

Among other American journalists who specialized in Olympic coverage—"Ringheads," as they were known, even among themselves—the Dream Team chroniclers were either an alien species or some version of the Rodney Dangerfield character in *Caddyshack*, an obnoxious trespassing outsider. A few of the Ringheads made a statement by refusing to watch the Dream Team play, so it must've made them gag when International Olympic Committee president Juan Antonio Samaranch, who didn't know a three-point shot from three-card monte, was a conspicuous Dream Team observer at the Palau Municipal d'Esports de Badalona. "There was a lot of jealousy and pettiness about this from the Olympics press," said ESPN's Michael Wilbon, who covered the Games for the *Washington Post*. "It was like their show was taken away from them and, suddenly, there was a bunch of non-amateurs in the Olympics. Like [sprinter] Michael Johnson was an amateur, right?"

At one level, I could understand how ridiculously overblown the Dream Team scene was, how absurd that so much of the world's attention was focused on a group of men who put a ball through a hoop. True, that is the sports journalist's game, but this was the game times a thousand.

But there was a serious side to covering the Dream Team. The possibility that something could happen was always there, and not just because the memory of the massacres at the Munich Games was only two decades old. The world was coming apart in the early 1990s. War and revolution had torn apart Yugoslavia and the Soviet Union, whose teams in Barcelona bore those scars. Basque separatists, whose MO was placing bombs in parked cars outside public buildings, were a constant threat. Spain itself was a country not even a generation removed from the military dictatorship of Francisco Franco, and I could not help thinking that some of those itchy-fingered *policía* brandishing weapons outside the Ambassador had worked for him. With the first Gulf War still fresh in everyone's mind, there was no clearer target than the Dream Team if one wanted to make a political statement about millionaire Americans.

This same kind of dichotomy was later captured by David O. Russell in *Three Kings*, a thriller set during the latter part of the first Gulf War. Outside was the constant threat of war, death, and destruction. But inside the bubble there were hijinks and insults and soldiers riding to war in luxury vehicles as Chicago's "If You Leave Me Now" played on the radio, the sappy sound track of the war.

Years later, when I talked to retired NBA security chief Horace Balmer, he still sounded relieved that nothing had happened in Barcelona. "Biggest assignment of my life," said Balmer, unnecessarily.

"But in the end, Atlanta was much worse." Balmer was on duty when a bomb went off in Olympic Park at the 1996 Games.

Not coincidentally, the McDonald's Open had been played in Barcelona in 1990 (it was an Olympics testing ground with the New York Knicks as the NBA entrant), so Balmer knew his way around. He says that he had worked for months with the State Department and various Spanish agencies to coordinate security and that even the French government had been involved, obligingly locking up hundreds of Basque separatists to keep them from coming to Barcelona. (That doesn't sound legal.)

Still, when Balmer saw the crowds outside the hotel, he decided that reinforcements were necessary from local law enforcement, which was already stretched thin by the demands of security at the Olympic Village. "They had the attitude of, 'Why can't these guys stay in the Village like everybody else?'" says Balmer. So he convened a meeting at the hotel and had Jordan, Barkley, and Malone drop by to offer their opinion that more was better. And so did it happen.

(Balmer grew so close to the local authorities that eventually a pickup basketball game was arranged between the NBA group and the Spanish police. During that game, which was good-naturedly refereed by Barkley and Drexler, assistant coach Lenny Wilkens tore his Achilles tendon, the fifty-four-year-old Hall of Famer thus becoming the most seriously injured member of the Dream Team.)

Inside the hotel was "a soft security presence," as Balmer put it, consisting of well-dressed undercover forces. But outside the presence was *hard*. Snipers crouched on top of the buildings surrounding the team hotel, and no vehicles could be parked within two blocks of the Ambassador. When Dupree and I had our dinner with Malone, the first thing he said was, "There's helicopters up there. This shit is *serious*." Balmer said that "these were the most protected guys in Barcelona," and I don't doubt that for a minute.

On game nights, two buses pulled out of the Ambassador en route to the Palau Municipal d'Esports in the suburb of Badalona, one bearing the players, one a decoy, the same technique the feds use to get a Mafia don to trial. Routes were constantly changed. Roads and freeways were cleared when the Dream Team bus headed to practice and tip-off. Stockton sheepishly remembers the police pulling over the bus of that night's opponent, Puerto Rico, so the Dream Team bus could get by; Stockton caught a glimpse of his Utah Jazz teammate Jose Ortiz, a starting guard for Puerto Rico, as he roared by.

"That night, when we lined up to exchange gifts, Jose and I were across from each other," said Stockton. "I could see all the Puerto Rican team angling to shake hands with Magic, Michael, or Larry. That's the way it always was. And I motioned to Jose, 'You better come over here.' We hugged, and I felt a little better about it."

Daredevil police motorcyclists were omnipresent. European police forces love their bikes, and I can only imagine the intramural clamor to get that gig. The cyclists in front of the bus went so frightfully fast that Bird eventually urged officials to tell them to slow up with the provision that the team would leave fifteen minutes earlier.

Besides trips to games, the Dream Team was largely tethered to the Ambassador, locked in a golden, twenty-four-hour-room-service prison that had been constructed by their own collective fame, *prison* being a curious term since the mob outside would've given a year's salary just to get inside. On at least two occasions, players (Magic, Stockton, and Mullin for sure) got off a caught-in-traffic Dream Team bus and grabbed the metro, driving security out of its mind.

Stockton, in fact, was the only Dream Teamer who was able to get around normally, being, as he puts it, "a six-foot white guy who looks like everybody else." He even filmed a segment for NBA Entertainment that centered around his anonymity. As Stockton held a camera, he spotted a tourist wearing a Dream Team T-shirt, and he asked if she had seen any of the players. "Well, we saw Charles Barkley," she said, having that in common with thousands of others.

"Anyone else?" asks Stockton before two of his children pointed to her shirt and said, "There's Daddy!"

Enticing invitations were tossed out like confetti at a wedding, but most fell to the ground ungathered. Michael Douglas, most recently seen bedding Sharon Stone in *Basic Instinct*, something that had to impress even these guys, wanted to entertain the team, but the Dreamers said no thanks. They did take up the offer of Miami Heat owner Micky Arison for an afternoon on his yacht. When they arrived, they were informed that the air-conditioning was down, so Arison was bringing over his other yacht.

"That was a valuable day for me, a lesson in life," Magic told me years later. "The difference between being rich and being wealthy. The man had a *backup yacht*. I never forgot that."

If a Dream Teamer wanted to go somewhere special with family or friends, he was supposed to inform Balmer or another member of security, who would either give them a lift in a van or accompany them surreptitiously. "Sometimes they didn't even know we were there," says Balmer.

Magic and Mullin knew they were there. When they run into each other these days they still talk about the afternoon walk they took with their families, both of the Dream Teamers pushing strollers.

"We had a couple bodyguards in front and a couple bodyguards in back," remembers Johnson, "and they all were carrying these bags. We asked what was in them but they never said. Finally, near the end of the Olympics, they showed us. Machine guns. *That's* what was in them."

Balmer says it all worked out pretty well and that the players were largely cooperative, themselves realizing the security risks of famous millionaires out on the town. "Well, all except Charles," says Balmer. "Charles had his own ideas on this."

I feel fairly safe in declaring that there has never been, and never will be, a media gathering like the Dream Team introductory press conference in Barcelona. Some twelve hundred of the unwashed, including me, jammed the auditorium, and, when the team walked in, the room rose to applaud, American reporters excepted. It was as if a giant box of action figures had been opened and out tumbled a parade of superheroes, some blessed with extraordinary speed, others with X-ray vision, all with super charisma.

That kind of reverential treatment should've been old hat by now, considering that we had seen opponents snap photos before and even during games. But I kept trying to get at why—beyond the obvious fact that the Dream Team was a collection of immortals gathered in one place at one time—the phenomenon was so large. "An awful lot of it had to do with Michael," says Wilbon, who postulates that Jordan, at that time, was the most famous person in the world. "Oprah was not nearly as big as she got. Bill Clinton wasn't president yet. Muhammad Ali was a relic. There was no Barack Obama. Who else you got? It was Michael."

The NBA's Kim Bohuny has a theory to explain the Dream Team's fame. "There had been an air of mystery about these guys for a long time, and suddenly they came to life," she says. "Always, across the pond, the NBA was that faraway thing they would never see live. Then, suddenly . . . it's here! And all of these guys are together."

Before the press conference, I caught the eye of Brian McIntyre, the NBA's head of public relations, and we exchanged head-shaking glances. He and his other staffers had already held a draft, complete with "territorial picks," to determine who would handle the media requests for which players. McIntyre, who had begun his professional life with the Bulls, got Jordan. Josh Rosenfeld had started with the Lakers, so he had Magic. "My next two picks were Harry and Larry," says Rosenfeld, "because I figured they wouldn't do anything anyway."

Terry Lyons, who was at St. John's with Mullin, took the lefty. USA Basketball's Craig Miller took Christian Laettner, the amateur guy, and, since there wouldn't be that many requests for America's twelfth man, Miller was also assigned to Barkley, a nerve-racking job but at the end of the day an easy one since Charles, as Balmer put it, "had his own ideas" on being handled. Pistons PR man Matt

Dobek took, of course, Daly, all he could handle since the Dream Team coach got so many requests.

I suspect that the Dream Team was hardly astonished when the room rose to greet them. By this time they must have been figuring, *Isn't this how everybody is supposed to act when we're around?* By this time, too, the gravity of the moment had begun to sink in. Nobody realistically entertained the notion that they would lose, but there was always that little sliver of doubt.

*We play like we should and nobody gets within 30 . . . but what if our jumpers start missing?*

*There's never been a team like ours . . . but what was that little island Daly was talking about in San Diego?*

So to maintain the highest competitive mind-set, they began to construct a bogus narrative, one fraught with we'll-show-them declarations and revenge leitmotifs. *We're tired of hearing how a bunch of All-Stars could never play together. We're tired of hearing that we should've stayed in the Olympic Village. We're tired of watching the United States get beat up by other countries. We're tired of hearing that we're just a bunch of millionaires on summer vacation.*

True, all of those points had been raised, but the Dream Team did what most athletes do in those situations—pore through the pile and cherry-pick the negatives.

Magic at the press conference: "We gave up our summer. We share the Olympic spirit like any other athlete. Basketball players from other countries have been getting paid and nobody said nothing, and now we come over and we get paid and everybody is making a big deal out of it."

Barkley: "None of these foreign athletes will admit it, but they don't like Americans."

Stockton: "The Olympic spirit for me is to beat teams from other countries, not to live with them."

The most ginned-up subject was the one about Brazil overcelebrating a victory over the United States in the 1987 Pan Am Games. "They were throwing coaches in the air and high-fiving," said Malone, always ready to don some metaphorical army gear. "It looked like a little rubbing in the face." In truth, nobody on the Dream Team cared a damn about the 1987 Pan Am Games, and anyway, Brazil celebrates days that end in *y* the same way.

But there were light moments, two of which have endured through the ages. Malone deftly fielded a question from a Japanese reporter who wanted to know "why it is that sometimes you shoot and it is worth two points and other times it is worth three points." Said Malone: "That's just how we do it, my man."

And Barkley, asked about the Dream Team's first opponent, Angola, offered: "I don't know nuthin' 'bout Angola. But Angola's in trouble." The quote has lived on, and anyone with a decent Barkley impression can get a laugh out of it. From time to time, Wilbon will just up and text Barkley: *I don't know nuthin' 'bout . . .*

Some of the most underrated lines came from Bird. "I felt pretty good," he said when asked about his health, "until I sat here and listened to all this BS." And this to a question about his possibly imminent retirement: "I've been retired for four years, but nobody's noticed it yet."

# CHAPTER 30

# THE JESTER AND THE ANGOLAN

. . . . . . . . . . . . . . . . . . . . . . . . . . . . . . . . . . . . . . . . . . .

## "I Did Not Know That He Would Make Violence with Me"

Las Ramblas is one of those streets that couldn't exist anywhere but in Old Europe, "the only street in the world," wrote poet Federico García Lorca, "I wish would never end." It was a 24/7 carnival, a place for the high and mighty and the low and low-down.

Charles Barkley loved it. So let's do the math: live chickens, unicycles, pickpockets, open containers, prime hashish from Amsterdam, lithe and callow señoritas with dewdrop eyes, and a famous American who's not afraid to drop-kick drunks. What could possibly go wrong?

Early on in the competition Barkley told Balmer, the NBA's director of security, "Dude, the notion that I'm going to be at the Olympics and stay in my room is crazy. This is the greatest sporting event in the world. I'm going out." His itinerary generally went like this: Begin a card game with Magic, Michael, and Pippen around ten. Play for an hour or two, then slip out the back door of the Am-

bassador, walk a couple of blocks, meet an elderly Spanish gentleman, slip him a couple of hundred dollars, and declare, "Okay,
you're my security for tonight. Let's go."

And off he went. Along the way, Charles picked up crowds of
anywhere from ten to fifty, the Pied Piper of Barcelona. His nocturnal divagations drove the NBA security people nuts for a while,
particularly when others were involved. One night special arrangements had been made for Magic, Ewing, and Barkley to attend the boxing venue, but Charles insisted on leaving the hotel
early and the plans for a special entrance at a special time got all
messed up. But, eventually and inevitably, the security folks got
used to it and gave up, praying all the while that they would not
receive a predawn call from the *policía*.

The best beat for any reporter in the '92 Games was the Charles
Barkley beat. I was on it for a couple of nights, trailing him down
Las Ramblas, where I would've been in any case, getting paid for
hanging out, the journalist's dream. Other players visited Las
Ramblas—that's where Stockton found the tourist in the Dream
Team shirt who didn't recognize him—but rarely in darkness, when
the place was teeming with night crawlers and the potential for
trouble was everywhere. On the nights I followed Barkley, there
were some strange moments. An older man, speed-freak skinny and
crack-pipe crazy, walked in front of him for a while, pointing and
laughing like a hyena, but Barkley just kept going, sipping his *cer-
veza* and eventually outlasting him. On another occasion a kid on a
bicycle kept weaving in and out of his path until Barkley had to
stare him down. Either one of those guys would've been put on a
Homeland Security watch list these days. On one particularly
glassy-eyed evening, Barkley asked a couple of kids if he could get
on their motorcycle. He gunned the engine and the bike started
forward, Barkley jumping off in horror. Charles pushed the social
envelope, to be sure, but he wasn't a thrill-seeker—witness his pro-
testations about mountainside driving in Monte Carlo.

The hardest job of tracking Charles belonged to David Dupree,
since he was ghostwriting Barkley's daily journal for *USA Today*.

Universally recognized as the journalist least likely to keep night hours, teetotaler Dupree nevertheless found himself at every nightclub in Barcelona, receiving notes from bartenders, bouncers, and strippers on where he could catch up to Barkley. He always did. You can always find Charles because there are always lots of clues.

It's a distinct art, this Barkleyian ability to make eye contact, mingle, and keep going forward, never stopping long enough to get really mobbed. "It's not hard, but players think it's hard," Barkley told me years later. "I have two main principles. Don't travel with security, because that's what makes people mad and that's when bad stuff happens. And don't travel with an entourage, because that puts people off, too. I rolled alone. Still do."

A few words about Charles Barkley and alcohol. He is familiar with it. But so am I, though probably not as familiar as Charles. Some of my fondest nights on the NBA beat involved having drinks with Charles somewhere in the immediate vicinity, so I am not the one to say whether or not he drinks too much. But drinking is part of the Charles Barkley story.

On December 31, 2008, he was famously pulled over in his hometown of Scottsdale and arrested after failing a field sobriety test. He was found to have a blood alcohol level of 0.149 percent, nearly twice the legal limit of 0.08 percent in Arizona, and later spent a weekend in prison. The typical story is to say that he came out of the experience a changed man, but that would not be accurate. Charles came out of it exactly as he went into it. There were those who wanted to see more public groveling and behavior modification from Barkley, those who have long felt that the media, seduced by the man's antic charm, let him get away with far too much. Perhaps. But I saw Barkley shortly after the arrest and before he went to prison, and—I'm sorry if this comes out wrong—I had to respect the fact that he refused to offer up a bunch of phony platitudes. Yes, he had done his scripted act of contrition on TNT after serving a network-mandated suspension. But he would not cop to the I-found-God-and-now-I'm-a-teetotaler attitude that would be predictable for others in his position.

"Look, drinking and driving is a very serious thing," he told me. "It is unacceptable, and I embarrassed a lot of people who care about me." (For the record, they were more embarrassed that he told the police he was looking for oral sex at the time he was pulled over.) "But come on now—everyone wants to be overly dramatic about it. I'm going to prison? Okay, big deal. For most people, when you go to jail, it's a terrifying thing. You come out and you don't have a house and you don't have any money. When I get out, I'll still have everything."

It was his way of saying: *I'm still going to drink. I'll be more careful and I'll try not to get picked up by the police. But I'm still going to drink.*

And he still does. On a January night in 2011, I met him for dinner at a Phoenix restaurant to discuss the Dream Team. After exchanging greetings with practically every patron, he took a look at my chicken entrée and said, "I should've gotten that. Black people love chicken."

So it went. We had a great time—the cell phone photos Brett Favre sent of his penis were a popular subject, at least with Charles—because you always have a great time with Charles. I almost performed a classic spit take as he delivered the punch line on a story he told involving an encounter with the boyfriend of his daughter, Christiana.

"The young man said to me, 'Mr. Barkley, Christiana said that if I treat her bad, you'll kill me.' And I told him, 'Son, that's just not true. I don't want to go to prison. I'm gonna *hire* someone to kill your ass.'"

For all I know, Charles has said that in a hundred other venues. Maybe he has said it on the air. As I was going through the reporting for this book, any number of people asked me: *How were your interviews with Charles Barkley?* And my answer was always: *They were great. Just like your interviews with Charles would be.* One truism of journalism is that the more the public knows a person, the worse it is for the interviewer. I suppose there is a hidden Charles to write about, but, more than any other Dream Teamer, the man is out there.

The one thing that may have changed a little for Barkley is that he has a greater appreciation—make that a greater cognition—of Arizona's Draconian drunk-driving laws. As he watched me sip my first vodka, he said, "You know, you're already over the legal limit. You can't drink anymore because you have to drive me home."

"Didn't you bring your own car?" I asked him. "And how can I be over with one drink?"

"Man, I don't drive around this city now. I take cabs. When you're in jail, it's a long fucking weekend. And yes, you're over. Trust me on that."

A couple of hours later, he climbed into my car. "Don't be too far under the speed limit," he said. "They look for that, too. Just nice and steady."

We were about two miles from Charles's house when he said suddenly, "Turn in here!"

"This doesn't look like home, Charles."

We were in the parking lot of a bar.

"I have to go in for a while," he said. "You wanna come?"

"I gotta go, Charles. Anyway, I'm over the limit, right?"

"All right, Jack," he said. "You be good."

"You gonna get another ride home, right?"

He waved as he went off into the night. I should've guessed that I wouldn't have been taking him home.

While Charles was rambling on Las Ramblas, his teammates were almost always back in the family room of the hotel, playing cards and goofing on one another. But it's not like Barkley missed that. He would get back to the Ambassador by two or three in the morning, maybe four, and there would still be a gang of them in there, usually Jordan, Pippen, Magic, and Ewing. Even when he was in his room there was a commotion. "Charles would come in at all hours, talking to himself or talking to somebody on the phone, loud as anything, and Liz and I could hear everything he said," remembers Mullin, who had the room next to his. "Singing, taking a shower, all of it. I went up to him one day and said, 'Charles, I don't know whether you care or not, but this place has thin walls.' He really didn't care."

Barkley wasn't the only Dream Team ambassador; he just handled the majority of the nocturnal and predawn duties. It became part of the journalistic landscape in Barcelona to dutifully report whenever a Dream Teamer showed up at a venue. Most of those stories had an annoying reverential tone to them, as if Zeus had come down from Mount Olympus to purchase an apple at the corner store, but then, that was the tone of most stories about these guys. And NBC never failed to zoom in on any Dream Team members who happened to be spectating, as if their very presence conveyed importance upon the proceedings.

The team had made friends early with the women gymnasts. Bird spotted several of them at the airport during accreditation check-in and invited them onto the bus, and the players gave them USA Basketball trading cards. Later in the competition, after the gymnasts had finished a rotation, they spotted Pippen, Stockton, and Laettner in the stands, reached into their bags, pulled out the cards, and waved them at the players, like the pom-pom girls flirting with the varsity.

Early on, Bird found a side door out of the Ambassador that he used to avoid the crowds. He was and still is a baseball fan, and he took in a couple of U.S. games, once riding the metro—riding it and riding it, in fact, since he missed his stop—to the venue. He exchanged autographs with the players in the dugout. Malone was a fixture at the U.S. women's basketball games and became buddies with U.S. boxer Oscar de la Hoya. Pippen was a mensch. He was everywhere, out of the Jordan shadow, a hero in his own right. Ewing took in a lot of events, too, including women's track and field at the Olympic Stadium, where he screamed like a grade schooler for his Jamaican homegirl, Merlene Ottey, who won a bronze medal in the 200 meters.

Not surprisingly, no one played the role of diplomat better than Magic. He spoke often of his love for the Olympics, how as a thirteen-year-old he'd run home to see if Mark Spitz was going to win another gold medal in Munich, how he'd gotten goose bumps watching the athletes cry on the podium, how he'd hesitated for just a minute about turning professional in 1979 since that meant he would never be an Olympian. Each morning that the Dream Team was not in action Magic would peruse the schedule and pick his events, like a man at the track handicapping his horses— reminiscent, in fact, of the way he planned his assignations: *Okay. I'm going to boxing in the afternoon, then take in a little gymnastics, and finish up at the track.* At every site, cries of "Ma-jeek" would roll through the stands, and each time it happened one had to marvel, again, at the ever-turning cycle of that man's life: presumably dying of AIDS in November, accepting worldwide acclaim in August.

The same cries would erupt before games, when Ma-jeek would be announced last, so happy that he had taken Rosenfeld's suggestion to wear number 15. He wouldn't be the only one cheered, of course, for nary a disparaging sound could be heard during pre-game introductions . . . except, of course, for the smattering of boos directed at the Jester, both the King of Nighttime and the Ugly American.


Years later, Barkley clings to the story that he was elbowed not once but three times by Angolan forward Herlander Coimbra before Barkley elbowed him back in clear view of everyone. This happened on July 26 during the Dream Team's first Olympic game at the Palau Municipal d'Esports.

"I warned him to stop elbowing me, and he didn't listen," Barkley told me during our 2011 dinner. "So I elbowed him back. Sure, it bothered me. But they weren't all innocent in this thing."

I can't verify that Coimbra elbowed Barkley, since game tapes are incomplete—NBC frequently cut away from Dream Team games as the carnage escalated. Karl Malone backs up Barkley. "I mean, you going to give somebody four chances before you do anything?" said Malone years later. "In the States, normally, you get one chance." I'll take the Mailman's word, but it should be noted that he loves Charles.

Jordan sees it differently. "Charles was an idiot in that case," he says, taking the sting off the words with a chuckle. "He said that was his way of intimidating, and I said, 'Charles, they're getting our autographs before the game. You think they need to be intimidated?'"

Whatever Coimbra may or may not have done, everyone watching in the stands or at home that day clearly saw Barkley throw what seemed to be an undeserved elbow as he headed upcourt after scoring a layup. What some forget is that minutes earlier Barkley had shoved an Angolan forward named David Diaz, so evidently Barkley was already in a bad mood.

Justified or not—I'm going with not—the Barkley elbow crystallized, early in the competition, everything that seemed to be wrong about NBA players competing in the Olympics. Angola was a struggling war-torn nation with three gymnasiums in the entire country; the Dream Team represented an imperial power. Coimbra weighed 174 pounds; Barkley was built like a fullback. Coimbra studied economics; Barkley studied flight attendants. Barkley was Coimbra's favorite player, a man he searched for when he got snippets of NBA games back in his hometown, Luanda; Barkley didn't "know nuthin' 'bout Angola." After the game Coimbra said he was astonished that Barkley would "make violence with me"; Charles was unrepentant, saying, "If somebody hits me, I hit 'em back."

The Dream Team, with the exception of Malone, always found that humorous. "It wasn't the elbow that got Charles in trouble," Mullin said years later, "as much as it was trying to explain it."

Then there was the game itself, which ended in a 116–48 U.S. victory. At one point, the Dream Team went on a 46–1 run. Daly had decided weeks earlier that he was never going to call a time-out during the Olympic competition—"What am I going to say that these guys can't figure out themselves?" he reasoned—but at times he felt like he should've called for one just to stanch the opposition's bleeding.

Given the thin public relations line that the Dream Team was walking, the elbow was a big deal. Though his public stance continued to be that Coimbra deserved it, Barkley apologized to his teammates even before Magic, Jordan, and Robinson gave him quiet talking-tos. "We said, 'Charles, what we want to do is destroy these guys, but not destroy the love they have for us,'" Magic told him, as only Magic could.

The biggest reaction came from USOC officials, who, fed up with the Dream Team in the first place, pondered for a short moment if Barkley should be sent home. Wisely, they let him stay. Whenever the USOC sends anyone home, as it did in 1968 after track stars Tommie Smith and John Carlos raised black-gloved fists in Mexico City, the fallout is worse than the offense.

As the years rolled by, *l'affaire* Coimbra folded comfortably into the Barkley narrative, right along with the unfortunate spitting, the fight with the drunk, the verbal insults directed at teammates, and all the rest of it. Anyway, for every one who turned anti-American after the elbow, Barkley probably gathered a hundred to the Dream Team's bosom with his personality, talent, and nocturnal ramblings. Barkley is always at his best when nestled within the comfortable cocoon of a family, cast as the impish delinquent who has to be chastised once in a while. These days on TNT, he is surrounded by Ernie Johnson, Kenny Smith and Shaquille O'Neal, the counterparts to Michael and Magic, the nice big brothers who keep him (somewhat) in line or at least render his transgressions less meaningful.

After the Angola game, Jordan steered the conversation toward the Dream Team's second game, the following night against Croatia, and not purely for diplomatic reasons. "If defense is ever going to be played," he warned, "it will be Monday night." Jordan and sidekick Pippen, see, were about to show the acceptably diplomatic way to terrorize, intimidate, and utterly emasculate an opponent.

# CHAPTER 31

# THE KUKOC GAME

. . . . . . . . . . . . . . . . . . . . . . . . . . . . . . . . . . . . . . . . . . . . . . . . . . .

### "They Were Like Mad Dogs on Toni"

To his fellow Yugoslavs, Drazen Petrovic was Michael/Magic/Larry all wrapped up in one. He was the player who had lifted Yugoslavia to international basketball prominence, like Magic and Larry; he was the most talented and showiest player, like Michael; and he was the most competitive, go-for-the-jugular player, like all three of them. Reggie Miller once paid Petrovic the ultimate Reggie Miller compliment: "Drazen could talk trash in four languages," said Miller, himself a world-class trash-talker.

In the wonderful documentary that NBA Entertainment produced for ESPN, *Once Brothers*, teammate Toni Kukoc says of Petrovic the same thing that was said about Jordan a hundred times: other players got so caught up in watching him perform that it sometimes distracted them from their game. "Drazen was a killer," said Dino Radja, another Yugoslav, who, like Petrovic and Kukoc, played in the NBA. "He was the only man I know who could beat somebody himself."

But the Dream Team's focus in Game 2 against Croatia—the sovereign nation that more or less represented the painfully crippled and "old" Yugoslavia, which could not play since it was on international sanction—was not point guard Petrovic, whom they knew and respected from his three years in the NBA with the Trail Blazers and Nets. It was forward Kukoc, whom they really did not know but reviled anyway.

Well, really, only Pippen and Jordan reviled him, steamed that Kukoc seemed to be the pet of Bulls general manager Jerry Krause, who had used the twenty-ninth pick to select Kukoc in the second round of the 1990 draft and badly wanted him in Chicago. That was one thing. But Krause went so far as to not extend Pippen's contract because he wanted to save money to offer $3.7 million to Kukoc. That was quite another. You must understand this about the NBA: You can insult a player, even insinuate that someone is better than him, and maybe throw in an insult about his mama. But when you mess with a man's wallet, you're asking for serious trouble.

And you must understand this about Jordan: if Jerry Krause said that George Washington was our first president, Jordan would argue that, no, it was actually Trooper Washington, a 6'7" forward who played in the old ABA. Without the addition of Krause into the volatile mix, I'm not sure how far Jordan would've carried the water on this one, for it was clearly Pippen's issue. But Jordan was by this point almost fully invested in Pippen as a worthy teammate—*almost* being the operative word, because they did have their moments.

Pippen had played shakily against the Knicks in the '92 playoffs, prompting Jordan to comment: "I think he [Pippen] is at the point now where maybe he is a little unsure of himself in certain games." In Game 6 of that series, Xavier McDaniel, one of the Knicks' many musclemen, was all over Pippen, taunting him, pushing him around, getting into his head. That went on until Jordan got in McDaniel's face, and that was that. And as far as Pippen had come since his uncertain early years, he still demonstrated from time to time how difficult it was to be a teammate of the greatest player in the world, as when he turned down a TNT interview request in the postseason. "You wanted Michael, not me," he sullenly told the NBA's broadcast partner. That could serve as Pippen's epitaph: *You wanted Michael, not me.*

But they had come together to win another championship—Pippen was almost as good as Jordan in the Finals against Portland—and they were clearly comfortable together in Barcelona. And so Jordan kind of sympathetically reviled Kukoc, or at least the *idea* of Kukoc. Krause had given Jordan game tapes of Kukoc, hoping that he would see the same brilliance; though Jordan would watch scouting tapes of Kukoc, looking for weaknesses to exploit, he had about as much chance of screening Krause's tapes as he did of watching Kurosawa's *Rashomon* in the original Japanese.

In the bus on the way to the arena, Jordan and Magic sat across the aisle from each other, as they usually did, figuring out margins of victory. They called each other M.J., a kind of joint masters-of-the-universe thing.

"M.J.," Jordan said to Magic, "I want to be up 20 by halftime."

"You got it, M.J.," Magic said back. "We'll do it for you and Scottie."

Since Scottie and Michael were doing some reviling, well, that was enough to get everybody else amped up, too. Even artificial challenges were hard to come by in the summer of 1992. The other Dreamers picked up on Pippen and Jordan's adrenaline burn and came after Kukoc the way the Samuel L. Jackson character, Jules, went after his victims in *Pulp Fiction*: "And I will strike down upon thee with great vengeance and furious anger those who would attempt to poison and destroy my brothers!"

Years later, I was surprised to discover how vividly the Dream Team and anyone associated with it remembered what came to be known as "the Kukoc game." Virtually everyone mentioned it before I brought it up.

Ewing: "They dogged Kukoc so bad. That was the best defense I ever saw Michael and Scottie play. By far. And they played a lot of great defense."

Barkley: "Dude, it was scary what they did to Kukoc. And beautiful to watch."

Mullin: "Scottie and Michael were like mad dogs on Toni, almost to the point that they lost sight of the game."

Malone: "You ever see a feeding frenzy? That's what it was like."

NBA international liaison Bohuny: "Scottie kept talking it up in the meal room—how Jerry Krause had screwed him to try to get Toni."

NBA PR man McIntyre: "I distinctly remember Scottie talking about it, and I can still hear him saying, 'I don't want Kukoc taking my money. That's *my* money.'"

Over in the Croatian locker room on that night, the young target was blessedly unaware of the vendetta against him, as well as how personal money matters could get in the NBA. "It was a strange time," Kukoc told me in the spring of 2011. "It was a strange time for all of us, just to be competing for Croatia after all that had happened in my country. We were happy to be there, but we were also sad about the war." That wasn't all—Kukoc's wife, Renata, was about to go into labor, and his son, Marin, would be born days later. "So my mind," says Kukoc, "was on many other things besides the game."

Kukoc doesn't remember much pregame strategy in the Croatian locker room. "It was just kind of 'Do your best against these guys, try to be competitive, try to not let them embarrass you,'" he says. "What would be the use of coming up with a game plan? There was none possible anyway."

Kukoc was a gifted player who with a little more straight-up quickness could've been the second coming of Magic. All right, the Dream Team will strike me down with great vengeance and furious anger for even suggesting that, so forget I said it. But Kukoc was damn good. As an eighteen-year-old in the 1987 Junior World Championships, he had played on a Yugoslavian team that twice beat the United States. In one game he made 11 three-pointers and scored 37 points; it was then that Krause first noticed him.

Still, Kukoc always *looked* a little soft. He was pale and skinny (his playing weight was listed as 192 pounds, which means he was probably 182), with a handsome, sleepy-eyed, boyish face. Petrovic was four years older than Kukoc and, beyond that, far more constitutionally suited to the kind of challenge that would be presented by the hunters in heat named Pippen and Jordan. Kukoc would go on to have a thirteen-year NBA career with four teams, most memorably the Bulls, and finish with averages of 11.6 points, 4.2 rebounds, and 3.7 assists. But on this night he was a distracted twenty-three-year-old lamb being led to slaughter.

At the time, the Celtics were courting one of Croatia's starters, center Stojko Vrankovic, so franchise player Bird and team president Dave Gavitt visited with the big man before the game. Other than that, the night had a kind of Cold War feel to it.

Daly was more than happy that his team was amped up and more than happy to give Pippen the hammer. The day before the game Jordan came to Daly and said, "Scottie and I want to play big minutes." What's the coach going to say, no? Daly started Pippen along with Jordan, Ewing, Barkley, and Magic. Daly never tipped his hand that he favored one starting team over another, but privately he knew that his three most important players were Jordan, Pippen, and Barkley. Barkley was important because he could always score, no matter what the opponent, no matter what the situation. He didn't have to depend at all on the vicissitudes of outside shooting—Charles would simply plow his way to the basket and get in position for an easy score. Jordan and Pippen were key because they could both cover the floor on defense and initiate the offense, either as shooters or as distributors. And there was a subset even within that subset. "Give me Michael and Scottie," Daly would tell his confidants, "and it really doesn't matter who else is out there."

As soon as the game began, Pippen latched on to Kukoc, who still managed to wriggle free early and slip a clever pass to Radja for a basket. That infuriated Pippen and represented the only Kukoc highlight of the night. At the other end, Daly called for a rare isolation play, stationing Pippen at the top of the key with the ball while his other four teammates spread the floor. He managed to draw a foul on Kukoc.

Everyone looked for Pippen to get open; twice Mullin slipped him clever passes for dunks over Kukoc. At times, Pippen face-guarded Kukoc all the way up the floor, like Kukoc was a junior high rival who had stolen Pippen's girlfriend. At times, early on, Kukoc slapped away Pippen's hands, but—ultimately and inevitably—Pippen stole his will. Jordan was all over the place, picking up Kukoc when Pippen overplayed him, clogging the passing lanes, even blocking a Kukoc layup. He had an incredible seven steals in the first half and Pippen had four.

*They just moved Chicago Stadium to Barcelona. That's all they did.*

Even breaks in the action were lively, which was not normally the case. "Time-outs for us were funny more than anything," Magic said years later, "because there was nothing to really talk about. We'd stare at each other and maybe say something about a back screen, and Chuck would stare at us for a while and finally just say, 'Okay, keep doing what you're doing.'" But on this night Jordan and Pippen made sure that everyone stayed in focus. The Bulls duo was so amped up that Barkley played the role of peacemaker, lifting Kukoc up after he had been knocked down and making a palms-down take-it-easy sign to his teammates at one point. Of course, Barkley still managed to collect a technical for talking to the crowd, a no-no in international ball.

Some of the Croatian players would later concede that their goal was to keep the margin at 25, which they failed to do, losing 103–70. Pippen was blunt in his postgame appraisal of Kukoc, who made only two of eleven shots, committed seven turnovers, and in general looked like a Roman spectator who had been mowed over in a chariot race. "Toni Kukoc could be a good player," says Pippen, "but he's in the right league right now."

"I played a terrible game that night," Kukoc tells me now. "Well, let's just say a very bad game."

The most lasting Croatian impression was made by Petrovic, who battled throughout, never intimidated, always going nose-to-nose with whomever was guarding him. He hit two back-to-back fuck-you three-pointers near the end of the first half, one of my enduring memories of that game. Alas, Petrovic would play only one more season in the NBA, the 1992–93 campaign, when he averaged 22.3 points per game for the Nets and seemed to be coming into his own, ready to be the first international player to really make an NBA splash.

On June 7, 1993, Petrovic was asleep in the front passenger seat of a car driven by his girlfriend, Klara Szalantzy, when it crashed into the back of a truck on a rain-drenched section of the autobahn in Bavaria. He was dead at twenty-eight. Some 100,000 of his countrymen attended his funeral in Zagreb. Kukoc was one of the pallbearers. Back home, his Nets coach, who had been with the club for only one season, was one of the mourners. That was Chuck Daly.

Years later, over breakfast, Pippen and I talk about Kukoc, a subject of which he has grown tired over the years, mostly because the Croatian was a central character in Pippen's lowest professional moment. That happened in the 1994 postseason (the one when Jordan was off playing minor-league baseball) when Pippen refused to re-enter a game after coach Phil Jackson had designed a last-second shot for Kukoc, not him.

"I was always cool with Toni," Pippen tells me, but their coexistence was uneasy, owing first to Krause's contract offer and second to the playoff game, which dogged Pippen for the rest of his career. To an extent, it still does. Whenever any athlete refuses to go into a game, Scottie's name is the one that is raised. "Sittin' Like Pippen" was the headline run by one New York newspaper after Yankees catcher Jorge Posada refused to enter a 2011 game because he had been moved down in the batting order during a slump.

"You know how I felt about that," says Pippen. "It was an insult that I wouldn't take the last shot. I regret that it happened, sure, and it was the wrong thing to do. But I always considered that [Jackson's strategy] wrong since I was the franchise player at that time."

Pippen's resistance to Kukoc was not personal—it was professional. What basketball people praised in Kukoc was his versatility, his ability to be a perimeter package of shooting and playmaking even though he was an interior-sized player. That was Pippen's calling card, too, and he deeply resented it when Krause said the Bulls needed another do-everything player.

Kukoc, for his part, looks back on the '92 Games with mixed feelings. "My son was born, we made a good statement for European basketball, and Croatia, my country, got to compete," he said. "All that was good. But then I think back on Drazen, how great he played and how spirited he was in Barcelona and what happened later . . . and I get very sad."

Kukoc also swears that he didn't think anything unusual was going on that night with the Dream Team defense. "I thought that was the way they guarded everybody," he said.

Trust me, I tell him, it wasn't—and it certainly wasn't the way they guarded everyone in the Olympics.

"Well, I'll take that as a compliment, then," he says. "Or at least figure that it helped me when I got into the league. I got the toughest first."

Kukoc eventually made peace with both of his teammates in Chicago, though he has a more enduring friendship with Jordan because they have something to do together. "I became a golf addict, a golf fool, a golf degenerate, whatever you want to call it," he says. "Like Michael." Kukoc even emerged triumphant in the tenth annual Michael Jordan Celebrity Invitational in the spring of 2011. His partner? The tournament host.

Still, there is no record that Jordan ever looked at the tapes of Kukoc.

# CHAPTER 32

# THE COOLEST ROOM IN THE WORLD

· · · · · · · · · · · · · · · · · · · · · · · · · · · · · · · · · · · · · · · · · · · · · · · · · · ·

### "Charles, We're Sorry, but This Is a Ring Table. . . ."

After the win over Croatia and the systematic stripping of Kukoc's manhood, the Dream Team games took on a numbing sameness for players, coaches, fans, and press alike. After each rout, one story nugget of interest might present itself, just enough to write a "game story," although any sort of upset possibility was gone by six or seven minutes into the game. We had assumed that the low-hanging fruit had been dispensed with in Portland and that Barcelona would present a higher competitive plane. It turned out that, for the Dream Team, it was *all* low-hanging fruit.

Germany fell 111–68 on a night when Bird (game-high 19 points) looked like he was young again. Brazil went down 127–83 on a night when Oscar Schmidt finally got to play against his idols, though his stat line revealed an essential truth about true greatness and offensive efficiency—Schmidt scored 24 points on 25 shots, while Barkley ("Ooh, Oscar Schmidt; I'm shaking in my boots") scored 30 on only 14 shots.

Spain was next, making a 122–81 sacrifice on a night when Stockton's healing leg finally allowed him some playing time—he scored 4 points in six minutes. And as the United States entered the medal round, Puerto Rico went down in the quarterfinals, 115–77, on a night when the outside shooting of Mullin (21 points) was the big story.

The team was by then a cliché—a well-oiled machine—turning it off and on at will, handing out points, rebounds, and assists according to some notion of democracy of which they were aware but couldn't really elucidate. "It became kind of like playing your little brother," Drexler told me years later. "You knew you were going to kill him, so it became only a matter of how much pain you wanted to give him."

By the time they would finish, five players would average in double figures (Barkley led with 18 points and shot an absurd 71 percent from the floor) and three others would average 9 points or more. Laettner, predictably, was the only low scorer, with a 4.8 average. Nobody would average more than 5.3 rebounds (both Ewing and Malone), but everybody would get some. The only jaw-dropping number was Pippen's assist total—he had a team-high 47 over eight games, and it's hard to even remember him playing long stretches as a traditional point guard. Jordan had 37 steals and Pippen had 23 in the eight games, but here's another remarkable number: Barkley had 21, demonstrating both his instincts and the extent to which he could play the passing lanes if so inclined.

None of the Dream Teamers ever glanced at a stat sheet—it just wasn't important because the game *felt* right. Besides, it would be gauche, and if someone got caught doing it, well, it would've been all over. Their own stats didn't matter and the opponents' stats didn't matter, so for the Dream Teamers the only way to measure oneself was against a teammate. Years later I would be surprised at how much they said they got from one another.

From Jordan and Pippen, Malone learned about single-minded mental focus. "When those guys honed in on their competitors," said Malone, "you could just forget it. That time they were watching films of Kukoc? You could've walked in front of Michael and Scottie a thousand times and their eyelashes would've never moved."

From Malone, Pippen learned physical preparation. "You'd see Karl's physique during the season, but until you're with him you don't realize that it's not an accident. I started working out with Karl during the Dream Team, and that really pushed me."

From Stockton, Jordan learned the value of synergy. "Karl Malone was a great player," said Jordan, "but he could not play without John Stockton. John was his left hand to Karl's right. That's how important he was. That's how important some teammates can be to others."

From Michael/Magic/Larry, Robinson learned the lessons of leadership. "The Spurs had not been a championship team at the point when I went to Barcelona," Robinson said, "so what I wanted to pick up on was, what do you need to do to be a leader, to lift your team up? And I took that commitment and focus back to San Antonio. Sure, I did the physical and mental work, but those guys made me understand that you have to require the same thing of everyone around you. You have to *demand* excellence from your teammates or you will not win a championship."

And from the entire collective experience, Mullin learned something about himself. "I don't think I realized this until years later," he says now, "but the Dream Team turned out to be a very positive reinforcement about the way I was living my life. To come from where I was [alcohol rehab] to make that team . . . man, that really helped me beyond basketball."

More specifically, Mullin remembers—indeed, treasures—the shooting games he had against Bird. The team rarely held formal practices in Barcelona, but a bus took volunteers to casual workouts. And on one such off-day afternoon, an hourlong game of H-O-R-S-E turned into an unseen masterpiece, something like the morning scrimmage in Monte Carlo.

"Larry and I would play for a hundred dollars a shot," Mullin told me in the summer of 2011. "You shoot, you miss, just normal shots, not this crazy, bounce-the-ball-off-the-wall commercial shit."

(Such a trick shot made by Mullin at the Bristol campus of ESPN when he was working as a playoff commentator has become a You-Tube classic.)

"The stakes get up to about a thousand. I'm up considerably. I couldn't miss. I remember looking over and David Robinson has stopped working out and he's watching us. I don't know, maybe I started letting down. Maybe I started thinking, 'Holy shit, I'm kicking Larry Bird's ass.' But little by little Larry starts coming back, all the time telling me, 'You know, I never lost one of these.' Finally, he gets even and he says, 'Okay, that's it.' He tosses me the ball and just walks away."

Bird had been concerned even before the game began. "I needed to take lots of shots to prepare," he told me in 2012, "and I hadn't been doing that because of my back. When I got back to even, I knew that had to be it."

Mullin is positively beaming as he finishes the story. "You know, before that . . . I mean, I knew I was a good shooter, better than most. But one of the guys I always thought was better than me was Larry. Of course he was better. It was *Larry Bird*. And that day, when I shot even with him, even though I didn't really beat him . . . that day helped my career a lot."

More and more, the center of the team became the family room at the Ambassador, their polestar. "By the time the Olympics were over," said the NBA's Kim Bohuny, "nobody cared what they looked like. Flip-flops, sweatpants, probably a pair of pajamas or two. You wore anything in there."

At the beginning of the Games, Krzyzewski's oldest daughter, Debbie, was overwhelmed the first time she was introduced to Magic, her favorite player. "She just burst into tears," remembers her father. "Strangest thing." But by the end of the Games, Debbie and Magic were simply friends.

The room was located on the second floor of the Ambassador, one flight up from the regular lobby, accessible either by stairs or by elevator. I visited a couple of times, but, as was the case in the Monte Carlo casino, I felt a little hesitant about hanging around, almost like I was rummaging through someone's bedroom. I remember looking in one afternoon and seeing Stockton and his sons horsing around. It figured that Stockton needed to get out of his room—he, his wife, and their three kids were all encamped in there, mattresses spread out on the floor like a slumber party.

The room was designated primarily as a gathering place for players and their families, though NBA and USA Basketball people were all over the place. The two "outsiders" who had carte blanche were Jordan's guys, Ahmad Rashad and Spike Lee. Payne Stewart wandered in from time to time in between his high-stakes golf games with Jordan. So did Will Smith, a guest of NBC, whose executives were staying at a nearby hotel.

As was the case with the casino in the Loews Monte Carlo, the family room had a peanut gallery aspect to it: if an interloper somehow managed to elude security and gain entrance to the hotel, he could stare into the room, since the side facing the lobby was all windows and the door was frequently open.

By day, the family room was abuzz with the noise of beeping video games, the crack of pool balls, the rhythmic *plonk . . . plonk . . . plonk* of a ping-pong match, and the sound of a music video coming from a TV, usually Cypress Hill, since the selection of videotapes was small. The room functioned as a kind of drop-off center, where athletes and wives left their kids so they could attend other Olympic events. To this day Larry and Dinah Bird and Clyde and Gaynell Drexler greet Bohuny warmly as "our babysitter."

Don Sperling, then the head of NBA Entertainment, remembers scooping up Jeffrey Michael Jordan seconds before the young boy would have tumbled down the elegant marble stairs into the lobby. Jordan gave him a grateful nod. Not so lucky were the pool balls thrown by Bird's son, Connor, which from time to time clattered lobbyward.

C. M. Newton remembers with fondness the afternoon that his late wife, Evelyn, sat down to play a video game in an effort to improve her skills so she could play with her grandchildren. Her partner was Patrick Ewing's young nephew, Michael, and they were playing against Patrick Ewing Jr. and someone else. Mrs. Newton eventually blew the game, and she turned to apologize to Michael.

"I'm so sorry," she said. "Next time you'll have to get another partner."

To which Michael replied: "That's all right, Mrs. Newton. We'll get those motherfuckers next time."

Says C.M. today: "That was one of her fondest memories. She really felt like one of the boys."

In the early evening, after golf, it might be ping-pong time, which meant Jordan time, which meant life was miserable for everyone if the man lost. Any number of people (including me) can relate horror stories of playing ping-pong against Jordan, who was very good but not great, beatable on paper but generally not in reality since he wore almost everyone down with his relentless aggression and psych game. At one point Steve Mills was playing him even until Jordan put down his racket, stared him in the eye, and announced, "I will *not* let you go home and tell your friends you beat me." From that point on, his lacerating competitiveness simply rolled over Mills.

One major exception was Laettner, an outstanding player who repeatedly beat Jordan, at one point prompting the world's most famous athlete to throw his paddle in disgust and storm out of the room. Later, one of Jordan's buddies was tasked with finding a ping-pong table in Barcelona so Jordan could set it up in his room and practice, but it never came to pass.

(The identity of Laettner's biggest rival, though, might be a surprise. "I could usually beat him," remembers Laettner, "but Commissioner Stern was my toughest opponent by far.")

I was glad Laettner had his table-tennis moments because the Olympic experience, while a pure joy for the Dream Teamers who had come from the NBA, was a mixed bag for Laettner. No matter what he said then or says now, he felt like a tag-along. Barkley, Bird,

Mullin, and Drexler went out of their way to befriend him, but Laettner was no fool—he knew he only half belonged.

Not his mother, though. Bonnie Laettner positively plunged into the Olympic experience, trading pins and cheerleading like mad at the arena. She developed a close relationship with Drexler's wife and at one point almost got involved in fisticuffs at a game to protect Gaynell's seat when she left to change a diaper.

It was after midnight when the family room achieved legendary status. Not everyone was a part of it. David Robinson, for example, floated blessedly above the fray, sometimes literally so, as when he and Branford Marsalis traded sax licks on the roof of the Ambassador. But most of the Dream Team was in there at one time or another, the hours moving steadily to dawn, the card game in full swing, the beer bottles and the glasses of vodka and lime (purchased at the nearby corner bar) starting to stack up, along with the empty pizza boxes, snuffed-out Jordan stogies, and, most of all, one-upmanship rhetoric.

There were moments of high comedy, as when one Dream Team member burst into the room and demanded, "Who's got a rubber? I need one quick." (That demonstrated, more than anything, that the NBA had officially joined the post-Magic HIV awareness era.) And Drexler's ears are still ringing from the abuse he took in the room for mistakenly bringing two left sneakers to practice one day. ("I was dressing in the dark that morning," he told me years later.) Clyde actually tried to get away with wearing them until Barkley stopped practice and exclaimed, "Wait a minute, Clyde's got two damn left sneakers on."

The room regulars were Jordan, Magic, Barkley, Pippen, and Ewing. They *owned* it, the first three in particular, of course, owing both to their personalities and to their status within the game. But Pippen and Ewing were full-fledged members as well. Pippen's inclusion in the charmed circle was easy to understand. He was good company, he had proven himself to be Robin to Michael's Batman, and he was now a champion. At first glance, Ewing might not seem to belong, but there was never a question that he was one of the main guys. That rarely came across to outsiders. Ewing's agent, David Falk, was always trying to convince me that Patrick was an engaging personality whose name sold a lot of shoes, but I never bought it. Ewing was never exactly rude, but to outsiders he was more or less dismissive, his postgame comments blander than broth. Whenever I wanted a one-on-one interview with him at practice, for example, I always had to do it as he got a post-practice rubdown from the athletic trainer, his version of multitasking.

"This doesn't work when there's somebody else around, Patrick," I used to complain.

"Works for me," he said. "I'm not going to change any answers because somebody else is around."

"That's because you never say anything," I'd remind him.

*Take it or leave it* was his position. Yet I, like many others, genuinely liked Ewing because, at the very least, he was consistent in his dismissiveness.

I was secretly happy years later, though, when Ewing told me, "The only thing I'd change about my career is that maybe I should've been a little more accessible to the media." He also admitted that he regretted the four-team deal that sent him to Seattle late in his career, one that came about largely because he wanted out of Gotham. "After hearing rumblings for fifteen years that the team was 'better without Ewing,' I just got tired of it," Ewing told me. "I reached my breaking point." He tacked on a forgettable free-agent year in Orlando that ended his career in 2001–2, but his legacy remains as a New York warrior who couldn't quite get his team to the finish line. I do believe that, even for those who didn't appreciate his game, he was a respected player.

On non-game nights, the cards in the Coolest Room in the World came out around ten. Tonk fit their style—a form of knock rummy, it's played at a high rate of speed, concentration helpful but not essential, so part of the brain could be devoted to insults.

The go-to insult for both Jordan and Magic was championships, as in who had won some and who hadn't. Malone and Stockton got a pass—they weren't particularly close to either player and woofing on those who are not return woofers is kind of like drowning puppies, even for those guys. Now, had Jordan known then what would transpire later—Finals victories over their Jazz teams in 1997 and 1998—perhaps he wouldn't have been so kind.

Ewing was a favorite target of Jordan's, owing to their long friendship. Years later, Ewing would tell me, half amused and half angry, that Jordan was relentless. "Michael never let me forget that I couldn't beat him," Ewing says, shaking his head. "Michael never let me forget *anything*. Michael has been talking trash from the first day I met him at age seventeen, and he's never stopped. Hell, yeah, it bothers me that I never beat him. And I gotta hear it from him every day I see him. 'You didn't beat me in college, and you didn't beat me in the NBA. You're out of chances, Patrick.' That's the kind of shit I gotta hear from him until my dying days." (Ewing couldn't even bring up the 1994 Eastern semis, when his Knicks finally beat the Bulls—Jordan was off playing baseball.)

Drexler, whose Finals frustration was freshest, got drawn in once in a while, and he would try to go back at them, particularly Magic.

"I used to tell them, 'Let me play on your team and you play on mine,'" Drexler told me. "'Let me play with Cap [Abdul-Jabbar], Worthy, Byron Scott, and A. C. Green, and you play with my team, and let's see how many rings you'd have.' Or, 'Let me have Scottie. See how I do then.' That would shut them up real quick." (Drexler deserves his say, but it should be noted there is little anecdotal evidence that either Magic or Jordan shut up "real quick.")

Jordan and Magic were particularly ruthless toward Barkley, who might sit down to join them only to hear, "Sorry, Charles, this is a ring table." Magic would say something similar to Barkley or Ewing when he and Bird shot around together. "This is a ring basket" was Magic's comment. Now, Jordan and Barkley were tight. A well-honed dialogue passed between them from time to time in Barcelona. Jordan would say, "Hey, Charles, who's the best two-guard in the world?" and Barkley would answer, "That would be Michael Jordan." Then Barkley would ask, "And who's the best power forward in the world?" and Jordan would answer, "That would be Charles Wade Barkley." It was their own little poke at Drexler and Malone.

And Barkley could go at Jordan, one of his favorite topics being what he considered to be Jordan's fraudulent sex appeal. "Man, you are so damn black," Barkley would tell him. "And you ain't the best-looking guy in the world either. Any guy has $500 million looks good. If you were a fuckin' plumber, you couldn't get a date." Jordan would laugh because what else could you do? Only Barkley would choose to make a fellow African American's skin color an issue.

But there was *another* circle, the supercircle above friendship that excluded Barkley, one in which only Michael, Magic, and Larry were members, the ones who had won nine straight MVP awards (three each) from 1984 through 1992. Even Pippen, who had won the same number of championships as Jordan, was not allowed. Back in San Diego, Jordan and Magic had been asked to appear on a *Newsweek* Dream Team cover. "Not without Larry," they said, and so Bird was included in the portrait, too. ("I'm still signing those covers today," Magic says.) Michael/Magic/Larry was special. They could say anything to anybody.

Bird wasn't much of a card player and tended not to be the first one into the conversation. He would watch where it was going for a while—"Kind of like the father figure," Mullin said, "just waiting around until someone said, 'What do you think, Dad?'"—then jump in with both feet, an enthusiastic needler and debater when the subject interested him. He and Ewing, Harry and Larry—"the Odd Couple," as Magic called them—would always share a beer or two or three or four. "Or twelve or thirteen," Jordan added.

In Jackie MacMullan's *When the Game Was Ours*, the author recounts a long, late-night dialectic among the principals when they debated both which team was the best ever and who was the best one-on-one player.

"Obviously one of our Laker teams," said Magic in response to the first question. "We won five championships. More than all of you."

Jordan had won two and had something to say about it. "You haven't seen the best NBA team of all time yet," Jordan said. "I'm just getting started. I'm going to win more championships than all of you guys."

Ewing and Barkley tried to join in, the former offering up Bill Russell's Celtics as the best of all time and Barkley offering up himself. "Michael, I'm going to steal at least one of them from you," said Barkley who by then had gotten his wish and been traded out of Philadelphia.

It is fascinating to hold up that conversation in the light of the history that unfolded over the next few seasons. Barkley would get the chance to steal one of them from Jordan the very next season, but, like so many others, he would fall short. And Jordan would prove correct in his assessment—he would go on to win six titles, one more than Magic, three more than Bird.

Bird was never a chest-beater in the same way that Magic and Jordan were, but he had a cold heart when it came to winning. On this night he was feeling no pain. Others who were there remember Bird reclining on the floor—his back made it tough for him to sit—with empties all around him.

"You ain't won nuthin', Charles," Bird said to Barkley after Charles made his I'm-going-to-steal-one-from-you claim. As Mac-Mullan writes, Barkley, chastened, slumped away.

At another point in the conversation, the principals started musing about what ultimate victory in Barcelona (now all but guaranteed) would mean.

"If I get this, then I'll have two gold medals, two championships, and one NCAA championship," said Jordan.

And Magic said, "Yeah, and I'll have an NCAA title, five championships, and one gold medal."

And Ewing said, "I'll have two gold medals and an NCAA championship, and when I get my NBA title I'll be right there with you."

Jordan would have none of that. "Until you learn to pass out of a double-team, Patrick," His Airness said, "you won't have to worry about that NBA ring."

It was classic Jordan, moving the needle beyond the gentle-jab point because Ewing's weakness was indeed that part of his game.

Jordan was always more respectful of Bird than he was of Magic, probably because Bird had always been so respectful of him. The Greatest Game Nobody Ever Saw in Monte Carlo affords a snapshot of that, Jordan and Magic going tonsil-to-tonsil while Michael remembered Bird's lone basket of the game as absolutely crucial to victory, which it was not. Jordan's affinity for Bird dated back to the 1986 postseason, when the second-year Bull laid 49 and 63 points on the Celtics in Boston Garden, although the Celtics won both games. "He is the most exciting, awesome player in the game today," Bird said then, sounding very un-Bird-like. "I think it's just God disguised as Michael Jordan."

The interplay between Magic and Michael had more bite to it. A couple of variations of it played out in Barcelona. Magic was not ready to give up his treasured spot at the top of the NBA hierarchy. And while Jordan was amenable to, even grateful for, ceding the outward leadership to Magic—at the Tournament of the Americas he had proclaimed the Dream Team to be "Magic's Team"—he wanted it confirmed, at least within the tight architecture of the team, that *he* was the Man.

Which, to confirm a point that has been made before, he was. "Michael was the leader," Ewing said years later. "Yeah, Magic said all the things that Magic says. But Michael is Michael. We knew who the real leader was."

Jordan kidded Johnson about not bringing his whole family out to L.A. to watch the Bulls beat them "out of respect for you." Johnson countered by bringing it to Jordan's attention that he felt sorry for Jordan since he would never have a rival like Bird. "We went two weeks without sleep knowing, if we made one mistake, the other guy was going to take it and use it to beat us," MacMullan quotes Johnson in her book. "Who do you measure yourself against?"

Jordan had no answer for that one. He was indeed sui generis, which worked for him and against him. But he would not give in when Magic pressed the one-on-one argument.

"You've got no chance on this one," Jordan said. "Larry, you don't have the speed to stay with me. Magic, I can guard you, but you could never guard me. Neither one of you guys can play defense the way I can. And neither one of you can score like me."

Jordan went on and on, piling up points because he was right and everyone knew it. Everyone except Magic. As MacMullan writes: "'There were plenty of years when I knew in my heart I was the best guy in the room,' Bird said. 'That night I knew in my heart it wasn't me anymore. And it wasn't Magic either.'"

Years later, I am astounded at the degree to which that ongoing dialectic stuck with Jordan. Maybe I shouldn't be, since we saw Jordan's astonishingly long memory at work in his Hall of Fame induction speech, when he seemingly conjured up every slight that had ever come his way during his gilded career. But it bothered him that Magic would not recognize what he saw as plain truth. And he had an interesting riff on the Magic-Bird relationship.

"See, Magic really thought that it was his and Bird's team, that the whole moment belonged to them," Jordan told me in 2011. "Bird didn't see it that way, and you know what? I learned as much about their relationship on that trip as anything else.

"Bird went along with that whole we-go-back-to-'79 relationship, but he was never into it the way that Magic was. He just kind of pulled Bird into it. Even today, sitting and talking with Larry, he knows that he will always be remembered for it, but it's not necessarily something he wants to promote." (We can assume that Jordan would not have been first in line for tickets to the production of *Magic/Bird*, which at this writing was scheduled to hit Broadway in 2012.)

"And the one time Larry stood up to Magic was in that room. He said: 'Let's just ride off into the sunset, Magic, we've had our time.' He was able to say, 'Okay, you and Pippen are better than we were, offensively and defensively.' He gave out those rewards, whereas Magic would challenge them."

Jordan acknowledged that it was Magic's competitive nature at work, which he understands. But it still nags at him that in the summer of 1992—with Magic a few days from his thirty-third birthday, suffering from a virus that most of the world thought would turn fatal, and having been swept up like everyone else in the one-man tornado that was Jordan—Magic still believed he was the better player and would not surrender an inch.

But I wonder, too, if in some small way Jordan, who had conquered so many worlds, was indeed resentful, or at least envious, of the relationship that Magic and Bird did have, that whole "we-go-back-to-'79" bit, as Jordan put it. The one thing Jordan never had was a doppelganger, a friendly rival to measure against himself, a combatant with a shared history, "the only NBA super-duper star without a relative equal driving him to remain on top," as Bill Simmons put it in *The Book of Basketball*. Jordan did have a beloved companion, one who shared his hopes and his dreams and even his DNA. But that man left far too soon.

# THE CHOSEN ONE

. . . . . . . . . . . . . . . . . . . . . . . . . . . . . . . . . . . . . . . . . . . .

## "I Know My Father Was Up There Watching Me"

*Charlotte, North Carolina*

I'm perusing a magazine story about the human time bomb named Charlie Sheen when Michael Jordan enters the conference room at the Charlotte Bobcats offices.

"I'm reading about your boy," I say to Jordan, who's wearing a Bobcat-blue Nike shirt. He and Sheen did Hanes commercials together what must now seem like a thousand years ago.

"Charlie's not *my* boy," says Jordan. "I haven't talked to him in a long time. Man, I don't know what's going on there."

I wonder how easy it would've been for Jordan to do a Sheen. He was one of the most famous people in the world for a while, if not *the* most famous. Everywhere he went, people offered themselves up like human sacrifices, clutched at him, jostled him for just a moment of his time. It's not much different now. Plus his personality seemed prime for addiction—the thirst for competition, the gambling, the desire to always come out on top and crush the opposition.

Yet for the most part Jordan seemed to keep his rampaging impulses reasonably in check. He's enjoyed the company of Lord knows how many women and his marriage broke apart because of it, yet, aside from several small incidents—there he is grinding away with a couple of young things in Cabo, a huge phallic cigar protruding from his mouth—in recent years he has stayed away from being a tabloid headline, kept the greatest part of himself in isolation. (At this writing, Jordan is planning to marry Yvette Prieto, a Cuban-born model.)

There is Magic, here, there, everywhere, one arm around Janet Jackson, the other around a nameless CEO from Asia, closing deals, chasing franchises, spreading the Gospel of Johnson. And Jordan is . . . somewhere. A golf course? Hiding in the Bobcats offices? Cabo?

Over the years David Falk, no longer Jordan's agent but still a confidant, would say to him: "Let's do a movie, something fun, *Lethal Weapon 17* or a James Bond type of thing. You're well dressed, gadgets and stuff, play some kind of cool character. *Space Jam* did $400 million worldwide at the box office. Four hundred million in 1996! You could stay visible for the rest of your life." But always Michael says no. No, no, no. No to almost everything. He claims that, more and more, as he gets comfortable running the Bobcats, he even says no to alluring golf invitations.

"I'm more of a mystique person, and Magic is more of a show-man," says Jordan on that afternoon in Charlotte. (I didn't even bring up Magic; Jordan did it himself.) "Magic is out there, 'I own this, I got this. I got real estate.' To me, if you have to say all those things, you feel like you haven't gotten the respect and it worries you. He's a master at maximizing his Magic Johnson name. I wanted to *control* my name.

"Look, my most valuable asset is my time. I could make a lot of money and have my name out there, but that doesn't drive me the way it drives Magic. The fact that I've only given exactly what I've wanted to, as opposed to giving everybody everything, is one of the reasons I've been able to sustain popularity."

There are many metrics through which to judge that popularity, none better than the Google Alerts I had set up to keep tabs on these guys. Rarely did a day go by when a Dream Teamer was not mentioned, in some context, once or twice. Magic, Bird, and Barkley came in somewhere around four to six items daily because of, respectively, business deals, running the Indiana Pacers, and exercising his vocal cords on TNT and wherever anyone else was holding a mic.

Jordan's daily count was more like forty items, relatively little of it having to do with his stewardship of the Bobcats. Unless you check these almost every day, as I have been doing for the purposes of research, you simply wouldn't believe how often "Michael Jordan" is mentioned in police reports from all over the country, either because a piece of Jordan apparel has been stolen or because a suspect is wearing Air Jordans. In any given week, there are more stories about Jordan footwear than there are about most of the Dream Teamers. For three weeks in the summer of 2011, Scottie Pippen's Google Alerts went way up. Why? Because that's when Pippen hinted that LeBron James was as good a player as Jordan; essentially Pippen's hits were about Jordan.

"Michael Jordan plays basketball better," author Scott Turow once wrote, "than anyone else in the world does anything else." I don't know whether that's true, but Jordan is indeed a frame of reference unto himself. Someone wrote recently—and wrongly—that Miles Davis "was the Michael Jordan of his time," when, in fact, Jordan was the Miles Davis of his time. But a quick roundup from various newspapers and magazines over a four-month period reveals Jordan's primacy as a cultural touchstone.

Patricia Zhou from the Royal Ballet of London will be the Michael Jordan of ballet. Jordan's own guy at Nike, Tinker Hatfield, is the Michael Jordan of shoe design. Itzhak Perlman is the Michael Jordan of the violin. A character on ABC's *Happy Endings* (author's obligatory note: never saw it) is the Michael Jordan of ruining relationships. Joey Chestnut is the Michael Jordan of eating hog dogs. The Large Hadron Collider is the Michael Jordan of particle accelerators. Ira Pressman is the Michael Jordan of Ponzi schemers. Yelena Isinbayeva is the Michael Jordan of women's pole vaulting. Dr. Drew Pinsky is the Michael Jordan of televised addiction treatment. The HTC ThunderBolt 4G is the Michael Jordan of mobile phones. Kelly Slater is the Michael Jordan of surfing; keeping it in the water, Dallas Friday is the Michael Jordan of wakeboarding. Human resources guru Bill Taylor is the Michael Jordan of hiring. Donnie Burns is the Michael Jordan of professional ballroom dancing. BroLoaf is the Michael Jordan of hardcore; keeping it hardcore, Anderson Silva is the Michael Jordan of mixed martial arts. Lionel Messi is the Michael Jordan of soccer. Bill Clinton and Joe Biden are the Michael Jordan of schmoozers. Cesar Millan is the Michael Jordan of dog whisperers and Buck Brannaman is the Michael Jordan of horse whisperers. Doyle Brunson is the Michael Jordan of poker. Jan-Ove Waldner is the Michael Jordan of table tennis (though there is little doubt Jordan thinks he could beat him).

Trust me, that's not the end. There are thousands and thousands of Michael Jordan Google Alerts left in my email, and I'm just not going to get to them. I am the Michael Jordan of Not Getting to Google Alerts About Michael Jordan.

Oh yes: Yale's Susan Gibbons is the Michael Jordan of librarians. That's my favorite.

Jordan and I talked about a lot of things—the old Bulls, the Dream Team selection, Magic and Larry—and some of his comments have been peppered through this manuscript. The conversation edges toward the events surrounding his first retirement in 1993, a year after the Dream Team phenomenon. I had never had a protracted discussion with Jordan about the gambling revelations. He went away from the game and joined up with the Birmingham Barons, got into an epic dispute with *Sports Illustrated* over a cover line that read "Bag It, Michael," suggesting that he was disgracing baseball with his minor-league career, and I left the NBA beat for a while. I wrote neither the inside story nor the cover line that Jordan hated, and Jordan wasn't mad at me. But he was furious with *SI*, to which he never gave—and never will give, he says—another interview, his legendary intransigence and competitiveness in full locomotion.

"I never had to meet with the league about gambling because I never did anything illegal outside of gamble when I golfed," Jordan says, bringing up the topic himself. "But David Stern never corrected the record. It was never addressed. I felt like I had given my heart to the game of basketball and it helped the NBA's business. But they let all the articles come out, all the speculation continues."

I felt that Jordan was putting it too strongly and told him so. "I thought the commissioner did try," I said. "At least when I asked him about it, he just about took my head off and—"

Jordan interrupts me. "You know that David Stern's voice commands respect. David Stern says, 'Don't even go there,' and nobody goes there. But we *did* go there. He allowed it to fester, and all those ideas came out that were totally bogus. They allowed all this peripheral stuff to happen. They knew I never had a connection with any kind of crazy thing. They knew there was no Mafia hit on my father. Yet they never defended me." (Stern, obviously, does not agree with Jordan's opinion.)

Jordan continues: "So that was a big part of why I said to myself, 'I'm tired of this game.' And then my father died and that made it worse and I knew I had to get away.

"And you know what? I'm *glad* I got away. I wouldn't have traded those nights in minor-league baseball for all the world, all my championshlps. People thought it was failure. Well, I thought it was the winningest thing I ever did."

Ever so carefully, I ask him about James Jordan. "I can't imagine what you went through," I say. "A brutal death. You were close. We later found out the autopsy was botched. And some people thought your gambling might have something to do with his death. You must've felt . . . violated. I always wondered if you think you've dealt with it or if you ever felt you needed help."

"I dealt with it and I don't need help," he snaps. "In my own way I dealt with it. These guys, they had my father's championship rings that I had given him, a lot of other personal stuff, a watch inscribed with 'Love from Michael and Juanita.' When they found out who they had killed, they videotaped the whole scene. The police tracked them because one of those idiots was showing the tape to his friends."

"That's what I mean," I say. "That is incredibly hard. You know that one of the suspects was wearing—"

"I know," Jordan interrupts. "He was wearing a Michael Jordan T-shirt when he was arrested." He's silent for a moment.

"So, how *did* you handle this whole thing?" I ask.

Jordan's answer is emphatic.

"It was baseball," he said. "The Barons. There were a lot of lonely nights out there, just me and George [Koehler, who has been his driver and loyal companion from his first day in Chicago in 1984] on the road, talking. And I'd think about my father, and how he loved baseball and how we always talked about it. And I knew he was up there watching me, and that made him happy and that made me happy, too."

At that, he stood and we shook hands and he left the room, the best basketball player ever (I'll argue anyone who says otherwise), still an icon, the reference for a librarian from Yale and a violinist from Tel Aviv, the once and future king, the Chosen One, but sometimes just a kid who lost his father and his best friend way too soon.

# CHAPTER 33

# THE TIE-DYED DARLINGS

. . . . . . . . . . . . . . . . . . . . . . . . . . . . . . . . . . . . . . . . . . .

## Sabonis Wins Bronze, Then Sleeps It Off

There was one other hugely popular men's basketball team in Barcelona—Lithuania. It was one of three countries that had come to the Games under trying political circumstances but was clearly the only one that engendered almost universal sympathy. Croatia was torn apart by a horrible civil war, but the roots of that conflict tested the understanding of most on the outside. Similarly, few could get a handle on what exactly the Russian entry was. Officially called the Commonwealth of Independent States (CIS), it had been hastily patched together in 1991 by leaders from the Russian Federation, Ukraine, and the Republic of Belarus. It came to be known as the Unified Team, but to many—especially the Lithuanians—it represented the old, repressive Soviet Union.

Lithuania's struggle and ultimate independence from the Soviets, by contrast, was something we could all throw our arms around. Plus Lithuania had something else going for it: marketing, baby, marketing. Yes, the shirt bearing the likeness of all the Dream Team members, the one the tourist was wearing when Stockton met her on Las Ramblas, the one that swelled the bottom line of Magic Johnson tees, was only the *second*-best-selling shirt at the Barcelona Olympics.

The Lithuanian tie-dyed T-shirt, a stoned-out psychedelic masterpiece splashed with the nation's official colors of green, red, and yellow and anchored by the Grateful Dead's skeleton symbol, was the one to have. (Mine, now threadbare, still rests in the bottom drawer of my dresser, probably my most prized sports memento. The competition is not strong.) Whenever I glance at it, I don't think of the Dream Team–Lithuania semifinal game, which ended in the predictable rout. I remember the remarkable story behind the genesis of the T-shirt, the competitive spirit of the great Sarunas Marciulionis, and the legendary talents of the bloated giant Arvydas Sabonis, who, owing to an engagement with Comrade Vodka, could not quite roust himself for the medal ceremony.

Lithuania had declared its independence from the Soviet Union on March 11, 1990, but massive inflation and unemployment plagued the new nation, which was in fact divided from within, a conflict manifested in a schism between the chairman of the Parliament and the prime minister. In January 1991, Soviet military units made their presence felt in Vilnius, the capital of Lithuania, allegedly to quell internal dissent but mostly to reestablish its hold on this small runaway republic.

To patriots such as Marciulionis, who early in his career was obligated by the conditions of his "release" from the Soviet Union to give about half of his Golden State Warriors salary to various Russian agencies, the reasons didn't matter. A free and independent Lithuania, without a Soviet military presence, was all that mattered. Lithuanians took to the streets, some of them brandishing primitive weapons such as pitchforks and ax handles. Inevitably, armed conflict erupted, Soviet tanks rumbled through the streets, and soldiers killed thirteen Lithuanians on January 13, 1991, a day that the Lithuanians refer to as "Bloody Sunday."

Strong anti-Soviet reaction from the West helped force a treaty—remember that Mikhail Gorbachev, a relative peacenik, was the head of the Soviet state, which was itself crumbling. Marciulionis, by then a solid NBA player with the Golden State Warriors, was one of the new nation's best-known figures, and he convinced the government that it should organize a team that would attempt to qualify for the Olympics.

His suggestion was met favorably. The problem was, the country was bankrupt.

Marciulionis had already tapped his good friend Donnie Nelson, a Warriors scout, to be an assistant coach, and, as the 1991–92 season got under way, coach and player also began the arduous task of fund-raising in the Bay Area. Marciulionis would handle some of the funding from his $1.28 million Warriors contract but more was needed. "We'd go to great lengths to make speeches at a hundred dollars a whack," remembers Nelson. "We talked to season-ticket holders and told them about Lithuania. We'd call *anybody.* 'Hey, what if Sarunas and I showed up at your Key Club? You got any money?'"

Eventually they got a call from a representative of the Grateful Dead, whose members had been inspired by Lithuania's struggle for independence. Nelson and Marciulionis showed up at the address they were given in San Francisco, which was a small, nondescript garage. "I thought we were the victim of a practical joke until we opened the door and there was a state-of-the-art recording studio," says Nelson.

"I still remember the Dead were trying out Beatles covers, doing stuff like 'Here Comes the Sun' and 'Hey Jude,'" Nelson recalls. "But they were just kind of working through things and sounding kind of nasally and, well, maybe there was a little pot going on. So Sarunas pulls me aside and says, 'Donnie, no way these guys are famous. They're terrible.'" (Marciulionis grew to like them a little more, but he was speaking as a musician; on a memorable evening, sitting on a dock on the Black Sea in the summer of 1988, I had listened to Marciulionis knock out Lithuanian folk songs on his guitar. He wasn't half bad.)

Nelson treasures the memory of that first meeting. "Can you imagine that today?" he says. "In the Internet age? Sarunas in the pot garage with the Dead? He would've failed every drug test in the NBA handbook."

Eventually Jerry Garcia sat down with them and said to Marciulionis, "Man, you're all about freedom and liberty and that's what we're about and we really dig you guys and we're going to support you." If that sounds like a caricature of Jerry, well, that's how Nelson remembers it.

The Dead wrote Marciulionis a check for $5,000, but, most important, gave Lithuania the rights to a T-shirt that had been made for a concert in Boston. Sales of the Dead/Lithuania T-shirt in Barcelona all but financed Lithuania's sojourn to the Atlanta Olympics in 1996, where they won the bronze, the same finish as in 1992. And as much as anything, that T-shirt turned the Lithuanians into folk heroes and their heroic struggle for independence into mainstream sports fodder. At "Lithuania Day" at a Warriors game, Dead guitarist Bob Weir was in the locker room before the game, learning the chords to the Lithuanian national anthem from Marciulionis.

Consider this: the United States had raised millions of dollars to send million-dollar pros to Barcelona, where one room at the Ambassador cost almost a grand a night. Lithuania sent a team that had to raise its own money, the equivalent of Little Leaguers selling magazines door-to-door.

I'm not passing judgment. I'm just saying.


On the day that the United States played Lithuania in the semifinals, Jordan was so concerned about the challenge ahead that he played thirty-six holes of golf. The team bus was idling in front of the Ambassador, Daly muttering a few "Omigods," before Jordan finally showed up, having instructed his wife, Juanita, to retrieve his basketball shoes from their suite.

Going into the Olympics, remember, Lithuania was Daly's principal worry. He knew that four of the five Lithuanian starters had been on the Soviet team that beat David Robinson and the United States in 1988 in Seoul. He respected the hard-bodied, tough-minded Marciulionis. And he worried about the mysterious giant Sabonis, who at his best was a better center than either Robinson or Ewing. Of course, Sabonis's best had been a decade earlier.

Not long ago, as we sat by the tennis courts at a country club near Marciulionis's home in southern California, I asked Sarunas what had been going on in the Lithuanian locker room before the semifinal.

"We were not thinking about winning the game, if that is what you mean," he answered.

"But was there any talk of going zone or making the U.S. shoot from the perimeter?" I asked him. "Donnie told me that you wanted to keep them out of the paint and—"

Marciulionis began waving his hands to stop me. "It did not make a difference," he said. "It did not matter what Donnie said, and I do not even remember what that was. We just wanted to—how do you say it?—not lose face."

Jordan, meanwhile, may have made Daly uneasy, but he understood the challenge. "I got Sarunas," he told the coach. "Don't worry about it."

Jordan hit an early jumper and Magic hit a three-pointer. Jordan made a layup off a steal, then he scored on a stutter-stop jump shot, and it was over by the time the United States built a 31–8 lead and Lithuanian forward Arturas Karnisovas had instructed a team manager to take a photo of him guarding Barkley, his favorite Dream Teamer. The final score was 127–76. Nine of twelve U.S. players scored in double figures, led by Jordan's 21—who knows how well he would've played if he'd gone only eighteen holes—and, in a statistical anomaly, Bird, Drexler, Malone, and Mullin all finished with 10 points. In retrospect, it might've been the Dream Team's most devastating performance.

A couple of things from that game resonate with me. At one point a loose ball happened to hit an official, keeping it inbounds and enabling Lithuania to retain possession. Less than a minute later Bird grabbed a rebound with his left hand, glanced at that same official, who was standing nearby, and bounced the ball off him, scooping it up a split second later. In that brief span of time between when he grabbed the ball and saw the official, Bird's basketball mind took a snapshot, developed it, and determined that he could have a little fun without giving up the advantage. He used to talk about how he was able to freeze the action, get time itself to almost slow down, so he could make a split-second decision.

The other one involved Jordan. For about a six-minute stretch he simply decided that Marciulionis wasn't going to do anything. He guarded him so zealously that on most possessions this most determined and resilient of players couldn't even get the ball. "I remember that," Marciulionis told me when I brought it up. "It just changed everything for us. My teammates were used to me controlling the ball, and now I couldn't get it, and now somebody else had to make decisions. We were lost, all because of Michael." Jordan remembered it, too. "Sarunas was so strong with the ball that the best thing to do was not let him get it," said Jordan. "You can't do that for the whole game, but you can do it for a while." Jordan was so into the idea that Marciulionis was going to be contained that after the Lithuanian scored a basket right before halftime, Jordan, who was on the bench, reamed out the defender, Drexler.

Jordan's defense on that night was one of Daly's favorite Olympic memories, too. On more than one occasion—it could've been fifteen years later—I'd say to him, "Chuck, how about the night you put Michael on Marciulionis and—"

"Michael didn't let him get the ball," Daly would say, finishing my sentence. "He wouldn't even let him *get the damn ball*."

Lithuania's defining moments of the Games took place two nights later against the Unified Team, the bronze medal at stake. The game got lost in the hubbub of the Dream Team–Croatia gold medal game, which was played several hours later, but it was absolutely one of the most significant political games in the history of the Olympics.

"I never felt any pressure like that in my entire life," remembers Donnie Nelson. "To the Lithuanians and anyone associated with them, even an outsider like me, the Unified Team represented the Soviet Union. We were playing the country that had killed our citizens and ruled over them for decades. The feeling was, 'We *cannot* lose this game. There is no way we can lose this game.'"

The game was ragged and intense, tightly played throughout. Sabonis, who hadn't been able to do anything against the United States, screamed at his teammates, imploring them to battle harder. He played with a stiff-kneed magnificence, which was a revelation. To much of the Western world, Sabonis had been a basketball Sasquatch, spotted from time to time outsmarting some centers, stomping on others, an eternal man of mystery who had been throttled by the Soviet hierarchy and who drowned his anger and frustration in his nation's favorite beverage.

Sabonis's teammates included Alvydas Pazdrazdis and Gintaras Einikis, who were among those who had joined hands to stop the Soviet tanks rumbling through the streets of the capital. Marciulionis was all over the place, as he always was, and in the end, his brilliance and the play of Sabonis won the day. The game ended with a score of 82–78, touching off a wild celebration.

The president of Lithuania, a dignified man named Vytautas Landsbergis, was doused with champagne. He had brought only one suit to the Olympics, so he changed into one of the Grateful Dead tie-dyes and began squirting champagne himself. When that celebration was over, Marciulionis retired to the shower and stood under the water for a long, long time in his uniform, all the while thinking, *What if we had lost to the Soviets? What if we had lost?* He told me this years later: "Thinking about what *could've* happened almost took away the joy of winning. That's how much we needed to win."

Eventually, though, the celebratory mood returned, and the Lithuanians went back to the Olympic Village. "We had several hours before we were due back at the medal stand," said Nelson, "and that's way too much time if you're a Lithuanian." Sabonis, who had been kept in a virtual basketball prison for years—as a thirty-one-year-old, he would finally get to play in the NBA in 1995 with the Portland Trail Blazers, where he had seven fairly productive seasons—was a particularly avid celebrator. He took on and vanquished all comers—boxers, weight lifters, discus throwers—in arm-wrestling contests, all the while downing shots. When it was time to return to the arena, as the Dream Team was playing Croatia in the gold medal game, Sabonis was sleeping it off somewhere. Legend has it that he was found a couple of days later in the women's dorm of the Unified Team, having beaten the Russians on the court but then doing his best to spread his own version of *glasnost*.

The Lithuanians were supposed to wear the logo-emblazoned collared shirt of a sponsor to the medal ceremony, but at the last moment Marciulionis handed out the skeleton T-shirts and told his teammates to put them on. "The Grateful Dead believed in us when we were nothing," he said, and out marched the Lithuanians in their garish T-shirts, displeasing representatives from the IOC—a fascinating tableau that was not the only medal-stand kerfuffle of the evening.

# CHAPTER 34

# THE GOLD, THE FLAG, AND THE CHOSEN ONE

Some Wear Old Glory . . . Though Not
in the Service of Patriotism

On the night before the United States was to play Croatia for the
gold medal, the card game in the Coolest Room in the World was
especially animated. All the regulars were there, including Jordan,
who was scheduled to do a video shoot the next morning for NBA
Entertainment. It was not a small thing, a commitment of several
hours for what would become *Michael Jordan: Air Time.* To be honest, I can't separate one Jordan video from another, but they were
big deals in the sports world, exquisitely produced moneymakers.

This was classic Jordan—commit to something, let it hang in
the air for as long as possible while the other party goes apoplectic
with anxiety, then pull it off at the last moment, like a buzzer-beating
jump shot. Magic does things the same way.

It was one in the morning, then two, then three. Jordan was
smoking his phallic stogies and the guys were ripping on one another, and Don Sperling of NBA Entertainment was circling the edge

of the group like an overwrought den mother, trying to remind Jordan about the morning shoot and how Michael should also figure in the small matter of, you know, the gold medal game that night. Then it was four o'clock, then it was five. The players knew that this was the last card game, for the team was leaving Barcelona as soon as the gold medal had been secured and the arena celebration dispensed with. This round of tonk was something special, a ceremony of sorts, a parting of the ways before they all became enemies again.

At six-fifteen the game finally broke up. Sperling followed Jordan to one of his two rooms (a Jordan perk), where Jordan was to take a shower.

"Don't crash on me, Michael," Sperling begged.

"I told you I'll be out," said Jordan, "so I'll be out."

True to his word, Jordan reemerged twenty-five minutes later, showered, bald head glistening, decked out in a bright, orange-tinted shorts set that made him look like a Zambian exchange student. And for the next several hours the crew followed him through Barcelona, filming on the streets and at the Olympic Stadium. "What you have to understand is that it's ninety-six degrees and 100 percent humidity and he had no sleep," said Sperling. "And when you see that video, he looks as fresh as if he'd just gotten out of bed after eight hours."

When they were finished, in midafternoon, Jordan asked for a favor.

"Could you take me to the golf course?" he said. "My clubs are out there, and I'm going to try to get in a round."

Jordan played eighteen holes at the Real Club de Golf El Prat on the outskirts of Barcelona, as he did most days, got a ride back to the hotel, went to his room, changed, waded through the crowds at the Ambassador (they had only gotten larger as the Games went on), climbed aboard the team bus, and, eight years after his first, went off in search of his second gold medal.

"Michael tried to get me on his schedule over there, and I just couldn't do it," Magic says today. "I got so I could play cards all night, and so did some of the other guys. But then to go out and play eighteen, thirty-six holes of golf? Then come back and get 20 in the game like it's nothing?

"Man, nobody could do that. Michael Jordan is the strongest, and the strongest-willed, athlete ever. I don't care what anybody says."

No matter how the story is spun two decades later, the United States Olympic Committee deeply resented the attention that the Dream Team received in Barcelona. That resentment had started way back in Portland and continued from the first days in Barcelona. NBC's Dick Ebersol had made special arrangements for the Dream Team to arrive late for the opening ceremonies and be deposited into the middle of the U.S. procession in an effort to lessen the chaos. It didn't matter. As soon as the players were spotted, athletes of every size and stripe broke ranks and ran to the Dream Team, particularly to Magic.

And you know what? It couldn't have been a better scene if NBC had orchestrated the choreography of it.

But it didn't matter to the USOC. The special accommodations, the extra security, the demand for tickets for a sport that in some years was barely on the Olympic radar—all of it angered the organization deeply. Mike Moran, the head of PR for the USOC, went after Barkley for the journal he was "writing" (it was more like a dictation with David Dupree cleaning it up) for *USA Today*, concerned that he was getting paid. The pettiness boggled the mind. Barkley was of course not getting paid, and if he had been, the sum wouldn't have covered the amount that accidentally spilled out of his pockets on Las Ramblas every night.

The lead bureaucratic jihadist was LeRoy Walker, one of the officials who had gotten under the Dream Team's collective skin in Portland. He was the titular head of the U.S. delegation as well as the next USOC president. Midway through the Games Walker caused a firestorm when he told a tale of stopping to watch a televised Dream Team game with a bunch of other U.S. athletes only to hear them root against their countrymen, the presumption being that they were fed up with the Brahmin treatment given the basketball team. "I may be from the old school," the seventy-four-year-old Walker told several news outlets, "but when I find Americans pulling against Americans, it bothers me."

"Old school" doesn't begin to cover it. Walker conjured up the master-of-Trinity character memorably portrayed by John Gielgud in *Chariots of Fire*, who complained that a sprinter was "playing the tradesman" for daring to use a professional coach. Walker was lost in the past, holding on to the idea that the pros should've stayed in the Olympic Village and that a U.S. college team could still win gold "if we choose the right ones." He ignored the fact that other highly compensated U.S. athletes, such as track stars Carl Lewis, Mike Powell, and Jackie Joyner-Kersee and tennis player Pete Sampras, were lavishly bungalowed outside the Olympic Village also, and that American collegians would no longer have a chance in an emerging new basketball order.

There is little doubt that the USOC saw it as a larger fight, one for the very future of the organization; even the eminently reasonable Harvey Schiller bought into that idea a little bit. "There was a real concern about the NBA taking over," Schiller, the chairman of the USOC in 1992, told me. "The NBA had already put people on the USA Basketball board, so what was to stop them from putting people on the USOC board? Some people saw this as the beginning of professional sports consuming the Olympic movement."

So the bureaucrats did what bureaucrats do—kvetch.

At the end of the day, the USOC dug in its heels on the one issue where it seemed to hold the hammer and one that seemed substantive enough to cause a civil war—the Dream Team's podium garb at the medal ceremony.

No governing body can control the "competitive attire" of an athlete, though what constitutes competitive attire can get tricky. In hockey, for example, a player can't be told what stick or skates he can use, but his gloves are up for grabs. In swimming, the cap is considered "competitive attire" but trunks are not. Basketball is like track and field—the USOC cannot dictate footwear, but it can mandate that a certain uniform be worn. There was never a whisper of complaint from anyone about the Dream Team game uniform, which was made by Champion, probably because the logo is small and Nike isn't in the NBA uniform business anyway. But the Reebok-sponsored platform suit, which featured the company patch on the right shoulder? That was something else again.

In accepting the invitation to play on the Dream Team, Jordan and his agent, David Falk, had told the USOC, USA Basketball, and whoever else was listening that he wouldn't wear Reebok. As much as anyone wanted to paint Nike as the bad guy—I'd be more than willing to do that if it were the truth—it wasn't the company making the stink. Swoosh chairman Phil Knight had all but checked out on the issue, other than to offer a memorable one-liner at the expense of the USOC chairman: when he heard Schiller insist that the basketball team would not be allowed on the podium if it did not wear the Reebok suit, Knight said: "Who does Harvey Schiller think he is, Janet Reno?" (History lesson: she was attorney general at the time.) It was Jordan and Falk—mostly Jordan—who were most insistent.

The Reebok story had substantial legs in Barcelona partly because there was almost nothing to write about once the Dream Team took the court and began dismantling the opposition. The USOC's Moran was always able to work up a nice froth when asked about the Dream Team anyway, and in this case he insisted that the players would not be able to take the medal stand unless they wore "the patriotic clothing approved by the USOC."

Now, we may raise an eyebrow about what Jordan believes to be principle, but by that time he had at least been in a protracted contractual relationship with Nike. As for the USOC's position, there was nothing intrinsically "patriotic" about the Reebok suit, nothing red, white, and blue, only green. Reebok had paid the USOC about $2 million to be a platform sponsor. But it was easy for the USOC to play the star-spangled-banner card, painting itself as protectors of the Republic and the Dream Teamers as greedy self-promoters.

"I got two million reasons not to wear that shit," Charles Barkley proclaimed, thereby releasing the terms of his deal with Nike.

But this wasn't about Barkley. It was about Jordan, whose annual Nike take at the time was exponentially larger than what Barkley got. The team would follow Jordan's lead. Players such as Malone, who had his own deal with LA Gear ("I'm an off-brand guy," Karl used to say), weren't crazy about always being a minor character in someone else's play, and it would've been interesting had Jordan declared, "We're not going out for the medal ceremony." I have the feeling that Malone would've wrestled him to the locker room floor on that point. But the Dream Team functioned according to a hierarchy that had Jordan and Magic on top (and Bird when he cared), and the rest of the team would take its cue from Jordan.

Jordan's loyalty to Nike sometimes reached a psychosis that went well beyond the objectionable *Republicans buy sneakers, too.* One of his good friends, Fred Whitfield, now team president with the Bobcats, remembers Jordan taking a knife to the Puma footwear that Whitfield had in his closet. One day Jordan, authentically indignant, looked at my piddling $50 New Balances and said, "What are you wearing that shit for?"

(When I interviewed Jordan in the summer of 2011, I wore loafers so he wouldn't get a gander at my standard-issue Asics. I make no apologies for that. Jordan had that same insane loyalty about his alma mater. He once told Falk that he would fire him if the agent sent his daughter to Duke, which is where she ended up going. Falk was honestly worried for a while that Jordan would follow through, but he didn't.)

So was it about loyalty or money? Both, really. The obvious comparison is to the Lithuanians, who wore their of-the-people-by-the-people-for-the-people Grateful Dead T-shirts out of loyalty. But, really, that had something to do with bucks, too—the Dead had written them a check.

Behind the scenes, Schiller played his trump card: the organization held all of the passports, and he told USA Basketball reps, "We won't give them back." Schiller knew that he wouldn't strand twelve of the world's best-known athletes in a foreign land—the Spanish government would've waved them through customs anyway, collecting autographs and photos along the way—and it was never going to come to that. But Schiller did see this as an issue that, unlike most involving the Dream Team, could be won.

As the years rolled by, it has become increasingly difficult to deconstruct this platform episode, to find out who knew what and when they knew it. Understand first there are two threads to the story—the pin-back and the flag. Schiller says that a few days before the gold medal game he attended a luncheon that featured U.S. tennis player Mary Jo Fernandez, who had won a gold medal in doubles and a bronze in singles. "Mary Jo was wearing the award jacket and had it zipped about two-thirds up," says Schiller. "And with the flaps opened up, it covered the Reebok logo. As soon as I left, I called Dave Gavitt, told him to get an awards jacket and zip it part of the way up, see what happens."

Meanwhile, a couple of days before the gold medal final, some of the Dream Teamers had decided that they would wear the jacket but get something—maybe tape or a strip of cloth—to cover up the logo. They didn't know about the pin-back idea, and Jordan swears that he believed they wouldn't have to wear the jacket at all. What is most incredible is that situation was allowed to go on as long as it did, right up until the gold medal game against Croatia on August 8.

On that morning, Daly read a note that had been slipped under his hotel room door. It was from NBC's Ebersol, inviting Daly to send someone to pick up a videotape of a piece the network had run the night before about the controversial U.S. defeat in the 1972 Munich Games. Daly dispatched a manager to get it, and he and P. J. Carlesimo reviewed it, agreeing that it might serve as motivation to get a tired team amped up.

The tape player wouldn't function at the pregame get-together at the hotel about four hours before tip-off. The Prince of Pessimism did not consider this a good omen. He made sure that the video came with them to the arena, and it did work in the locker room. On the way to the arena . . . another omen, though no one knew whether this was good or bad. As with Puerto Rico, the Croatian team bus was pulled over to the side so the Dream Team could pass. Bird was already on the practice court, going through his pregame retinue of shots, when the Croatian players arrived. "Laslo, what is this?" said Stojko Vrankovic, his Celtics teammate. "We cannot even be on the same road with you?" "Wasn't up to me," said Bird, suppressing a laugh and thinking, *I hope this doesn't work against us.*

Once in the locker room, the Dream Teamers watched the 1972 tape attentively, fascinated by the appalling compound of double-dealing and bureaucracy that enabled the Soviets to get three chances to win the game. None of the Dream Teamers believed that they could get themselves in a position to lose by referee incompetence; that only happens to teams that can't build a double-digit lead. But it was a wise move for the Prince of Pessimism.

Still, there was an anticlimactic feeling to the evening that was helped along by Croatia's coach, Petar Skansi. After his team had beaten the Unified Team to reach the final, he had declared, "This was our final today." The Dream Teamers were tired of Barcelona by then—even Barkley had stopped going to Las Ramblas—and thinking only of resting their weary bodies before NBA training camps began eight weeks hence. They came storming out of their locker room, stopped to take a pathetic snapshot (see the prologue), struggled for a few uneasy minutes (Croatia actually led 25–23), then continued on their merry, inexorable way, dispatching Croatia 117–85. Petrovic (24 points) was his usual defiant self, and Kukoc was a lot better (16 points) than he was in the first meeting. "I got my greatest respect for Toni Kukoc the second time we played them," Jordan told me. (Let's be clear that he said this in 2011; that's not the way he acted in 1992.)

That left only the suspense of what the U.S. team, having defeated their eight opponents by the absurd average of 43.8 points, would wear to the medal ceremony.

Plans had been made at the pregame meal, according to USA Basketball's Tom McGrath, to pin back the lapels of the Reebok suit on the players so that the logo wouldn't show; this was the Schiller

plan. I have no doubt that McGrath's memory is correct because
dozens of safety pins had to be gathered, and they were indeed there
for the players after the game. But either the pin-back idea never
caught on with the players, it wasn't communicated clearly enough,
or the players simply tuned it out.

"There kept being no solution and no solution and finally we're at
the gold medal game," says Jordan, still able to work up a fire-eyed
fury about the issue twenty years later. "So I thought we were just
going to wear our game uniform, which I thought would be great. But
then we were told, 'You can't go out there unless you wear Reebok.' "

Jordan stood up and said, "I feel like I'm dissing America, that
we're making business bigger than that America on our jersey." If
that sounds hypocritical since his fear was of showing disloyalty to
his own business interests, well, that's how he felt.

I ask him if he ever considered not going out for the medal ceremony.

"Of course not," he says. "I wouldn't have done that to my
teammates. And they knew that. They had me in a corner."

Then Jordan had another idea. "Can you find some American
flags?" he asked McGrath.

Out came the tie-dyed Lithuanians, hungover and happy, Sabonis-
less, looking for all the world like a gloriously pie-eyed band of pot
smokers who had beaten Alpha Tau Omega in the intramural
championship final. They were followed by the U.S. team. Magic
Johnson, wearing a wide smile, was in the lead, an American flag
draped over his right shoulder, his left hand holding it in place. Barkley was next, a flag around both of his shoulders. Mullin, Stockton,
Malone, and Drexler followed. None of them wore flags, but all had
their jackets zipped so that the Reebok logo was hidden. Jordan,
blowing a bubble, was next, a flag on his right shoulder, clearly covering the Reebok logo. Pippen, Bird, Ewing, Robinson, and Laettner
followed. (Only three flags had been procured from spectators.)

From his seat near midcourt, NBA commissioner David Stern
watched with mixed emotions. He was proud (in general) of the

way the NBA players had comported themselves, proud that they never seemed to rub it in (Barkley's elbow notwithstanding), proud that eight grind-the-other-guys-into-dust routs had been accomplished without an international incident. But he was also a businessman, schooled in the art of the deal, and was disappointed in the flags and the artfully zipped jackets.

"In retrospect, I would've been much more forceful with our players for their sake," Stern told me years later. "But unfortunately, as was our style in Barcelona, we [the NBA] deferred, and it tainted our players a little bit. We would've told Reebok and Nike, 'Okay, fellas, let's be above this.' But we let USA Basketball handle it."

That rings false. With Jordan's legendary stubbornness in play, only a powerhouse on the level of the commissioner had the power to do anything, and he, like everyone else, let the issue fester, and after the game, the players had to deal with the matter.

"Everyone agreed we would not deface the Reebok [logo] on the award uniform," said Jordan. "The American flag cannot deface anything. The American dream is standing up for what you believe in. I believed in it, and I stood up for it. If I offended anyone, that's too bad." As if to punctuate that, Jordan took off his Reebok suit and tossed it to Brian McIntyre. "I certainly don't want it," he said.

Magic sounded more contemptuous. "They could have come to us and treated us like men and talked this thing out," he said. "Instead they had to be the big shot, be the big man." Years later, Schiller would wryly note that Magic became an Olympic spokesman, securing sponsorships from the people he trashed.

On press row we noticed the flags and the zipped-up jackets, of course, but I doubt if anyone in the stands that night said, "Oh, look, the players covered up the logo." As with most issues related to money, nobody cared except the people involved.

No, the fans were watching the smiles and the pure joy on the faces of the players, who turned around and around, waving to all sections of the cheering crowd, searching the seats for their loved ones. Several of the Dreamers beckoned for Daly and his assistants to join them on the podium. They had grown quite close to the staff over the weeks together and had universal respect for Daly. They loved his staccato speech, his sweat-only-the-big-stuff philosophy, his command of the game, and his habit of occasionally touching up his hair and smoothing his collar ever so subtly, even in the heat of the game. "Every time I went out on the floor," Malone said years later, "I'd look back and there would be Coach Daly doing all this . . ." Malone mimicked a man grooming. "Everything had to be perfect."

True to fashion, Daly and assistants demurred, players-first guys to the end. From the press area, I wanted to scream: *Chuck, get up there! You'll be coaching the New Jersey Nets soon! Enjoy this!* But he *was* enjoying it, as Wilkens later made clear. "Chuck grabbed my arm and just held on, and I looked over and there was a tear coming out of Chuck's eye. That said it all for me."

Malone put his arm around Drexler. Harry and Larry, now bound for life, exchanged high fives. Barkley blew a kiss to the crowd. And Magic Johnson, a man who was supposed to be dying, pumped his right fist, then his left fist, and took Barkley in his arms.

I remember staring at Magic and Bird and wondering whether we had just seen the last time that either would ever play in a basketball game. Magic's status as a returning NBA player was in doubt, and Bird had seemed paralyzed with stiffness in the gold medal game, having failed to score in twelve minutes. Was it over for the two men who had saved the NBA a decade earlier?

Then, suddenly, they were all gone, back to America on their chartered plane, which had practically begun idling during the second half. The lights dimmed, the Palau Municipal emptied, workers picked up trash, and it was like the day after your birthday, when the world seemed a little less bright, the fine edges of joy scrubbed flat.

The Dream Teamers continued their card games and their celebrating on the way home, but when they stepped off the plane it was like a curtain closed behind them and a malevolent stage crew began rearranging the scenery. No more Never Never Land. The "basketball heaven" that Stockton talked about was gone, to be replaced by realities, harsh and unforgiving.

# CHAPTER 35

# THE AFTERMATH

. . . . . . . . . . . . . . . . . . . . . . . . . . . . . . . . . . . . . . . . . . . . . . . . . . . . . .

### Michael/Magic/Larry . . . and Then There Were None

#### The Legend

A couple of days after Larry Bird returned to Boston from Barcelona, he went in to see Dave Gavitt. They hemmed and hawed about the Dream Team experience, hemmed and hawed about what the Celtics' prospects were for the upcoming season, and then hemmed and hawed some more before finally Bird had had enough of hemming and hawing.

"That's it, Dave," Bird said. "I'm done."

Gavitt had figured that was coming. But he needed Bird to say it.

Bird's wife, Dinah, team trainer Ed Lacerte, and physiotherapist Dan Dyrek had some idea of what Bird had gone through during those summer months with the Dream Team. But only he truly knew how many nights he'd lain awake in pain, how uncertain he'd been that this movement or that movement wouldn't send a breath-stopping electric stab through his body. True, guys with arthritic knees and ruined hips climb telephone poles and wrestle with jackhammers every day, and women with aching bunions make beds, cook dinners, and carry babies in their arms, so let's not go overboard in turning Bird into a working-class hero. But what he did during those summer months of 1992 had a kind of last-gasp grandeur to it, and the Dream Team wouldn't have been the same—wouldn't have been *nearly* the same—without him.

"Larry . . . Larry just *had* to be there," Magic told me years later, struggling to find some way to put it. "Just *had* to. How could you have something called a Dream Team without Larry Bird?"

Bird had two years left on his Celtics contract. If he played sixty games of the 1992–93 season, he would make about $8 million. He was due to receive $3.75 million of that, in fact, on August 15, which was only a couple of days hence, not enough time for Bird, with the attendant red tape, to get his official retirement letter prepared. But he backdated that document so he wouldn't get the money. Where Bird came from, you didn't take money for nothing.

Earlier in his career Bird had joked that upon retirement he would become the "fattest man driving out of Boston." But in later years, after injuries and wear and tear had made him feel like a mere mortal, he had a change of heart. He realized that he liked his body when it was in tune and humming, and he wanted to keep that feeling in civilian life. With age, he realized he had lost the ability to shed excess weight, and it gnawed at him because he loved to eat. After he sat out most of the 1988–89 season following Achilles tendon surgery, he described to me what a bored and injured Larry Bird was like to be around. "I'd sit around the house, drive my wife crazy, and eat and eat," he said. "In two and a half weeks once I ate ten gallons of ice cream and seven wedding cakes. I ate wedding cakes because you knew they were gonna be good. I mean, who would screw up a wedding cake?" As I wrote at the time, that was Bird's philosophy at its most crystalline.

Fishing, golf, and French Lick home repairs such as building fences, bricklaying, a little roofing—that's what Bird envisioned for retirement. Plus more fishing. That's what he said publicly, anyway, and I have no reason to doubt him. But things changed during his exit meeting with Gavitt, which went something like this.

GAVITT: So what are you going to do now?

BIRD: Do? I might do nuthin'.

GAVITT: You know you're going to need back surgery in Boston. So why don't you come work for me as a special assistant. See a few college games, give me your opinion on players. It will be a big help having you around.

BIRD: Okay.

GAVITT: What do you want to get paid?

BIRD: More than you.

GAVITT: That's not going to happen.

They settled on $350,000.

"You know what it came down to?" Bird told me in 2012. "I wanted to hang around Dave Gavitt. I love that man. He was one of the smartest human beings I've ever been around. And he wanted to hang out with me. So I signed on. It was that simple."

So Larry Bird became the most famous special assistant in history, giving his opinion on players, attending some Celtics functions as an official representative (man, did he hate that), and being a kind of éminence grise around the Garden—a junior one, since Red Auerbach, the senior éminence grise, was still alive and kicking. Bird was in the job for five years, during which the Celtics followed a 48–34 season with records of 32–50, 35–47, 33–49, and finally an egregious 15–67. For one who played the game the way Bird did, his acid reflux must've been as bad as his back had ever been.

And so he left the city where he had become a legend.

### The Magic Man

When the Dream Team was practicing in San Diego, Bird pulled Magic aside and said, "You look great." In Barcelona, Magic's eyes would light up the brightest when he talked about the reaction of his fellow Dream Teamers to how well he had played considering his months of inactivity and, well, his condition.

"They'd say to me, 'You're coming back, right?'" Magic said. "'Do you have to go back to the Lakers? Can't you play for us?'" It made him feel . . . whole. All the worldwide adulation from fans meant nothing next to the validation of his peers.

I assume that most of the comments from his fellow Dream Teamers were genuine or at least proffered in the understandable spirit of Barcelona bonhomie. But I did detect hesitation from some members of the team when I would ask about Magic. They would all say the right things about his skills, but on the subject of his future as an NBA player, I never heard the will-you-come-play-for-us? sentiment expressed.

And once they were back in the States, all hell broke loose. Credit goes to Harvey Araton of the *New York Times*, who, at a preseason game between Utah and the Knicks at Madison Square Garden, interviewed Karl Malone about the prospect of Magic coming back to play full-time.

Here's some of what Araton wrote in the November 1 issue of the *New York Times*.

"Look at this, scabs and cuts all over me," Malone, the Utah Jazz All-Star forward, said last Tuesday night in the visitors' locker room at Madison Square Garden before a preseason game against the Knicks. He pressed a finger to a small, pinkish hole on his thigh that was developing into a scab. "I get these every night, every game," he said. "They can't tell you that you're not at risk, and you can't tell me there's one guy in the N.B.A. who hasn't thought about it."

Others leaped into the fray, some without attribution—*Players are scared. I could see myself backing off when I'm guarding him. Players don't know what to think. Players need more information*—and some with. Phoenix Suns general manager Jerry Colangelo said, "I have a son-in-law who does surgery every day, and he wears gloves, goggles, masks, and lives in mortal fear." Gerald Wilkins of the Cleveland Cavaliers, brother of a superstar, Dominique Wilkins, who had been spurned by the Dream Team committee, said that some players were "scared" to be playing against Johnson but, because of Magic's celebrity and overall popularity, "are handling it with white gloves."

It turned out that a *rubber* glove was the tipping point in the Magic controversy. A couple of days after Malone made his comment, the Lakers were in Chapel Hill, North Carolina—Jordan country—playing an exhibition game against the Cleveland Cavaliers, one of those spread-the-game-to-non-NBA-towns events that players and coaches detest. Johnson suffered a small cut on his right forearm, and under new medical guidelines that had been set up specifically to allay fears about Magic—"the Magic rule," as it had been inevitably christened—he was forced to come out of the game for medical attention.

Gary Vitti, the veteran Lakers trainer who was extremely close to Magic, came over to check it out. Vitti—one of those unsung heroes of the NBA, a guy who kept everything humming in Laker Land and never sought the spotlight himself—had made it his business to study up on the disease. The medical literature was not voluminous at the time, but from everything he could glean the risk of Magic's passing on the disease was small, smaller than the cut itself, which Vitti later said he could barely see.

The trainer reached for a cotton swab and appeared to be reaching for the rubber gloves in his pocket, which was the newly instituted policy for dealing with blood. But then Vitti decided against it and tended to Magic barehanded, applying a cotton swab and bandage.

There was a stunned silence when fans realized that Magic was the one who was about to get treatment, and then a small collective gasp as everyone stared at the tableau before them: a man touching the bloody arm of someone with the AIDS virus. The story and the photo made national headlines the next morning and continued to have legs for weeks afterward. To look on the positive side, it did initiate a dialogue about what was safe and what wasn't. It was a bit like the stories that would follow in the wake of a nonfatal accident at a nuclear plant—the story was not what happened but what *could* happen. On the negative side, the sensationalism dominated the conversation, and there were more than a few tabloid stories exaggerating the danger of what Vitti did or didn't do. One medical doctor even filed a complaint with the Occupational Safety and Health Administration about the trainer.

"By putting on gloves, I would have been giving my players a mixed message," Vitti explained later. "I had told them there was no danger [of scrimmaging against and dressing next to Magic]. Yet here I'd be putting on gloves when the injury was only a scratch. The point of wearing gloves was not to protect me and other players from Magic, but to keep *him* from getting an infection."

To gauge what happened psychologically to Magic on that autumn evening, you have to understand how the man thought and still thinks. He had done his due diligence about the disease, gotten himself into shape and changed his diet, come back, entertained the public, captained the Dream Team, heard the encouraging words from Bird, and gotten the (apparent) support of the other Barcelonians—in short, turned on the old charm and the old game, and now it was business as usual, the Magic Man back in form. So what could possibly be the problem?

But then came the visceral reaction from the fans in Chapel Hill. Magic's face said it all. He was shocked and dismayed, and others saw it, too, particularly Cavaliers coach Wilkens, the Dream Team assistant who had grown close to Magic over the eventful summer months. Wilkens actually thought for a moment that he was going to have to coax his team back onto the floor.

Magic reentered the game, but he wasn't the same, his joy devoured by that silence, that gasp, the attendant attention given to a small cut and the comments of Malone, his brother in gold.

"Just because he [Magic] came back doesn't mean nothing to me," Malone said. "I'm no fan, no cheerleader. It may be good for basketball, but you have to look far beyond that. You have a lot of young men who have a long life ahead of them. The Dream Team was a concept everybody loved. But now we're back to reality."

Over the next couple of days, Magic got some support, too. Of his fellow players on the Dream Team, Drexler spoke the loudest. "If Magic wants to play," said the Glide, "I have no problem playing against him."

Against much opposition, David Stern, from his bully pulpit in the commissioner's office, remained solidly behind Magic. Whatever Stern's legacy might be in terms of marketing and television deals, do not forget also that the man stood tall against those dark-ages diatribes about HIV.

But in the end, even the positive-minded Magic heard Malone loud and clear on the subject of reality. He told Lon Rosen to convene a press conference to announce his second retirement. Magic didn't even show up, which revealed the depths of his sadness about the whole thing. He walked away from the game he loved and the game he saved, an outcast angel.

Magic says that Malone's comments did take him aback. "We were in the process of educating the players and the public," Magic told me in the summer of 2011. "The Olympics had given me the platform to show that a guy with HIV could still play at a high level and you weren't going to get HIV by playing against me. So I come back and when Karl said what he did, yes, it did set back the message."

Magic believes that Malone had another agenda, too. "Karl didn't want the Lakers to be strong again with me on the roster," Johnson said. "Karl saw the opportunity to win and he wanted to take advantage of that."

To this day, Malone has never apologized to Magic, and in fact the two have never had a conversation about the Mailman's comments. Like most athletes, Malone generally steers clear of the trip wire of regret.

"You know it's not my style to take stuff back," Malone told me in 2011. "That's all that needs to be said about it. A lot of times I didn't say the things people wanted me to say. But I don't take anything back. As a writer, don't you all cringe when somebody says,

'I was misquoted'? I've never done that. I've stood behind what I said."

In the summer of 2003, Malone was considering taking a free-agent offer to become a member of the Lakers, a last-ditch attempt to win a championship. He called Magic, then a part owner of the franchise, and they talked, and Magic encouraged him to sign on, which he did. No other subject came up.

## The Chosen One

The 1992–93 Chicago Bulls, who won 57 games and who struggled at times in the postseason, were the least dominant of the six Jordan-Pippen championship teams, certainly nowhere near the caliber of the 1995–96 Bulls, who won 72 regular-season games and an astonishing 87 of 100 including the postseason.

But I always thought that the 1992–93 season represented Jordan at his best. Both he and Pippen returned from Barcelona physically and mentally exhausted. The repercussions from gambling, the revelations in Sam Smith's book, the burdens of being a global superstar—all had taken a toll on Jordan. Plus two other teams, Ewing's Knicks and Barkley's Suns, had come along to steal some of the Bulls' thunder, not to mention a couple of their wins, the Suns finishing with a league-best 62 and the Knicks with 60.

Barkley, in particular, was a revelation. Freed from what he considered the inhumane shackles of Philadelphia, he found new life in the Valley of the Suns and would play well enough during the season to win his only MVP award. Any reporter looking for easy copy could zip into Phoenix, spend a day or two sniffing around the Jester, dash something off, and go have a cold one.

As if it had been scripted, the Bulls and the Suns met in the Finals, Michael and his antic buddy Charles the leading men in what proved to be one of the greatest Finals in league history. Phoenix lost the first two at home, so the Suns were written off. Then they won an epic triple-overtime game in Chicago, so Phoenix was back. Then the Bulls won Game 4 to go up 3–1, so the Suns were dead again. Then Phoenix won Game 5 and, though trailing in the series 3–2, had the final two games at home. Then the Bulls won Game 6 and the championship. That's five home-court losses in six games.

Barkley was magnificent throughout the postseason, averaging 26.6 points and 13.6 rebounds. But in the Finals Jordan was epic. Immortal. Sick. Stupid good. In the six games he scored 31, 42, 44, 55, 41, and 33 points. Though a John Paxson jumper won the decisive Game 6, it was Jordan who put a rope in his mouth and hauled his team—not single-handedly but damn close—across the finish line.

After the game, Jordan and I made an arrangement to collaborate on a back-of-the-magazine column for *Sports Illustrated* about the pressures and strain, as well as the joy, of winning three straight championships, the first time that had been done since the Red Auerbach Boston Celtics, who won eight in a row from 1959 to 1966. By "collaborate," that means the subject gets interviewed, the writer writes it, and the subject either approves or disapproves.

In this case, Jordan—or, rather, David Falk—disapproved. The column was, to Falk's thinking, too dark, too replete with revelations about how hard it was and how sick Jordan was of the scrutiny, not celebratory enough, not Jordanesque.

But that's how Jordan was feeling at the time—ecstatic about the win and the three-peat accomplishment but ambivalent about the toll it had taken on his private life.

Before the Bulls beat Barkley's Suns in that epic Finals, it looked like they were going down. The powerful Ewing-led Knicks won the first two games of the Eastern finals at Madison Square Garden, and before Game 3 the *New York Times* reported that Jordan had been spotted gambling in an Atlantic City casino on the night before Game 2.

To those who knew Jordan, the story was along the lines of revealing that news anchors apply mousse. It was not Jordan being disruptive, contrary, or defiant. It was just Jordan being Jordan. But it seemed to be a story because it had the weight of the *Times* behind it. Would I have written the story in the way that it was written, as if it were an exposé (albeit one written in the subdued style of the *Times*)? No. Because I think it got blown out of proportion.

But the line is fuzzy. There are few laws in journalism, only judgments. Would it have been more of a story if Jordan had been at the casino until, say, 8:00 a.m. instead of 2:30 a.m. (the *Times* version) or 1:00 a.m. (Jordan's version)? Yes. Would it have been a story if Jordan drank to excess (something he rarely did and which I never personally witnessed) and made a commotion? Absolutely. If nocturnal casino trips began affecting his play? Absolutely.

And was it more of a story put in the context of past revelations of Jordan's gambling, *l'affaire* Slim Bouler? A trickier question to which the *Times* answered a resounding yes. But this is a legitimate question, too: should an adult be prohibited from indulging in recreation, on his own time and of his own free will, at a legitimate place of business just because it doesn't *look* right?

To me, it was more of a note in the larger story: *Michael Jordan didn't let a customary casino visit hamper his play last night as he scored 36 points, although his Chicago Bulls lost, 96–91, to the New York Knicks to fall behind 2–0 in their Eastern Conference final series.* Which is what happened. Then Jordan had a triple-double in a Game 3 victory, positively horsewhipped the Knicks with 54 points in a Game 4 win, and played another splendid all-around game in a Game 5 victory. In Game 6, however, he was less than super, appearing fatigued in the second half, as his "supporting cast" (Jordan's frequent and clueless description of his teammates) led the way to a series-clinching victory.

To believe that Jordan was fatigued because he had been in a casino a week earlier is absurd. To believe that Jordan was fatigued because of the collective strain of bad publicity (and carrying a team on his back) is not. Because before that Game 6 win, a Jordan golfing partner named Richard Esquinas climbed out of a Las Vegas sand trap and claimed in a self-published book that Jordan owed him as much as $1.25 million on bets. Esquinas further wrote that Jordan had negotiated the debt down to $300,000 but had repaid only $200,000.

Throughout his five minutes of fame, Esquinas presented himself, unconvincingly, as a kind of early Dr. Phil, a man on the edge who wrote *Michael and Me: Our Gambling Addiction . . . My Cry for Help* to help himself, to help Michael, to help *America*, for heaven's sake, with addiction. But nobody said that Esquinas was an outright liar, and he did raise the possibility that Jordan was, in gambling terms, "chasing," that is, doubling up on his bets to try to get even, the conventional road to ruin.

Jordan confirmed betting with Esquinas but called the amounts of money that he owed "preposterous" and said that he could not "verify how much I won or lost" because he did not keep records.

One can only imagine the firestorm that would've ensued had Jordan been mediocre in the Finals. But he put the bad publicity behind him, found some extra energy source, conquered Barkley and the Suns, and looked forward to . . . what exactly?

On August 3—about eight weeks after I last saw Jordan as he was sipping victory champagne and celebrating with his father—the body of fifty-seven-year-old James Jordan, the son of a sharecropper, was found in a creek near McCool, South Carolina, the cause of death a single gunshot wound through the right side of his chest from a .38-caliber pistol. James, who had been returning home from a funeral, had pulled over to sleep in his Lexus at a North Carolina rest stop. When his body was discovered, he had been dead for about ten days, and positive ID was made only through dental records.

About eight weeks after that, at a press conference in Chicago, Jordan announced that he was "stepping away" from the game. The atmosphere at the gathering was, in some respects, like Magic's press conference announcing his retirement, a jaw-dropping moment of *Holy Jesus Christ almighty, what the hell is next?* But it was different, too. While Magic's press conference was imbued with a kind of *Hamlet*-esque gloom, as if we were listening to a doomed man speak from a castle in Elsinore, an air of skepticism engulfed Jordan's midmorning affair. Were we getting the whole story when

Jordan said that he was exhausted and just needed some time away from the game? Was he really as sick of the media—"you guys," as he called us twenty-one times during the press conference—as he said he was? True, Bjorn Borg had retired from tennis at twenty-five. But how could someone as larcenously competitive as the twenty-nine-year-old Jordan, a man with a forest-dark competitive heart who would rip out your spleen to win a game of Parcheesi, possibly exist without basketball?

Not as much as some but more than most, I was aware of the toll that his fishbowl life had taken on Jordan. I had seen it coming even before all the gambling revelations, *The Jordan Rules*, and the murder of his father. (Had so many things happened to one person, even a famous person, in the course of a year?) At the same time, I, like every other NBA journalist, had to pursue the idea that David Stern had ever so quietly asked Jordan to step away.

There were so many questions. Had Michael lost too much money at the tables? Was he hanging with too many unsavory characters? Worst of all, did his father's death have something to do with Jordan's associations? With Jordan as an active player, the questions would be unceasing. If he stepped away, perhaps the temperature on the story would plummet.

I put in the dutiful phone call to Stern, who called me back and took my head off, calling such intimations "scurrilous" and "dangerous." We'd had a few disagreements over the preceding years, but nothing like that. At the same time, part of it had to be an act, since he knew that questions such as those would be coming and would never stop coming. At such moments we turn once again to *Hamlet*: could it be said that Commissioner Stern, like Queen Gertrude, doth protest too much?

Twenty years later, I still don't know. I've had numerous off-the-record discussions with players, coaches, and team executives who swear that Stern did make the request, and just as many who say that it was Jordan's decision alone. We have gone through the Jordan press conference and the subsequent Stern statements like amateur Kremlinologists, and at the end of the day we all begin our theories the same way: *Look, I don't know this for sure, but . . .*

The same arguments can be mustered to support both positions.

Jordan was so big, such a global star, that Stern couldn't risk any further revelations. He had to jettison him for a year. Or: Jordan was so big, such a global star, that Stern couldn't risk getting rid of him. He needed the Jordan buzz, the Jordan revenue.

It was Stern who always supplied the best barometer of Jordan's fame. He delighted in telling of a trip to a rural province of China, where families lived in almost prehistoric conditions, and meeting a farmer who, upon learning who Stern was, said, "Ah, the team of the Red Oxen." Or his visit to a refugee camp in Zambia when the residents swept the dirt floors clean and put on Bulls jerseys to welcome an NBA contingent. "It demonstrated to me," said Stern, "that the Bulls were the world's team."

And Jordan was, to a greater extent than anyone else besides Muhammad Ali, the world's athlete. But he left, for a while at least, riding buses and eating fast food with the Birmingham Barons, the minor-league team he joined for spring training in 1994, conjuring up nightly memories of his father, secure in the knowledge that James Jordan was looking down and beaming, even on those frequent nights when he went 0 for 4.

### The Writer

So as the 1993–94 season began, Bird was gone, Magic was gone, and Jordan was gone. The Dream Team was gone. Portland, Monte Carlo, Barcelona . . . all of it gone. I had signed on to do a book with a rookie named Shaquille O'Neal—cue requisite laugh track for the lunacy of telling the life story of a twenty-year-old—and my heart was only half in it. Shaq was, still is, a great character, a truly smart, funny, and unique individual. But I could see right away that this was new territory—the era of the fully hatched superstar, the guy who wanted to cut the line and get his just because, well, he could.

Shaq went on to be a great player, but for him it was never first and foremost about the game. It was about the other stuff that came with the game. For the guys on the Dream Team, these cut-out-your-heart-and-watch-it-beat-on-the-sidewalk immortals, it was always about basketball first and foremost. The other stuff just happened to come. I had been fortunate enough to catch them in the full bloom of their talent, maturity, and competitiveness, a team like no other.

I told my bosses that I needed to get off the beat for a while. It just wasn't going to be the same, couldn't be the same, and so I jumped off what had been the greatest ride in the world.

# CHAPTER 36

# THE IMPACT

. . . . . . . . . . . . . . . . . . . . . . . . . . . . . . . . . . . . . . . . . . . . . . . .

## "We Were Like Actors in a Play"

Dirk Nowitzki was a gangly fourteen-year-old German in the summer of 1992, simply another kid with big dreams. He had just taken up hoops in his native Würzburg in northern Bavaria, and he was getting a feel for the game, having discovered that he had a gift for shooting and an even greater gift for working hard, happy in isolation, shooting, fetching his own ball, shooting some more—the same repetitive choreography that had made superstars out of American players such as Larry Bird, Scottie Pippen, Chris Mullin, and John Stockton. Nowitzki was a good tennis player and an even better team handball player, a sport his father, Jörg, played, and one that Germany dominates worldwide; had Dirk not found basketball with the help of the Dream Team, it's easy to imagine that, with his height and athleticism, he would've represented Germany in team handball. Had that happened, he might today have a gold medal. And several million fewer dollars.

"For a long time I thought basketball was a woman's sport because my sister and my mom played," Nowitzki, the Dallas Mavericks star, told me in 2011. (His mother, Helga, was good enough to make the German women's national team.) "That doesn't make any sense, I know, but that's how I thought. I started shooting around when I was maybe twelve or thirteen and then—boom!—the Olympics hit and everything changed. It made me really want to play basketball."

Flashes of the Dream Team press conference and the Dream Team turning the opposition into chicken *Geschnetzeltes* were broadcast back to Germany. "I remember the other teams taking photos," says Nowitzki. "I remember the Dream Team locked in the hotel with throngs of people outside. I remember how easy it was for them to dominate. And I'll never forget the quote from Charles." Nowitzki breaks into a big smile, and we say it together: *I don't know nuthin' 'bout Angola. But Angola's in trouble.*

Like most young Germans, Nowitzki idolized his countryman Detlef Schrempf, who in the summer of 1992 had just completed his seventh NBA season and had led Germany into the Barcelona Olympics. But his favorite player was Pippen. "Scottie could do everything on the court, an all-around player, shot threes, posted up, passed, played defense. And it all looked so smooth. It really made an impression on me."

Had Nowitzki ever told Pippen that?

"No," says Dirk. "When I first came to the NBA my English wasn't good and I was shy. So I never got a chance to tell him how important he was. Guess I'm telling him now."

And so it went. *Boom*, as Nowitzki put it. Thousands of booms went off all around the world, the start of a revolution. In Argentina, Manu Ginobili, a fifteen-year-old with a wild, almost primitive athleticism, was watching. In Spain, twelve-year-old Pau Gasol, who had designs on being a doctor, and ten-year-old José Calderón, a budding point guard, were watching. In Turkey, two tall thirteen-year-olds, Mehmet Okur and Hedo Turkoglu, were watching. In France, ten-year-old Tony Parker, already among the quickest youngsters in his country, was watching. In Brazil, a pair of ten-year-olds, big, strong Nene Hilario and speedy Leandro Barbosa, were watching. Closer to home, two young athletic prizes, sixteen-year-old Tim Duncan in the Bahamas, a swimmer, and eighteen-year-old Canadian Steve Nash, who was about to begin what few saw as a particularly illustrious hoops career at Santa Clara, were watching.

The whole world was watching. The television audience was not nearly as fragmented by cable as it is today, so the sport never had a wider viewership, never *will* have a wider viewership, at least in terms of audience share. An eager international army of print journalists spread the word, too. "Many foreign journalists were already invested in our game by Barcelona," says Terry Lyons, the NBA's international PR man at the time. "They would come to All-Star Games and Finals, and they just got it quicker than our guys did over here. They saw what it was about, how this could grow the game."

"The Dream Team absolutely had massive impact," says Donnie Nelson, the former assistant for the Lithuanian team who is now general manager of the 2011 champion Mavs. "You can't really calibrate it, but you can imagine it. What effect did the Beatles coming to America have on music? It was the same kind of thing."

"The Dream Team was the single biggest impact of any team in any sport in history," says Lithuania's Sarunas Marciulionis. "How many kids around the world started playing? How many said, 'Oh, this is a great game. It is maybe better than soccer'?"

"We take a lot of research detail from our international players," says the NBA's Kim Bohuny, "and I can't begin to tell you how many of them say they started watching basketball at the '92 Olympics."

By 2011, there were eighty-six international players from forty countries on NBA rosters, a number that no doubt will only increase. Of the first seven picks in the 2011 draft, four were international players, from Turkey, Lithuania, Serbia, and Congo.

To those people who loved the sound of a ringing cash register, obviously, the revolution wasn't all about the game. "Based on the impact of the Dream Team around the world," says Rick Welts, the former NBA marketing genius now with the Golden State Warriors, "it moved our agenda ahead twenty years." By "agenda" he means, of course, "bottom line." If basketball didn't supplant *futbol* as the world's game after Barcelona, the NBA did turn into the world's league and David Stern became the world's commissioner.

That remains true today, the kick-start from '92 the principal reason that the NBA makes one-tenth of its revenues (about $430 million) from international operations; the reason that NBA games are broadcast in 215 countries and territories (that number was eighty-five before the Dream Team) and translated into forty-six languages; the reason that three hundred members of the international media now cover the Finals; the reason that Beijing will probably have an NBA team before, say, San Diego will; the reason the NBA has an office in Africa, the next place that Stern wants to plant his flag; the reason that the commissioner did a grip-and-grin with Al Jazeera Sport during the 2011 NBA Finals. "Not sure how Stern's Jewish owners feel about this," said one courtside observer, "but nobody can ever say the guy is asleep on the job."

It's not just the league that raked in money. Remember that the NBA shares revenue with its players, so people such as Charles Grantham, a USA Basketball committee member who was also head of the National Basketball Players Association, also cheered the business uptick in the years that followed the Dream Team. "The Barcelona Olympics generated more international interest in the NBA, more international TV contracts and more revenue," says Grantham, "so in the long run all NBA players benefitted from the Dream Team. It was a masterful triumph of timing. Unlike with other sports, the groundwork was there because basketball was at least being played in these other countries. It was the right time, the right place, and the right bunch of players to do it. Players talk about their 'brand' now. Well, I never heard anybody mention 'brand' until the Dream Team."

As for the game of basketball, well, most of us in America had it wrong. We failed to heed the sermons of the Inspector of Meat. We looked on at all those 40- and 50-point victims in Portland and Barcelona—gunned down, gutted, and field dressed—and we thought they would be discouraged. But for a whole younger class of competitors it had the opposite effect. Where others saw annihilation, the young foreign players saw revelation, a demystified process.

*Yes, Michael Jordan operates at a level a hundred times above me, but I do the same things. I fake right, go left hard. I post up and shoot a fallback jumper. I sneak down the lane and double-team a big man.* And if Jordan was a bad example, owing to his extraordinary athleticism, there was John Stockton. *I'm his size. I can learn to run a team like him. And look at Patrick Ewing. I'm seven feet tall and I never realized I could go out to the corner and shoot jump shots.*

Also, the Dream Team's whipsawed opponents were the ones who became the coaches and basketball missionaries back in their own countries, returning not only with stories and photographs but also with stratagems.

"True, back then we thought of the NBA as apart from us," said Juan Antonio Orenga, who played for Spain in the 1992 and 1996 Games and is now assistant coach of the national team. "They were gods. It was like an impossible mission to play them.

"But it was a good mission. Everyone in basketball was waiting for this because players—if they are serious—want to play against the best no matter what the result. Only by playing the best can you become the best."

We in the press, and the viewers back home, understandably want close games, tension, and some kind of buzzer-beating denouement. But whereas we looked down and saw scorched earth and carnage, the opponents saw lessons. Orenga remembers a major one from Barcelona.

"Before the game our coach [the respected Antonio Díaz-Miguel] tried to convince us that we could win," says Orenga. "'They are not great shooters and they will not be motivated,' he told us. So out comes the Dream Team and they make everything they shoot. And not motivated? Well, we were in a free-throw situation and I remember Scottie Pippen taking a look at the scoreboard and hollering to his teammates, 'Hey, come on! We're only up by 25 points. Come on!'

"It was not a fake. It was just that he thought they weren't playing good enough. Next thing I know they are up 40, and I don't even remember how. So I suddenly had the feeling, right out on the court, that they could do whatever they wanted, whenever they wanted. We were playing the game, but we were watching it, too." Orenga smiles at the metaphor he had been forming in his mind. "We were like actors in a play. We wanted to get to that level ourselves."

There had been the perception in the minds of some, too, that Americans were simply superior athletes, that their dominance was based primarily on size and speed. In other words, the same false conclusions held by some Americans were also held around the world. The Dream Team squelched that. "Yes, physically they were far above us," said Orenga, "but they were far better than us in basketball, too. It showed how much work we had to do."

The octogenarian Inspector of Meat, who never tires of studying the game, believes that the Dream Team altered what had been a flawed paradigm. "A lot of countries were doing it like the Soviets did it," Stankovic told me recently. "Too much emphasis on physical preparation and being strong and not enough on how to dribble and shoot. What we learned from this first American pro team was the skill set.

"And strategy, too. Zone defense was too prominent in the FIBA game. Americans made us think more about man-to-man, and the game just looks different that way, more intense, more . . . *energetic*."

The way the Dream Team played flowed organically from who they were as players. Nobody had to up his game or take it to the next level, as the clichés go. "The main thing that happens when the best get together is that the game speeds up and you have to make plays a little quicker," Bird said not long ago. "Basketball is so simple. You can run the pick and roll to perfection, work for the open man, and, if you don't have a shot, swing the ball. That's how you play. It doesn't always happen, but on this team it happened. It wasn't about scoring because we could've just got it in to Charles. It was about playing the game correctly."

There was something else going on, too. By dint of the Dream Team's collective maturity, its knack for domination without irritation, it offered a blueprint for professionalism, the lesson that Eddie Felson, the pool veteran played by Paul Newman in *The Color of Money*, tries to communicate to Tom Cruise's Vincent. "Pool excellence is not about excellent pool," Felson tells him. "It's about becoming someone."

Before Spain's game against the United States, Orenga remembers, he met some of the Dream Team members in the bowling area at the Olympic Village. Spain had had a tough Olympics by that time, having lost to Angola in the first game and never gotten its bearings, a humiliation for the host nation, which had been considered a candidate for the bronze medal. The players were feeling down when they met the Americans, but that changed quickly. "They knew us and told us how sorry they were that we had lost," Orenga said. "Charles Barkley, Larry Bird, Michael Jordan. And they *knew* us. They knew they would beat us, but they treated us with respect. No one on our team ever forgot that."

Marciulionis, who knew most of the Dream Teamers personally or at least competitively, put it more simply: "They didn't hold their noses in the air. They were who they were."

Watching it all as a somewhat awed college coach, Dream Team assistant Krzyzewski says: "There was more depth to the dream than the basketball. It was the type of people they were, what they had done together to build the NBA. So it was not only that they were responsible for the explosion of basketball around the world. It was that the game exploded in the right way."

Chris Mullin added this: "More than winning or losing, what I remember was the feeling of responsibility that we all had. We never talked about it. But we all felt it. How you handle yourself.

Play with class. Play at the highest level." He searched for another word. "Play, *ultimately*," he added.

Oddly, a kind of reverse reaction happened at home. Almost as soon as the Dream Team had finished its mission, USA Basketball was tasked with rostering a team to play in the 1994 World Championships in Toronto. It was out of the question that any of the reigning gold medalists would play so shortly after the splendid show in Barcelona, so the goal became to select young players who would—along with a few of the original Dream Teamers—form the basis of the 1996 Olympic team in Atlanta.

Now, think of the enormousness of the mission for these guys: all they had to do was follow the best and most popular team in history. They were doomed from the beginning, and the smartest of them, such as Alonzo Mourning, knew it and said so. "Everything we do is compared to the first Dream Team," said Mourning. "We can't win."

The Zeitgeist of that team was not to make nice while singing hosannas to the '92ers. No, this was, almost quite literally, a different generation, one disinclined to play the role of dutiful progeny. They would act in accordance with their own code of comportment, which was, say, 10 percent Barkley and 90 percent bark.

The results were predictable. If the 1992 Olympic team produced a perfect chemical reaction, an ideal blend of talent, tenacity, and maturity, the 1994 team, which was prematurely and unfortunately labeled (not by me) Dream Team II, was an unholy concoction of all the wrong ingredients, a basketball dystopia, defiantly christened by forward Larry Johnson as "the all-principal's-office team," crotch-grabbers such as Derrick Coleman and Shawn Kemp, preeners such as Mourning, talented but incomplete players such as Johnson, whose game basically consisted of posting up with his back to the basket and waiting for the ball to be thrown in to him. Don Nelson got the gig that he had originally wanted two years earlier, and because he wasn't the kind of coach who reined players in, he was as helpless as anyone else as the United States arrogantly rampaged through the tournament while making comments such as "We're basically taking a lot of countries to school" (Johnson again). Okay, that's what the first Dream Team did, too, but the idea was not to advertise it, "not be arrogant with the ass-whuppings we were handing out," as country boy Karl Malone put it.

A snapshot of the difference between the two teams came in the way that they spent their nocturnal hours. While the Dream Team hung around the family room in the Ambassador, playing cards and ragging on one another, DT II bragged about clubbing at all hours. That doesn't make them bad people and doesn't make them all that different from Barkley. But it does speak to a different culture and a different wellspring of team chemistry. Were an editorial cartoonist to put this on paper, one panel would show a bunch of young bucks out on the town, the other an old-folks' home with card tables, afghans, and wheelchairs, the geezers trading stories and lies, children and beer bottles at their feet.

"That 1994 team was a disaster," said Dick Ebersol, who got a migraine when he thought of what the 1996 Olympic basketball broadcast might look like.

"It was not a team to be proud of," said Dave Gavitt. "And you know what the worst thing was? It was noticed immediately by the international opponents."

"I don't know if *vile* is the right word or *disgusting*," said Andrew Gaze, a respected player who was the star of the Australian team that lost 103–74 to the United States. "There should be at least some pleasure in playing the game, some dignity."

So just like that, the world went from taking pregame photos with the American heroes to calling them vile. Dream Team II won the Worlds but went a long way toward losing the world.

One footnote: Isiah Thomas had accepted an invitation to be on that 1994 team, at long last getting the chance to represent his country. But he tore his Achilles tendon in a late-season Pistons game, an injury that ended his career. Would DT II have been more mature with Isiah leading it? Or even more dysfunctional?

A sea change can never be explained simply. Obviously, seeds had been planted for the game to change domestically even before the first Dream Team came along. Remember that Magic and Bird had come into the league way back in 1979. Drexler's rookie year was 1983, and Jordan, Barkley, and Stockton all came along in 1984. By 1994 and certainly by 1996, it was a new type of NBA player, tutored in a burgeoning AAU system that encouraged one-on-one performance art over teamwork. If you'll permit a metaphor to be stretched to the breaking point, the 1992 team, as spectacular as it had been, was a well-made play, grounded in the fundamentals, a kind of moderned-up *Cherry Orchard* or *Hedda Gabler*. The '94 team was a Cirque du Soleil show, an overproduced hodgepodge of high-wire acts, costumes, and over-the-top theatrics, a sexed-up mess.

I've long theorized that a major reason for the NBA's post–Dream Team decline was that the new generation was not sufficiently invested in the league as an entity. Magic and Bird had come into an NBA that was perched on the precipice. They didn't need to be sold the idea that it was in trouble, because the proof was manifest. And so they bought into the idea that they had to save it. Things had gotten better by the time Jordan came along, but he followed the Magic/Bird model and others followed him.

But the Shaqs, the Alonzos, and the Shawn Kemps had no such compunction about helping the game along. When they came in, everything was fine, the cash register was ringing, and the feeling was, *Just let me get mine.*

One could argue that Jordan, who called his teammates "my supporting cast" and whose singular appeal sold out arenas and created an empire out of a shoe company, had something to do with the attitudinal change in the game. Harvey Araton did argue exactly that in his 2005 book, *Crashing the Borders: How Basketball Won the World and Lost Its Soul at Home*. I can't begin to offer a complete and cogent summary of Araton's argument in these pages, so

I'm not going to try. Suffice it to say that what Araton says makes
some sense, particularly when he writes that, because of the
one-man cyclone that was Jordan, the NBA became more about individuals than teams.

"Even going back to the late eighties, David Stern and NBA
Properties, which was a machine by then, was doing a very good
job of marketing players as individuals and promoting individual
stars," says Grantham. "So, as part of a game plan, to the extent
that it was, the Dream Team fell right into that."

Grantham, whose job it was to promote players, sees it as a good
thing, a brand maker. Araton, whose job it is to question and cast a
skeptical eye on the deleterious effects of commercialism, sees it as
bad. Reasonable men can gaze upon the same inkblot and one will
see the secrets of the universe and the other will see a truckload of
turnips.

But certainly Jordan wasn't all to blame. In the summer of
1985, Converse, finally realizing that it had been years late to the
party, arranged for Magic and Bird to film what became an iconic
commercial that showed Johnson arriving, via limousine, in French
Lick. So there were those two grind-it-out competitors, always
about basketball first, blood rivals, locking arms in the name of
commerce. The concept of players being marketed ahead of teams
began with Magic and Bird, though there is no doubt that Jordan
finished it.

But whatever anyone thought or wrote about any of those
guys, they were always about basketball first. That's more than obvious with Bird, who has never been comfortable in front of a camera, but it was the same for Magic and Michael. I always considered
Jordan's ultimate achievement to be that he was better than his
hype, which is not easy when you're hyped the way he was. Those
who followed were passionate about themselves more than the
game, wanted what Jordan *had* without becoming what Jordan *was*.

"People have written books about how Jordan became Jordan,"
says David Falk, "but it can't be figured out logically. You have all
the individual components of his competitive personality. He had

the great coach at Carolina in Dean Smith. He was a late bloomer who wanted to prove himself. He came to an NBA that had gotten better with Magic and Larry but still needed him. And then you had to *ignite* that mixture somehow with something. You can't just re-create it.

"In a similar vein, the Dream Team will never be replicated. The U.S. might someday put together a team that would win by 80 points and it still wouldn't be the same. You wouldn't have this combination of great players who were also icons."

Only two players from the '94 Nightmare Team (which was also called the Scream Team and the Preen Team), Shaquille O'Neal and Reggie Miller, were allowed onto the '96 Olympic team, which won the gold medal in Atlanta. A sprinkling of original Dream Teamers—Barkley, Pippen, Malone, Stockton, and Robinson—also played. Lenny Wilkens was the coach and the team easily won the gold medal. But it wasn't the same. It didn't have the electricity, the magic (or the Magic). They knew it, too. They felt like the wife of Gus Grissom, the astronaut who flew the *second* Mercury mission, in the movie version of Tom Wolfe's *The Right Stuff*; she feels slighted that her husband didn't get the parades, the acclaim, and the plaudits from the Kennedys that had accompanied the return of the *first* man into space. "Where's Jackie now?" she wonders.

"I played because they called me and, honestly, I still considered it almost a duty," says Stockton today. "But I knew it wasn't going to be the same. You can call all the teams that followed Dream Teams, but the fact is that there was only one. Every guy was a rock star." Stockton suddenly realizes with alarm that he's just described himself as a rock star, so he self-corrects. "Well, maybe not everyone. But the first five or six. You line up next to someone on the court and they're saying stuff like, 'I just touched Magic Johnson,' or 'I just talked to Michael Jordan.' Now how are you going to match something like that?"

Barkley, also a '96er, put it in stronger terms. "It was a fucking nightmare," he told me recently. "I wasn't going to play when Lenny called me the first time. I said, 'Lenny, I loved 1992. It was such a great experience and I want somebody else to have it.' But he said, 'I need you to play, but I need you more for leadership.' So I said okay.

"I was just amazed at some of the things that went on," Barkley continued. "We had a couple guys skip practice because they didn't get to start and didn't play as many minutes as they thought they should. Can you imagine that? Michael Jordan didn't start some games in '92. Michael *freaking* Jordan!" Barkley wouldn't name the players, but they were Shaq and Penny Hardaway.

In some press reports, Hakeem Olajuwon, a native Nigerian who had just been granted U.S. citizenship, was presented as *the* model teammate on the '96 squad. Pippen said that wasn't the case. "Penny and Hakeem . . . there's two guys who will whine when things don't go their way. Hakeem got mad at Lenny because he didn't play against Greece. 'I've never had a DNP [Did Not Play] in my life!' he was shouting at Lenny. He was so mad that tears were coming out of his eyes. I'm telling you, it was bad. I enjoyed Atlanta, I guess, but it wasn't the same. And it wasn't a Dream Team."

Orenga was also on Spain's '96 team, and he recalls standing next to some of the U.S. team members at the Opening Ceremonies. "They looked at us and said, 'Who do you play for, and who do you play in your first game?' And we said, 'We are from Spain and we play you.' And it was like it was no big deal to them. Right away I didn't see the same maturity and dedication as with the Dream Team."

Remember that there was a fairly significant original Dream Team presence on the '96 team, thus demonstrating that the whole of the '92 team was greater than its individual parts. I stand behind no man in my affection for Sir Charles. But Sir Charles as team leader and Michael/Magic/Larry as team leader are two vastly different things.

"This is probably sad," says Grant Hill, "but Charles was our leader. He was probably the best player and the most natural guy to do it except for Scottie. But Scottie led more by example." Hill didn't mean *sad* as in "tragic"; he meant more like *sad* as in, well, "tragicomic."

Barkley saw himself as a legit leader, and to some degree he was. But somewhere in his heart of hearts, he knows that he was not the perfect man for a leadership job, not on a team that is to be judged by history.

In the gold medal final in 1996, Yugoslavia led the United States by 7 points in the first half, was down by only 5 at halftime, and was trailing by only a single point, 51–50, with 14:03 left in the game. The Americans got their act together after that and won 95–69.

But the chipping away had started. At the Sydney Games in 2000, the United States beat Russia by only 15 points, Lithuania by only 2, and France by only 10 in the gold medal game. A disastrous sixth-place finish in the 2002 World Championships in Indianapolis augured failure in the 2004 Games in Athens, and failure is exactly what happened there. The backcourt of Allen Iverson and Stephon Marbury couldn't guard an arthritic llama. Tim Duncan was disinterested and disinclined to be the leader he should've been, and callow stars such as LeBron James, Dwayne Wade, and Carmelo Anthony were ill-prepared to lead in his stead. Larry Brown, the coach, saw what was coming early and, as is his wont, tried to deflect blame away from himself and onto the team. The United States got blown out by Puerto Rico—*Puerto Rico!*—in the first game and won only the bronze medal.

To a world that hadn't been paying close attention, it seemed sudden and cataclysmic. But that wasn't the case. It was the product of gradual erosion in the American product and an exponential improvement in an international game that had been catalyzed by the Dream Team. Athens forced the United States to take seriously the idea of replacing the haphazard let's-see-what-we-got-every-four-years approach, which had been the operative model, with a structured national team. Veteran executive Jerry Colangelo became USA Basketball's CEO, and Krzyzewski, who years ago had learned so much as a Dream Team assistant, became the head coach.

"Barcelona was so important for my development as a coach," Krzyzewski told me. "I came back with a greater love for the game because I hadn't realized that NBA players could love the game that deeply. There is a certain percentage of college guys who believe with all their heart that we love the game more than anybody, certainly more than the NBA people. That was disproven by the Dream Team."

During the '92 Games, a veteran Brazilian guard named Marcel de Souza made this observation: "I will never play like Scottie Pippen, and my son will never play like Scottie Pippen. But perhaps my grandson will play like Scottie Pippen."

He was too conservative with that prediction. In the 2011 NBA playoffs, Dirk Nowitzki, that wide-eyed observer of the 1992 Dream Team, averaged 28 points a game, made almost 50 percent of his shots, converted 94 percent of his free throws, and won the Finals MVP award as he led his Dallas Mavericks to the NBA championship. All those not-that-long-ago perceptions about European players—*they're too soft, they don't grow up with the game like we do, they don't have the discipline, they don't have the athleticism*—were dashed on the rocks of Nowitzki's exquisite play.

De Tocqueville wrote: "In a revolution, as in a novel, the most difficult part to invent is the end." We are still waiting, one supposes, for the end of this revolution begun by the Dream Team, but we have certainly seen where it is heading and how much quicker it moved than most of us originally thought. But not the Inspector of Meat. No, not him, not this perceptive, far-seeing man who came to these shores nearly four decades ago to learn the lessons of an American game.

"I was not surprised," says Boris Stankovic. "I was not surprised at all."

# THE LEGEND

· · · · · · · · · · · · · · · · · · · · · · · · · · · · · · · · · · · · · · · · · ·

## "I Would've Liked to Have Touched Gold When I Was a Kid"

After I interviewed Larry Bird in February 2012, something he told me has stuck with me. It concerned the last game he played for the Boston Celtics, Sunday, May 17, 1992, at Richfield Coliseum, in Summit County, about halfway between Cleveland and Akron. The Cavs routed the Celtics 122–104, a Game 7 playoff victory that sent Boston home and Cleveland into the Eastern Conference finals, where (of course) they would be drummed out by Jordan and the Bulls, who went on to win the championship.

Bird's back was killing him in that game. He played 33 painful minutes and took only nine shots and, most tellingly, never got to the free throw line. He had almost nothing left and his first Dream Team practice was less than seven weeks away.

"I walked off that floor and I said to myself, 'This is it,'" Bird told me. "Maybe I had thought it before. But now I knew for sure."

After that game, we clustered around his locker, trying to figure out when to ask the question that was on everyone's mind, see if we could get an exclusive. Bird would've been most likely to reveal his decision to the *Boston Globe*'s Bob Ryan, but he told Bob: "I can't answer that right now. I've got the Olympics ahead of me."

Still, Bird said he felt peace on that afternoon. "It just felt right, ending it there, in Cleveland."

"I'm confused," I said. "Why did it feel 'right'? Why was Cleveland special?"

"See, I loved that building, Richfield," he answered. "The second game I ever played in the NBA [in 1979] we pulled up there and I couldn't believe it. Omigod, there was this beautiful, big arena in the middle of a cornfield. It's what I had always dreamed of." He nodded his head and smiled. "A big arena in a cornfield."

I went back to check Bird's memory, and he was of course correct. It was the second game of a season in which he would lead one of the most remarkable turnarounds in NBA history, a rookie orchestrating a Celtics revival that led to 61 wins after a 29-win season in 1978–79. In that memorable (to him anyway) first game at Richfield, he had 28 points in a 139–117 Boston rout.

"I usually played well there," he said. "Something about it just felt right."

Bird is ever the realist, rarely caught up in hype or given to bursts of sentimentality. Alone of the Dream Teamers, he expressed this caveat about all the Dream Team bonhomie: "If we would've been together another two weeks, we would've had some problems. You could sense it. You could hear it. 'Oh, man, I only got to play fifteen minutes.' 'Oh, man, Chuck didn't use me enough.' I always told everybody, 'Damn, it doesn't matter. We're winning by forty points. Hell, Michael Jordan's only playing twenty minutes.'" Bird smiled. "Yup, I was glad it was over when it was."

While it was going on, though, the experience meant as much to Bird as it did to anyone, and he enjoyed poring through the memories.

"I'll never forget [Dream Team assistant] P. J. Carlesimo coming up to me after I came out of one game and saying, 'Man, Larry, I didn't realize you could rebound like that.' I said, 'P.J., I know you're only a college coach, but you must have a TV, right?' The guys got on P.J. something terrible after that."

I ask for his memories of the Greatest Game Nobody Saw in Monte Carlo. "The talk started early because we figured we were going to scrimmage, and this might be the last one before we went to Barcelona," Bird remembers. "So there was all this chatter on the bus, Magic and Michael, of course, but I wasn't paying much attention because I didn't think I was going to be playing. My back was killing me that day.

"Now we get there, and I climb on the stationary bike and that was where the hell I was going to stay, and all of a sudden I gotta go the whole time because we only got ten guys. I just wish I had been feeling better that day, and if I have one regret from the whole experience it's that I was never in top shape."

I ask him about the memory of his steal from Magic and how Jordan remembers it as the key play of the game. Bird smiles, and you can tell he recalls every detail, but it is part of his code that he won't gloat about getting the best of Magic.

That's when I tell him about Jordan's opinion that the whole "back to '79 thing," (Jordan's words) is a torch held highest by Magic. Bird swats that away, too. "Hey, it is what it is. You know Earvin as well as I do. He likes to talk. But we came in together, we played against each other, and the history is real and it's been told millions of times. I would never run from it."

Years ago, when his capacity for nostalgia was lower, Bird might've run from *Magic/Bird*, the Broadway play that was due on-stage in 2012 (after this book went to press). But Bird is fully invested, and he is revved up over the opening when we talked. He has read the script and even suggested a few changes. "When I'm involved in something I just read my own part to see if it's accurate," Bird told me. "Whatever Magic says happened from his viewpoint, hey, that's fine with me."

Bird's response surprised me when I asked him if he, like so many others, took away any lessons from the Olympics. I expected he would say something like, *Sheet, I already knew everything these guys did.* But he didn't.

"I remember watching how Michael and Scottie played together," Bird says. "Michael would always play the point guard and put pressure on him, and I'd just be sitting there watching. Then Scottie would come, and next thing you know they've turned the guy and he would just throw the ball over his head. Anywhere. Just to get rid of it. The pressure that Michael put on these kids? Man, I could've got fifteen steals a game if I played with him.

"You know, winning by forty isn't fun. Maybe to some guys but not to this team. But watching Michael and Scottie together out there, suckering these guys into a corner, or right before the half-court line . . . that was fun."

Like almost every other Dream Teamer, Bird stood—still stands—in awe of Jordan's abilities. "He'd play thirty-six holes of golf, and we'd be heading to the bus and here comes Michael with his clubs. But he'd be back two minutes later ready to play. The energy that man had . . . never saw anything like it.

"That's why, when Magic started talking, deep down, he had to know that Michael had passed us. I mean, Michael was the best player in our league before Barcelona. I had no problem with it. I had my run. I said to Magic, you gotta be out of your mind if you think you can still compete with this guy. Let it go, man, let it go. Compete against him like you're going to kick his ass, but realize it's his time."

I wondered if Bird ranked the Dream Team experience as highly as did Magic, who put it at the top of his achievements.

"It's completely different," he answered. "I thought it was special in high school when I played against the Russians. In college I got to play in the World Games. Each of those was unique—they just *felt* different—because of the international connection. It was the same thing with the Dream Team except on a much, much higher level. You just can't compare winning a gold medal to an NBA championship. They are both great in their own way."

Bird does not display his gold medal. But, then, he doesn't display anything, his fingers bereft of championship rings. "The rings don't mean anything to me," says Bird. "Now, the banners in Boston Garden? They mean something because they'll be there forever." But don't think that his gold medal is insignificant to him. He knows right where his medal rests, and every four years he takes it out of a box for some show-and-tell.

"I'll take it to high schools just so kids can touch it, leave it there a few days, then get somebody to take it somewhere else," said Bird. "I took it to my kids' school and to my own high school back in French Lick. Just so kids, when they're talking about the Olympics, they get to see what the prize is, what it really means. I would've liked to have touched gold when I was a kid."

I ask him what he remembers most about the Dream Team experience. He doesn't even have to stop to think about it. He brings up his father, Joe Bird, that dark soul who took his own life and never got to see the boy he raised become one of the immortals.

"When I was a kid, my dad was big on the Olympics," said Bird. "He'd turn it on—we only got about two stations—and my dad would hear the national anthem and he'd turn to us and say, 'The United States won gold.' He didn't care whether it was track and field or gymnastics or whatever. He just cared that the United States won.

"So when we stood on that platform in Barcelona to get our gold medals, that was the most exciting thing for me. I was thinking back to my dad and remembering that when he heard that anthem he was happy. And I was happy, too."

Talking to Bird has a way of simplifying things. Our games, and our Olympic Games, have a way of getting wrapped up in money and bureaucracy and politics and petty squabbles. But sometimes they're about the simplest things, about an arena that arises like magic out of a cornfield and about fathers and sons and what they mean to one another.

# *ACKNOWLEDGMENTS*

This book would not have been possible without the cooperation of the Dream Team members, all of whom I interviewed face-to-face. Anyone who has ever dealt with pro athletes knows that rounding them up is like herding cats . . . if the cats were millionaires with handlers, busy schedules, and global fame. But the process was enjoyable (in some strange way) and, more to the point, rewarding when I got to them. They were not easy to pin down, but, once I had them in front of me, it was their memories of, and passion for, this team that most colors the tone of this book.

I spent hours with several of them in their own habitat: a long Long Island breakfast with Mullin and another with Pippen in Florida; lunch at Drexler's house; a tour of Spokane conducted by Stockton; a morning at his school with Robinson; a morning and afternoon staring at the taxidermied conquests in Malone's Louisiana home; dinner and drinks (not too many) with Barkley in Phoenix—these are all pleasant memories that also bore journalistic fruit.

I hadn't seen many of them in a while, but past patterns reemerged immediately. Jordan aired out some ancient grudges about *Sports Illustrated,* and Bird took one look at me as I waited for him by his office in Indianapolis, and said, "What are you doing here? Thought you'd be driving around Magic in a limousine." At least he didn't say anything more . . . graphic.

There are many others who helped, and I hope I haven't forgotten anyone, but four names stand out for their institutional memory about this team—Mike Krzyzewski, P. J. Carlesimo, Russ Granik, and Jan Hubbard. I went back to the well more than once with all four of them. Mike Wilbon, with a memory as sharp as his barbs on Kornheiser, was a great source during a long breakfast talk.

Pete Skorich, formerly a Detroit Pistons executive and the man who shot most of the Dream Team live footage, was of enormous importance. And a big shout-out to *Sports Illustrated* editor Chris Stone for encouragement, as well as to Mickey Steiner for editorial assistance.

My agent, Scott Waxman, and my editor, Mark Tavani, deserve tips of the hat, as does former Random House editor Paul Taunton and ESPN's Steve Wulf.

Here are others who were generous with their time and memories, organized by the way I remember them. They are basketball and TV executives, Dream Team committee members, coaches, public relations people, print journalists, photographers, and players.

David Stern, Boris Stankovic, Rod Thorn, Dick Ebersol, Kim Bohuny, Rick Welts, Steve Mills, C. M. Newton, Harvey Schiller, Bill Wall, Tom McGrath, and Horace Balmer.

Donnie Nelson, Rick Carlisle, and Lenny Wilkens.

Jeffrey Orridge, Donnie Walsh, Quinn Buckner, and Charles Grantham.

David Falk, Lon Rosen, and Fred Whitfield.

Brian McIntyre, Terry Lyons, Don Sperling, Julie Fie, Josh Rosenfeld, Craig Miller, Nat Butler, Andy Bernstein, Florian Wanninger from FIBA, and Dion Cocoros and Paul Hirschheimer from NBA Entertainment.

Jackie MacMullan and Sam Smith, both of whose books are conjured up frequently in the manuscript, and, to the best of my ability, were given fair attributional recognition. Also, I single out Bill Simmons, a much younger man than myself who is capable of writing much longer books and achieving much greater cultural relevancy. Also, David Dupree, my eternal courtside colleague, and Bob Ryan, the eternal "Commish."

Grant Hill and Bill Laimbeer shared their very differing experiences with the Dream Team, as did, with considerably more reticence, one of my all-time favorites, Joe Dumars. (This is the time to point out that Laimbeer and Dumars's erstwhile Detroit Pistons teammate Isiah Thomas, a non–Dream Teamer who is a big part of this story, declined my request for an interview.)

Of the international players, Dirk Nowitzki (well, he's more a Dallas Maverick these days), Sarunas Marciulionis, and Juan Antonio Orenga were terrific and candid, and Toni Kukoc also gamely offered his thoughts on the night that he got legally assaulted by Scottie Pippen and Michael Jordan.

Two people who were close to the Dream Team died as I was finishing this manuscript—Matt Dobek, who was a friend of mine, and Dave Gavitt, without whose steady diplomacy there might not have been a Dream Team, at least not in the form that finally transpired. I had already collected their thoughts and memories, and I remembered them often as I wrote these words.

Chuck Daly died before I began the project. Over the years we had talked often about his Dream Team experience, and I could feel his steady presence throughout.

# INDEX

## ABOUT THE AUTHOR

JACK MCCALLUM is the author of two previously critically acclaimed basketball books, *Unfinished Business* and *Seven Seconds or Less*, both of which chronicled the season of an NBA team, the 1990–91 Boston Celtics in the former, the 2005–06 Phoenix Suns in the latter. In 2005, he won the Naismith Memorial Basketball Hall of Fame's Curt Gowdy Award for excellence in basketball writing. A senior writer at *Sports Illustrated* for 30 years, he lives in Pennsylvania with his wife, and is the father of two and the grandfather of one.